The 50 Most Influential Women in American Law

For two of my favorite sister lawyers:
Lisa Danielson and Janalyn Edmondson.

And for the Schnarky.

The 50

Most Influential Women in American Law

BY
DAWN BRADLEY BERRY, J.D.

Lowell House
Los Angeles

Contemporary Books
Chicago

Other books by Dawn Bradley Berry:

Equal Compensation for Women
The Domestic Violence Sourcebook
The Divorce Sourcebook

Library of Congress Cataloging-in-Publication Data

Berry, Dawn Bradley.
    The fifty most influential women in American law / by Dawn Bradley
Berry.
       p.   cm.
    ISBN 1-56565-469-2
    1. Women lawyers—United States—Biography.   2. Women judges—
United States—Biography. 3. Women legislators—United States—Biography.
4. Women social reformers—United States—History. 5. Women—Legal status, laws, etc.—United States—History. 6. Women—United States—Social
conditions. I. Title.
KF353.B47 1996
340' .082—dc20   96-41614
                                                          CIP

Requests for such permissions should be addressed to:
Lowell House
2029 Century Park East, Suite 3290
Los Angeles, CA 90067

Lowell House books can be purchased at special discounts when ordered in bulk for
premiums and special sales. Contact Department TC at the address above.

Publisher: Jack Artenstein
Associate Publisher, Lowell House Adult: Bud Sperry
Managing Editor: Maria Magallanes
Text design: Laurie Young

Manufactured in the United States of America
10 9 8 7 6 5 4 3 2 1

ACKNOWLEDGMENTS

I am extremely grateful to everyone who assisted me in bringing this book to life, especially to Shirley Chavez for typing of astounding speed and accuracy; to Jana Edmondson for superb research assistance; to Willy Berry, Clarette Bradley, and innumerable friends for support and patience; to Charlene Giangola, Hinkle Law Offices, and archivist John Nichols of the Wyandot County Museum; and to the staffs of the University of New Mexico Law School Library, the Albuquerque Public Library (especially the Wyoming and East Mountain branches), and the Santa Fe Public Library.

Thanks also to everyone at Lowell House, especially my great editors Bud Sperry and Maria Magallanes; and to Laurie Young for design and photo assistance.

And a very special thanks to Cecelia Goetz, Ruth Bader Ginsburg, Gloria Steinem, Nancy Mintie, Sarah Weddington, and Sandra Day O'Connor for generously providing input, information, and assistance in setting the record straight.

Acknowledgments

The publisher gratefully acknowledges the following sources for providing photographs:

Arabella Babb Mansfield: Photo courtesy of the State Historical Society of Iowa.

Elizabeth Packard: Photo courtesy of the Illinois State Historical Library.

Belva Lockwood: Photo courtesy of the National Portrait Gallery.

Myra Colby Bradwell: Photo reprinted from *The Green Bag*, vol. II (1890) published by The Boston Book Company, Boston, Mass.

Clara Shortridge Foltz: Photo courtesy of The Bancroft Library, University of California, Berkeley.

Laura DeForce Gordon: Photo reprinted from *The Green Bag*, vol. II (1890) published by The Boston Book Company, Boston, Mass.

Lyda Burton Conley: Photo courtesy of the Wyandotte County Museum.

Esther McQuigg Morris: Photo courtesy of Wyoming Division of Cultural Resources

Mary Gysin Leonard: Portrait from *First Lady at Law: Mary Leonard, Oregon's Pioneer Portia*. Reprinted with permission of Fred W. Decker.

Mary Clyens Lease: Photo courtesy of Kansas State Historical Society.

Ellen Spencer Mussey: Photo courtesy of the Office of Alumni Relations, Washington College of Law, American University.

Lettie Burlingame: Photo reprinted from *The Green Bag*, vol. II (1890) published by The Boston Book Company, Boston, Mass.

Tiera Farrow: Photo courtesy of the Wyandotte County Museum.

Crystal Eastman: Photo courtesy of the Library of Congress.

Florence Ellinwood Allen: Photo courtesy of The Western Reserve Historical Society, Cleveland, Ohio.

Dorothy Kenyon: Photo courtesy of Sophia Smith Collection

Mabel Walker Willebrandt: Photo courtesy of the Library of Congress.

Carol Weiss King: Photo from *Carol Weiss King: Human Rights Lawyer* by Ann Fagan Ginger. Reprinted with permission.

Margaret Chase Smith: Photo courtesy of Margaret Chase Smith Library.

Eunice Hunton Carter: Photo reprinted courtesy of the Smith College Archives.

Fanny Holtzmann: Photo courtesy of the Holtzmann Family Collection. Reprinted from *The Lady and the Law: the Remarkable Life of Fanny Holtzmann* by Ted Berkman.

Rachel Carson: New York World—Telegram & Sun Collection, Library of Congress.

Gladys Towles Root: Photo courtesy of the Herald Examiner Collection / Los Angeles Public Library.

Contents

INTRODUCTION

Shakespeare's heroine Portia in *The Merchant of Venice* assumed the role of lawyer to defeat Shylock's claim for a pound of Antonio's flesh, and in so doing became—and remains—a model for the many women who have endeavored to use and shape the law throughout the centuries. The first women seeking admission to the predominately male domain of law were certainly in need of such role models. Involved as they were in the growth and evolution of American law since colonial times, virtually all who tried to make their mark faced opposition. The first female attorneys, especially, encountered a tremendous hurdle.

With a few notable exceptions, the walls guarding one of the most exclusively male career domains did not yield easily to females. Witness the opinion offered by Chief Justice Edward Ryan of the Wisconsin Supreme Court in 1875, which has become something of a classic for its emetic prose denying Lavinia Goodell admission to the bar:

> The law of nature destines and qualifies the female sex for the bearing and nurture of the children of our race and for the custody of the homes of the world and their maintenance in love and honor. And all lifelong callings of women, inconsistent with these radical and sacred duties of their sex, as of the profession of law, are departures from the order of nature; and, when voluntary, treason against it.
> [*In re Goodell*, 30 Wis. 232 (1875)]

For the earliest trailblazers, such stereotypical notions were the rule. Among these were that women were too timid, too indiscreet, too distracting to males, or else too genteel to enter into courtroom battle. Women were presumed to lack a logical perspective and to be ruled by sentiment. Some argued that women were too physically delicate or mentally fragile and susceptible to disability due to pregnancy and childbirth. Moreover, the role of battling attorney directly challenged a woman's proper persona of nurturing wife and mother. Law involved adversity, confrontation, public advocacy, crime, and other "unfeminine" matters. Women were viewed as unfit to participate in what the Illinois Supreme Court referred to as "the hot strides of the Bar" in its opinion denying admission to Myra Bradwell. In the same opinion, Justice Bradley expressed his shock at the thought that women would be permitted to mix professionally in the nastiness of the world that finds its way into courts of justice. He went on to list some of these "unclean issues" and "nameless indecencies," ironically including pregnancy in that litany.

Yet these dedicated and resilient women persevered. In 1882, there were only 56 officially recognized female attorneys in the United States. By 1890, numbers had risen to about 135 attorneys and law students. The National Association of Women Lawyers was founded in 1899. By 1914, when *Case and Comment* devoted its October issue to female lawyers, Department of Labor records showed 1,010 in America. As of 1920, 3 percent of the legal profession was female. A 1944 article in *Good Housekeeping* heralded a new breed of woman lawyer, already changing the face of the profession. Other than a slight drop following World War II, the percentages have risen ever since. The influx of women into law schools has been noted as the most dramatic of any professional school enrollment increase through the 1960s and '70s.

Today, the majority of the barriers have fallen. Female students make up nearly 50 percent of the nation's law school population. Women are found in virtually all spheres of the legal profession and have held nearly every judicial and political office. Many of the best known and most accomplished advocates of social change are female. Yet despite these gains, women building careers in law and justice are still thwarted. An American Bar Association report released in early 1996 revealed that on the whole, female attorneys still encounter gender-based harassment, earn less money, and receive fewer promotions than their male colleagues. Female attorneys today still face the paradox that traits considered most desirable in a male attorney—

self-assurance, a competitive and aggressive nature, and high ambition
—are considered by many to be "unfeminine."

So the efforts of women to achieve true equality for themselves
and their sisters must—and does—continue. Fortunately, many others
have gone before us as lawyers and in other roles that impacted might-
ily in shaping the law of the land especially as it pertains to women.
Their brave, innovative undertakings provide both inspiration and
practical ideas for the work still to be done today.

This book profiles the achievements of fifty women who had a
positive, lasting effect on the development of the legal landscape of
our country—its laws, legislative priorities, and system of justice.
Their work has spanned several hundred years—from "Gentleman"
Margaret Brent, the first female attorney in colonial America, to
Marcia Clark, who drew unprecedented public attention as the formidable yet feminine prosecutor in the most sensational murder trial of
the twentieth century. All have, in some enduring and significant way,
directly affected the development of both modern law and the role of
women in today's world. Many were motivated by a deep dedication
to social justice, working to expand and protect the rights of other
women, minorities, and children.

But the accomplishments of the women profiled here, and of the
many others involved in shaping our legal system, have by no means
been limited to the sphere of reform. While many women throughout history have naturally been drawn to work for human rights—in
part as an outgrowth of familiar caretaker roles, as well as traditional
expectations of where female talents best fit in the legal arena—
women also have had a profound influence in shaping business, labor,
industry, and laws.

Deciding which of the many accomplished women to include
among these fifty pathfinders was a formidable task. Many, many
women have worked to shape the legal development of our country.
Others have recently ascended to positions of considerable influence,
and will no doubt have a hand in the continued evolution of our legal
future—women like Roberta Cooper Ramo, first female president of

the American Bar Association; Anita Hill, who courageously spoke out against sexual harassment; Catherine Palmer, the Manhattan D.A. who fearlessly challenged heroin kingpins; and Illinois senator Carol Mosely Braun, the first black woman elected to the United States Senate. Deciding who among these remarkable women would be included was an extraordinary challenge.

So while I have endeavored to be fair in my choices, I make no pretense of objectivity. Naturally, I have included my personal heroines, along with others who appealed to me as accomplished, influential, and fascinating. In the end, the choice was unavoidably subjective, and entirely my own.

It is tempting to look for common threads among the many women who broke new ground to reshape the law. Yet each of these unique individuals had to find a direction that was largely unfamiliar to a woman of her day, and each managed in her own way, often inventing her life as she went along. Some accomplished their goals with force and fanfare; others managed with guile and grace. The women profiled here are different in many ways—in background, motivation, methods, philosophy, style, and politics. Among them are liberals and conservatives, eccentrics and conformists, wild women and nuns, rabble-rousers and quiet traditionalists. These are real women with flawed and remarkable lives. Perhaps the only characteristics truly shared by all are those that must naturally occur in any trailblazer: courage, energy, gumption, dedication, and a willingness to break the bounds of convention. For that, we owe them deep gratitude.

"Gentleman"
Margaret Brent

1601 – 1671

M ARGARET BRENT, THE FIRST FEMALE LAWYER IN AMERICA,
was a true original. She was born in England to titled parents,
her father a lord and her mother descended from King Edward III.
Little is known about her childhood except that she was one of thirteen children and that she received an education, an unusual advantage
for a seventeenth-century girl. Brent was already a lawyer when she
arrived from England to settle in Maryland in 1638, accompanied by
her sister Mary and two brothers. Her cousin Lord Baltimore helped
her get a start by writing to Governor Leonard Calvert of Maryland,
recommending she be granted land. Margaret and her sister Mary
began with a grant of about seventy acres, which they named Sister's
Freehold. Margaret soon acquired a thousand acres from her brother in
payment of a debt. This included a mill, a house, and grazing pasture
where she raised livestock. As the years passed, she continued to amass
vast tracts of land, as well as considerable influence and political power.

Brent was renowned for her shrewd intelligence. She was well aware of the power of land in the colonial political structure. She steadily increased her holdings for herself and her family, as well as for investment purposes, and frequently granted portions of her land to other colonists.

Brent was an eloquent and skilled lawyer. Not long after her arrival, she was appointed legal counsel to the governor. She soon became famous for her outstanding talents in both negotiation and litigation. For a woman to take such a role in colonial times was so unusual that others were baffled as to how to treat her or even address her. Judges and courtroom opponents sometimes referred to her as "Gentleman" Margaret Brent, and the nickname stuck.

When Governor Calvert was ordered back to England in 1643 to assist in the civil war between the Monarchists and Parliamentarians, two Virginians, William Clayborne and Richard Ingle, took control of Maryland. Their authority and reputations were equally dubious, with Ingle rumored to be a pirate. So when Governor Calvert returned, Margaret Brent helped him raise a legion of fighting men to recapture the government. His power was restored, but he died a short time later, and Brent became executor of his estate, according to his wishes.

Calvert's estate, however, was soon hit with lawsuits seeking to collect debt. Brent was thus forced to defend the estate without the customary records, which had been destroyed during the upheaval in Calvert's absence. The greatest challenge came from soldiers who had been promised payment by Calvert for their services in helping restore his government, but who had received nothing from the public coffers. The new governor, at his wit's end trying to appease the angry mob, relied on Margaret Brent to take charge of the fiasco and arrange for the soldiers to be compensated.

Brent employed diplomacy, patience, and courage in forestalling the soldiers' mutiny while she figured out how they would be paid. Maryland was experiencing a severe corn shortage, so she imported corn from Virginia to feed them. She even slaughtered many of her own cattle to add to their compensation. Once the soldiers were paid, they dispersed peaceably, many settling in the area.

Brent was a woman of remarkable energy. In addition to her political responsibilities, she maintained a thriving litigation practice. According to records from the period, she was involved in 124 court cases over eight years, including many jury trials—and she won them all. History suggests that she suffered little in the way of discrimination on account of her sex, partly because her activities were so unusual that others simply had no idea what to make of her. She steadfastly refused to accept the socially recognized limits on women's rights that prevailed in colonial times.

While she was no stranger to controversy, most of Brent's difficulties arose from her political activities rather than her gender. When she persevered, for instance, in her pledge to pay Governor Calvert's troops after his estate proved insufficient, her cousin Lord Baltimore, who vigorously opposed the plan, turned against her and sought a rebuke by the Maryland Assembly. Instead, the assembly praised her for preventing mutiny and guarding public safety.

Yet she occasionally encountered legal obstacles when she asserted herself before established political bodies. In her role as attorney to the governor, she felt it her duty to vote and be heard in the Maryland Assembly. She appeared before Maryland's House of Burgesses to demand two votes in the proceedings—one on behalf of her client, Lord Baltimore, and one in her own right as a freeholder of land. When her request was refused, she demanded that all proceedings of that session be declared invalid.

Brent also had a domestic side and became the guardian of an orphaned Indian girl. She remained active in her many endeavors until the age of fifty-six, when she retired from public life to live quietly on her estate in Virginia, settling into a manor house she called Peace. According to some reports, she continued her involvement in law by acting as a mediator to settle minor disputes between neighbors. Today Margaret Brent's memory is honored annually when the American Bar Association's Committee on Women in the Profession bestows its Margaret Brent Women Lawyers of Achievement Award upon outstanding female attorneys.

ARABELLA BABB
MANSFIELD

1846 – 1911

AFTER MARGARET BRENT RETIRED, OVER TWO HUNDRED YEARS would pass before the next female attorney would officially practice in the United States. But such records may be deceptive. Scattered reports indicate there was a handful of female lawyers throughout rural areas of the West in the mid-1800s.

During the nineteenth century, the more common route to a legal education was through apprenticeship rather than law school, especially in the Midwest and western states. Attorneys who practiced only within their own county did not have to be admitted to the state bar. For example, an 1869 article in an Iowa newspaper mentioned a Mrs. Mary E. Magoon, attorney at law who enjoyed notable success before juries. It is likely that other women practiced in similar settings, either on their own or in partnership with husbands. Yet it was Belle Babb Mansfield who became the first documented female lawyer in America, officially recognized by a state's bar.

Arabella Babb was born on a farm near Burlington, Iowa, in 1846. The homestead was maintained by her mother after her father followed the gold rush to California and then died in a mining accident when Belle was only four years old. Mrs. Babb, determined to see her daughter educated, moved the family to a region known for its fine schools. Belle's high school in Mount Pleasant, Iowa, was run by Samuel L. Howe, an active abolitionist and suffragist, who likely influenced Belle's views.

Women gained a circumstantial advantage in education during the Civil War. Many colleges and universities were forced to relax their admissions standards in order to survive economically. Mansfield thus enrolled in Iowa Wesleyan College in 1863, where she excelled in debate, studied the classics, and graduated as valedictorian of her class. After graduating, she began teaching at Simpson College in Indianola, Iowa. In 1868, she married John Mansfield, a history professor at Iowa Wesleyan. She joined him on the faculty, teaching English and history.

Belle became fascinated with law and began working as an apprentice at her brother's firm. She was encouraged by her husband in both her legal studies and her work for women's suffrage. Belle and John studied law together and applied for admission to the Iowa bar in 1869.

Mr. and Mrs. Mansfield were both recommended for admission. The examiners noted that Belle had passed with high honors, and that she gave "the very best rebuke possible to the imputation that ladies cannot qualify for the practice of law."

But Belle Mansfield faced an obstacle in entering the bar: the Iowa code in effect at that time specifically excluded females. Justice Francis Springer, however, a progressive judge who made a point of selecting bar examiners who shared his views favoring equality for women, was impressed with her record and sought a way to circumvent the exclusion. Springer located another Iowa statute that extended all statutory references to the masculine gender to women as well. Justice Springer went one step further in favor of expanding the rights of all women when he declared that statutes specifying the male gender could not be applied so as to deny rights to women. Thus, in June of 1869, Belle Babb Mansfield became the first woman to be formally admitted to the practice of law in the United States. In their feminist publication *Revolution,* suffrage leaders Susan B. Anthony and Elizabeth Cady Stanton heralded the news with great joy.

Unfortunately, although Mansfield fully intended to practice law, she never saw that plan through. Shortly after her bar admission, her husband was sent abroad to Europe. She accompanied him on what turned out to be a lengthy stay, enjoying the opportunity to study the legal systems of various nations. While the Mansfields were in Paris, Belle continued her legal studies for several months at the Ecole de Droit. She became fascinated with international law and frequently visited European courtrooms. Upon the couple's return to America, Belle again joined her husband on the Iowa Wesleyan faculty, where she became a popular lecturer. The Mansfields both became active community leaders, and Belle continued to work for suffrage and women's rights.

Shortly after the Mansfields transferred to Indiana DePauw University, John developed a serious illness, leaving Belle the family's sole support. She cared for him for almost two years before he was placed in a California hospital. She then returned to DePauw, where she served as the first dean of women and continued to lecture as a history professor. Eventually, she became dean of the schools of music and art.

Although she never revived her own legal career, Mansfield continued her work as a champion of women's rights and remained interested in female lawyers and the law until her death in 1911. She was purportedly pleased to have been a pioneer for other women in the legal field. She also worked with the Methodist Church and gave Sunday afternoon lectures on art, literature, history, and religion. In the early 1870s she became one of the founders of Iowa's Women's Suffrage Society. She was known for her close and devoted relationship with her brother's family, her love of travel, and her characteristic hats.

ELIZABETH WARE
PACKARD

1816 – 1897

ELIZABETH WARE WAS BORN IN MASSACHUSETTS TO AN intelligent, progressive, and loving family. Her father, a minister, delighted in hosting frequent visitors, who contributed to the lively discussions and free exchange of ideas in the home. The early 1800s, a time of much questioning of traditional religious doctrine, saw the emergence of a number of new philosophies. Gatherings at the Ware home often inspired respectful disagreements and open discourse on all topics, including theology.

Elizabeth Ware enjoyed an unusually good education for a girl born in the early nineteenth century. At the Amherst Female Seminary she studied science, literature, algebra, languages, and philosophy. She had a passion for learning and for exploring new ideas. Her teachers described her as the best scholar in the school.

Elizabeth began a teaching career at the age of sixteen, which was briefly interrupted by a bout of "brain fever" when she was nineteen.

"Brain fever" was a common diagnosis for a plethora of maladies at this time, especially when the illness was severe enough to bring on delirium, as it was in Elizabeth's case. Unfortunately, to be admitted to a hospital where she could be afforded treatment by a highly respected physician, her father had to sign a form declaring her to be a lunatic. The inadvertent label was to haunt her many years later. Yet when she recovered, her doctor made a final entry in her chart, noting, "She is an interesting and intelligent girl."

The man who was to become Elizabeth's husband, Theophilus Packard, was also the son of a minister, a well-respected man known as the "Sage of Shelbourne." Following in his father's footsteps, Theophilus attended the Princeton Theological Seminary. The school was a stronghold of strict Calvinist doctrine, a sect notoriously narrow-minded and fearful of any challenge to its dogma.

Theophilus Packard had long been friends with the Ware family. When he decided it was time for him to take a wife, he was drawn to beautiful, independent, twenty-two-year-old Elizabeth. Although fifteen years his junior, Elizabeth saw Theophilus as the "manly" type of husband she desired. After a brief courtship, they married.

The union was happy for both in its early years. Elizabeth enjoyed her duties and social position as a pastor's wife. She taught Sunday school, traveled for church assemblies, frequently entertained, and soon became highly admired in her community. When children were born, eventually totaling six, she found motherhood a joy. The family moved several times, eventually settling in Manteno, Illinois.

In Theophilus' view, the new ideas being raised in the church at this time were tantamount to heresy. But Elizabeth Packard found them fascinating. Her education had taught her scientific reasoning, and she began to apply it to church doctrine. Theophilus, horrified by any perceived questioning of his faith, flatly refused to discuss theology with her.

Elizabeth could not accept the doctrine of original sin, known in Calvinist dogma as "total depravity," which holds that human nature is inherently sinful. Elizabeth, well versed in Bible study and strong in her own faith, believed it defied both the Bible and common sense. She preferred to let her own conscience be her guide.

Her contrasting beliefs and natural curiosity, counterpoised with Theophilus' inflexibility, caused an increasing rift between the couple. The crisis came to a head when he journeyed to visit family members, leaving Elizabeth to teach an adult Bible class in his absence.

Elizabeth turned the class into an animated discussion group, urging open exchange of ideas on such controversial topics as spiritualism. She was charming, educated, and an instinctive leader, with the skill to support her theories with down-to-earth examples. The class soon grew from six members to forty-six.

Naturally, when Theophilus returned and discovered what she had been teaching, an uproar ensued. He asked her to step down from teaching and to tell the class the withdrawal was her own idea. She agreed to stop teaching, but refused to lie. Theophilus concluded that such disobedience was evidence of insanity, and he began a campaign to prove she was mentally unbalanced. Sparring with her, he watched for signs of delusion, and even invited others to the house to assess her mental state. Many observers believed that of the two, Theophilus demonstrated far greater signs of paranoia and obsession.

A law in effect at the time allowed married women and minors to be committed to a state mental hospital at the request of a husband or guardian, as long as the medical superintendent of the asylum found the woman or child "evidently insane or distracted." In other cases, evidence of insanity had to be presented to a court. Theophilus continued to build his case against Elizabeth, setting her up to look foolish. He forbade the children to spend time with their mother, made midnight searches of her belongings, and invited a doctor posing as a sewing machine salesman to come and assess her. Then, early one morning, two doctors and a sheriff arrived to carry Elizabeth away to the state hospital at Jacksonville. Friends, neighbors, and her children stood helplessly by as she was taken to the train. Many subsequently ostracized Theophilus, but to no avail. He was adamant that she remain hospitalized.

Elizabeth was determined to prove her husband wrong by giving him no evidence with which to challenge her sanity. She befriended the superintendent, Dr. Andrew McFarland, recognized as a pioneer in the effective treatment of mental illness. Elizabeth often dined with the McFarland family, took patients for rides in a carriage, and led visitors on tours of the asylum with her own set of keys. She appeared to many as an employee, rather than a patient. She carefully observed the workings of the asylum and noted many other married women in her ward who seemed to have no problems whatsoever with their mental health.

Eventually, Elizabeth and Dr. McFarland had a falling out. He became angry and sent her to a ward for seriously disturbed patients. In later writings, she remarked that the principles by which the asylum was run were "the best calculated to make maniacs that human ingenuity could describe." Meanwhile, Elizabeth was embarking upon a new course in life. Determined to maintain her own sanity, Elizabeth again went to work, cleaning the ward and caring for other patients. She often engendered McFarland's wrath when she intervened in the unjust treatment of other inmates. She instituted a system of daily work and maintenance, reading, Bible study, and exercise. Under her care the ward was transformed, and others soon followed suit. Elizabeth then set to work on several writing projects, including a book attacking the principles of Calvinism.

Elizabeth always enjoyed the support of many friends, though none were allowed to visit during her stay at Jacksonville. At one point a group held a "public indignation" meeting and tried to take legal steps to secure her release. Such efforts were, however, unsuccessful. Finally, her oldest son turned twenty-one and became legally qualified to take responsibility for his mother. After three years of involuntary commitment, she was at last released.

Elizabeth fully intended to embark on a campaign to change the laws and currently accepted views of mental health institutions. Yet her personal travails again intervened. Once she returned to the family home, Theophilus redoubled his efforts against her. He confined her to a cold upstairs nursery, refused to provide her with firewood or clothing sufficient to withstand the winter chill, and even nailed the window shut. Friends often gathered below and urged her to break out, but by then Elizabeth had become apprised that Theophilus planned yet another asylum incarceration for her, this time in Massachusetts. She finally slid a note to her best friend, Sarah Haslett, out a crack in the window frame, where it was found by a passerby and delivered. Haslett immediately went to Judge Charles Starr in Kankakee and reported that her friend was being held a virtual prisoner by her husband.

The judge requested sworn statements from those who knew of her imprisonment so he could issue a writ of habeas corpus and give her a day in court. Four men signed an affidavit, which outlined the circumstances of Elizabeth's ordeal. It added a complaint that the reverend was cruelly depriving his wife of winter clothing. The judge issued the writ, and Theophilus was ordered to bring Elizabeth to his chambers. In the initial hearing, Theophilus claimed his wife was incurably insane and denied the other charges of imprisonment or mistreatment. The judge told him he would be required to prove his charges before a jury.

At the trial, Elizabeth's intelligence, confidence, and optimism carried the day. It was also revealed that Theophilus had denounced Elizabeth from his pulpit, refused to let her join Bible classes or family prayers, and even managed to persuade members of her family in Massachusetts that she was insane. Although Elizabeth was deeply wounded by testimony from her former friend Dr. McFarland, her supporters far outweighed her detractors. Many commented that of the pair, Theophilus seemed the far less stable. Elizabeth's friends rallied around her, hiring attorneys, providing her with shelter, and even sharing warm clothing appropriate for court.

Some of the testimony offered against her was patently ridiculous. One doctor included in his list as to why he considered Elizabeth insane her aversion to being called insane, her rejection of Calvinist doctrine, and her calling him a copperhead "without proving it." Others testifying for Theophilus cited instances in which Elizabeth had committed such transgressions as gardening on a warm day; appearing disheveled in the early-morning hours after sitting up all night with her gravely ill daughter; or making biscuits rather than bread for dinner.

There were times when the spectators laughed hysterically. Several friends stated that the only sign of insanity they had ever noticed in Elizabeth was the fact that she did not seek a divorce from her husband! One doctor who had met with her for a period of three hours characterized her as the most intelligent lady he had talked with in years, and stated that he wished for a nation of such women. It took the jury just seven minutes to adjudge her sane. The verdict brought an outburst of cheers and applause.

Elizabeth did file for divorce soon after her trial, though the action was never completed. She promptly returned to Massachusetts to assure her family that she was indeed competent, and to regain custody of her children. She also prepared to embark upon her calling, to change the law so that others would never have to suffer a similar ordeal. She vowed to become self-supporting as a writer and to devote her life to winning justice for abused wives and better treatment for those who were truly mentally ill and confined to asylums.

When she completed her first book, she raised money by selling advance tickets to be redeemed when the book was published. She traveled throughout the Midwest by train, seeking sales at every stop, as well as on the train itself. Through Elizabeth's own powers of charm and salesmanship, plus the notoriety of the trial and the curiosity and chivalry of those she approached, she managed to pay for printing costs and turn a tidy profit. Meanwhile, Theophilus, who had sold the family property and fled back to Massachusetts with the children before the trial ended, refused to allow her to visit her children. But her father intervened. Through his efforts, along with the indignation of local residents, Theophilus finally relented.

As her sales efforts became more successful, Elizabeth's confidence in her power of persuasion grew. She decided to test it on the Massachusetts state legislature. At the same time, rumblings were being heard regarding reform of mental institutions. Yet the question of how and why people became asylum patients had hardly been raised before Elizabeth Packard began asking.

Elizabeth soon found a champion in Senator Samuel E. Sewall of Boston. At the time the two met, Sewall had been active in women's causes for twenty years. Known as a highly progressive politician, he had introduced into the Massachusetts senate a bill making married women the legal owners of their own property. He had worked to free a woman wrongfully committed to an institution by her husband and maintained a keen interest in expanding personal liberties.

At Elizabeth's suggestion, Sewall drafted a petition to change existing commitment laws. She canvassed Boston, gathering signatures from community leaders, telling her story, and selling books in the process. Finally, she and two other women who had been unjustly committed appeared before a select committee of the Massachusetts congress. The law was promptly amended and passed.

Elizabeth traveled on to Connecticut, where she encountered both support as well as personal attacks, including opposition from psychiatrists who feared for the autonomy of their practices. Meanwhile, she kept writing and arranged for publication of another book.

After a period of caring for her father before his death, she returned to Illinois with letters of recommendation from Senator Sewall and other renowned politicians. She quickly enlisted the assistance of Judge James B. Bradwell and his attorney wife, Myra Bradwell, publisher of the *Chicago Legal News*. They helped her draw up a petition to the Illinois legislature to change the commitment procedure. The law had been amended after her trial, possibly due in part to the attending publicity, but it lacked the teeth to guarantee its enforcement and was being violated frequently.

Again, Elizabeth gathered signatures and support from the press and distinguished citizens of Chicago, including the mayor. Governor Richard Oglesby assisted her in getting the bill before the legislators, in spite of his friendship with Elizabeth's old nemesis, Dr. McFarland.

The bill, which became known as "Mrs. Packard's Personal Liberty Bill," was subjected to hard lobbying both for and against, including organized opposition by Dr. McFarland and his cohorts. Eventually it passed. Elizabeth was so concerned about seeing it enacted that she physically followed the document through each step, carrying it from place to place, locating it when it was lost, and waiting while the governor signed it. She even followed the messenger to the secretary of state's office to witness the last required signature. The Packard Bill established that any administrator of a hospital or asylum who accepted or kept a person not declared insane by a jury was to be subject to a fine and imprisonment, and that those inmates previously confined without a trial would now be entitled to one.

Elizabeth's efforts in Illinois ultimately led to the passage of two additional personal liberty laws, enacted in 1865 and 1867. Myra Bradwell later took steps to make sure they remained on the books. She vigorously campaigned against a "private madhouse" bill introduced shortly after the personal liberty laws, which would authorize commitment of anyone to a state asylum without trial, upon the certification of two doctors. Bradwell, who wrote of the dangers such a law would impose, lobbied against it for twenty years as it kept coming up for vote. Primarily due to her efforts, the law was never passed.

Based again on her personal experience, Elizabeth next embarked upon a crusade for children. At that time, all children past the "tender age" were considered the property of their fathers, and no woman could get custody without going through a divorce that determined who was legally entitled to care for the children.

Her work for wives also took on a new direction. Through her writing, Elizabeth had earned enough money to buy and pay for a small home in Chicago, but under existing law it was legally the property of her husband. With the help of her son Samuel, who was now an attorney, she drafted one of the early married-women's property rights bills, entitling wives to retain rights in their earnings. She worked on another bill to establish equal rights in a marriage and between parents. Again she traveled to Springfield, where she became embroiled in the legislative battle. Eventually, versions of both her bills passed.

When she sought to introduce similar bills in Massachusetts, Elizabeth was pleased to learn that her old ally Senator Sewall was one step ahead of her. Massachusetts had recently granted equal parental rights to mothers, so she immediately sued for custody of the three Packard children who were still minors. With many prominent supporters, plus the help of Senator Sewall, Elizabeth was confident that she would emerge victorious. So, apparently, was Theophilus. He did not fight the suit and was in turn granted unlimited visitation rights.

Subsequently, the entire family relocated to Chicago, where the six children lived with their mother, and their father took up residence nearby. While the situation was not exactly idyllic after so many difficult years, the family maintained a courteous relationship and remained in close proximity until the 1871 Chicago fire destroyed a great deal of their property and the older children scattered to seek their fortunes elsewhere.

Her parenting duties put aside for awhile, Elizabeth returned to lobbying. Since two of her sons had moved to Iowa, she targeted it next. She had come to believe that an important element of justice for those confined in asylums was their right to write and receive uncensored letters. In this way, she reasoned, their true mental state, any instances of mistreatment, and other essential factors would not be concealed from those who needed to know.

Elizabeth approached Governor C.C. Carpenter, who became her champion, as did the chair of the Commission on Insane Asylums. The bill was passed, and the Iowa government went further to establish a committee to oversee its enforcement, as well as to monitor conditions of the state's institutions to assure compliance with regulations.

Elizabeth went on to New York, where charges of improper conditions of confinement and mistreatment had been highly publicized, much to the governor's concern. Through Elizabeth's efforts, a new law was enacted providing for the licensing of asylums, as well as for oversight and inspection.

The laws Elizabeth Packard helped establish were replicated in other states, as she continued to campaign nationwide, proposing bills, overseeing their metamorphosis, and presiding over their final passage and enactment. Her strategy was now established: She would seek out influential people and enlist their assistance, while simultaneously selling her books and pamphlets. She was savvy about locating a community's prominent judges, clergy, doctors, lawyers, and business leaders and rallying their support. The names of such sponsors were then printed in the pamphlets given to legislators as testament to the bill's popular and powerful backing. Elizabeth also spoke, lobbied, and wrote (sometimes anonymously) to the local press. She still suffered the occasional nasty personal attack that could reduce her to tears, but she persevered.

Eventually Elizabeth took her efforts to Washington, where she began by befriending the president's wife and winning Mrs. Grant's support for a national bill to require U.S. postal boxes in all asylums. Belva Lockwood, a successful Washington lawyer, offered her assistance. Although the drafted bill was never passed, various states subsequently enacted such laws for both mail and telephone communications. In many ways Elizabeth Packard carried on the work of Dorothea Dix, the well-known crusader for the mentally ill who also worked for prison reform.

Over the next fifteen years Elizabeth Packard went on to campaign in twenty-five more states. She visited asylums and spoke with inmates to learn of their problems and needs. She has been credited with directly effecting innumerable changes in the commitment and treatment procedures for those confined to mental institutions. Even when her efforts to change the law were not ultimately successful, she had a tremendous impact in raising public awareness and concern. In later years, it was estimated that she spent about half her considerable income on her own efforts to help the institutionalized. At least thirty-four bills were directly affected by her influence.

BELVA
LOCKWOOD

1830 – 1917

Belva Lockwood once asked, "Has God given one half of his creatures talents and gifts that are but a mockery—wings but not to fly?" Throughout her long life she proved over and over that gender need pose no limits on the heights to which any human being can soar.

Lockwood was the first American woman to complete a course of study at a university law school. Apprenticing remained the more common form of legal training for lawyers of both genders until the very late nineteenth century. This was an advantage for women and other minorities, who were frequently denied formal admission to law schools and bar associations. But it also led to lax standards for gaining legal credentials. Bar admission, for example, was rumored to be available to any Indiana man who could tell two funny stories (one for men only), one lie, and drink two glasses of whiskey. Thus, as the turn of the century approached, many states began to establish educational standards for bar admission.

Lockwood was born Belva Ann Bennett to a New York farm family. A fearless, curious, and precocious child, she read the entire Bible by the age of ten and once tried to walk on water. After eighth grade, she was forced to quit school because of a lack of funds and family opposition to her continued education. Like many young women she went on to teach, earning money to further her own education in the process. She married Uriah McNall in 1848 and had a daughter, at the same time working with her husband on his farm and at his lumber mill. She also continued to study, and wrote articles for newspapers and magazines.

Belva was widowed after five years of marriage when Uriah died after an accident at the mill. Left with a four-year-old daughter to support, she resumed teaching and again began to pursue her own education, although it meant a wrenching separation from little Lura, who lived with Belva's parents while Belva attended Genesee College. Her teaching career was successful, and she became preceptress of the Lockport, New York, Union Girls' School, where she sought to implement such progressive and controversial activities as gymnastics, public speaking, skating, and nature walks.

A meeting with Susan B. Anthony increased Belva's interest in women's rights. She continued teaching around the state of New York, then moved to Washington, D.C., in 1866. There she taught for a year before opening her own school, one of the capital's first private co-educational schools. She also lectured on suffrage, often enduring jeers, ridicule, and vegetables rolled up the aisle by hecklers. But it was at just such an event that she met her second husband, Dr. Ezekiel Lockwood, a dentist twenty-seven years her senior, whom she married in 1868 and who assisted her in supervising the school until his death nine years later.

Dr. Lockwood encouraged his wife's interest in the law and helped her run the school so she could pursue a formal legal education. In 1869 Belva Lockwood sought admission to Georgetown, Howard, and Columbian colleges (the latter to become Georgetown University). She was turned away by each institution, but the rejection by Columbian was especially ludicrous. In a letter to Lockwood, the president of the college predicted her admission would be likely to distract the attention of the young men in class. Finally, in 1871, she was admitted to the capital's new National University.

Gaining admission to law school was only the first hurdle faced by nineteenth-century women aspiring to a law degree. Female students were frequently subjected to humiliation and outright hostility by professors and classmates. When Belva Lockwood began classes at National University Law School, the fourteen women in the class were made to feel so unwelcome by the male students that only two remained by the end of the first semester. Moreover, she and her sister students were not allowed to participate in regular class discussions with men, but had to recite separately. After male students whined about the presence of women, the remaining two were not even allowed to attend the lectures, although they were still enrolled and paying tuition. Lockwood and Lydia Hall persevered through graduation, however, only to encounter more obstacles.

The male students threatened to boycott the graduation ceremony if the women were honored with the rest of the class—or if their names were so much as listed on the commencement program. The administration capitulated, removing the names of Belva Lockwood and Lydia Hall from the program and withholding their diplomas. While the women were outraged, they expected to receive their degrees by mail a short time later. Yet some professors wanted to withdraw the diplomas altogether to "save the school's reputation." This created a rift among faculty members. Additionally, Ulysses S. Grant, president of the United States, was also president of the law school and thus had to approve and sign all diplomas. There was speculation that Grant would not take sides in the controversy among the faculty but would delay his decision indefinitely.

At this point Hall gave up on ever receiving her diploma. But Lockwood, although fearful she was pursuing a lost cause, was determined to obtain what she had earned. Applying for admission to the Washington, D.C., courts, she campaigned on behalf of President Grant's opponent, the abolitionist Horace Greeley, and practiced in the lower courts, where Supreme Court admission was not required.

By 1873, she was tired of waiting for the issue to be resolved. She wrote a scathing letter to President Grant, challenging his authority as president of the university and demanding her diploma. She did not receive a written reply, but two weeks later her signed diploma arrived by mail.

The District of Columbia bar had changed its rules to admit women in 1871, so Lockwood had become a member upon her graduation in 1873. But she was refused the right to plead before the federal claims court or gain admission to the U.S. Supreme Court, based on the English tradition of only males becoming barristers. Myra Bradwell championed Lockwood's case in the *Chicago Legal News*, where her scathing indictment of the United States Supreme Court pointed out the absurdity of an American court relying on English tradition. Lockwood began her own personal siege against Congress, in which she invoked the assistance of pro-suffrage senators, including Aaron A. Sargent of California and George F. Hoar of Massachusetts.

Lockwood also campaigned directly to senators and spread word of her cause through the press, garnering widespread publicity and support. She persevered until 1878, when Congress finally passed a bill giving female attorneys the right to practice in the federal courts. The "Lockwood bill" was signed into law by President Hayes in 1879. Female attorneys could now pursue cases through the nation's highest court. In March 1879, Belva Lockwood became the first woman admitted to practice before the United States Supreme Court.

Lockwood went on to build a lucrative practice in the capital, passionately crusading for equality for all individuals. A year after her own admission, she sponsored the first southern black, Samuel R. Lowery, to be admitted to practice before the United States Supreme Court. One of the founders of Washington's first suffrage association, she remained active in the various conventions, addressing congressional committees and working for equal-pay legislation. She helped sister attorney Ellen Spencer Mussey and others involved with the district's Federation of Women's Clubs to secure passage of a law improving property rights for married women in the district.

She urged the inclusion of suffrage clauses in statehood bills for Oklahoma, Arizona, and New Mexico.

Lockwood's favorite cases involved suits against the United States government. She developed a specialty in soldiers' and sailors' claims for back pay. She also lobbied to change unfair laws, such as the one upholding a cap on the earnings of female government workers. Lockwood wrote a bill providing for equal pay and helped push it through Congress. She became well known in Washington both for her considerable skill in the law and for her habit of riding her tricycle to court.

Lockwood practiced for a time with two other female lawyers, Marilla Ricker and Lavinia Dundore. This trio, known as "the Three Graces," often raised the eyebrows of Washington's elite. One spring day they held a footrace through the suburban streets of the capital. Lockwood won.

Lockwood's law practice was both successful and lucrative. She was one of a team of lawyers that represented the Eastern Cherokee Indian Nation in a 1906 case which resulted in a $5 million settlement against the United States, based on violation of the treaty that led to the tragic "Trail of Tears" relocation of the tribe in 1838.

Lockwood ran for president on the Equal Rights Party ticket in 1882. During her campaign across the nation she shrugged off persistent ridicule. Newspaper stories charged her with such scandalous acts as wearing scarlet underwear and bribing judges with chocolate caramels. Yet Lockwood drew attention and widespread admiration from many sectors. In some cities, young men from local "Mother Hubbard" political clubs marched in long, baggy dresses and broad-brimmed bonnets to show their support. They took to the streets with brooms, advocating "a clean sweep with Mrs. Lockwood." She credited these goofy supporters with winning her a considerable number of votes in Indiana. Her platform emphasized equal rights for all, including blacks, American Indians, immigrants, and women. She also supported uniform marriage and divorce laws. When Lockwood became the first woman to make a serious run for president, she pointed out that although women could not yet vote, there was no reason they could not be voted for! She won over four thousand votes—all, of course, from men. A second run for president in 1888 drew fewer votes but increased her visibility. As Lockwood's career aroused public interest, she became increasingly popular on the lecture circuit, where she proved herself a forceful, distinguished, witty, and entertaining speaker. She continued to work for women's rights and other social causes, such as prison reform, lecturing until well into her eighties.

Lockwood was also an advocate of world peace and an early member of the Universal Peace Union, founded by Alfred Love. She served on the editorial board of its newspaper and became one of its chief lobbyists, working hard to advance the cause of peace on national and international levels. She even served on the nominating committee of the Nobel Peace Prize. True to her legal training, Lockwood urged the use of arbitration as a means of peacefully resolving problems among those embroiled in disputes, from individuals to nations. She attended the first World Peace Conference in Geneva in 1886, at the request of the U.S. State Department.

Lockwood is credited with single-handedly convincing the United States Congress to open the nation's highest court to female attorneys. Always willing to advise, help, and encourage aspiring female attorneys from all over the United States, she became an inspiration to many who were to follow her into a legal career.

She argued her last case in court at eighty-four, and participated in Woodrow Wilson's campaign at the age of eighty-seven. Near the end of her long life, she remarked, "I have not raised the dead, but I have awakened the living." Belva Lockwood was inducted into the National Women's Hall of Fame in 1983. Her image appeared on a U.S. postage stamp, part of the Great American Series, issued in 1986.

MYRA COLBY
BRADWELL

1831 – 1894

MYRA COLBY BRADWELL WAS A COLORFUL AND OUTSPOKEN character who became famous in the mid-nineteenth century for her work as the publisher of the *Chicago Legal News*. During her twenty-five years as editor-in-chief, Bradwell edited some 1,300 issues. Amazingly, she also found time to advocate, write, and work toward the enactment of many legal reforms in laws affecting women, children, and the allegedly insane.

Myra Colby was born in New England, but she moved to Illinois with her parents as an adolescent and always considered the prairie state her home. Both of her parents were active in the antislavery movement. As a child, she often heard the story of close family friend Elijah Lovejoy, a newspaper publisher and abolitionist who was murdered in Illinois in 1837 by a pro-slavery mob. This likely influenced her lifelong devotion to causes of freedom.

Myra Colby was popular as a young woman, enjoying the attention of many suitors. While studying at the Elgin Seminary, she met James Bradwell, a hard-working young man who was financing his education and study of law by doing manual labor. James was the son of immigrant parents, and most of Myra's family staunchly opposed the match. Finally the couple eloped, chased out of town by Myra's brother Frank as he brandished a shotgun. The Bradwells then traveled to Memphis, where they opened a private school and taught together for two years. During this period James passed the bar exam, and the couple started a family. Tragically, two of their children died in childhood, but a girl, Bessie, and a son, Thomas, survived to adulthood.

When the couple returned to Chicago, the Colbys welcomed them with open arms. James even became a partner with attorney Frank Colby, and Myra soon began to "read law" in her husband's office. When the Civil War started, she became active in many programs to support the effort, serving as president of the Chicago Soldiers' Aid Society for a period of years. The Bradwells became friends with Abraham Lincoln and his wife during this time. Both Bradwells were ardent suffrage supporters.

Meanwhile, Myra had identified a need in the legal community and orchestrated a plan to fill it. The *Chicago Legal News* debuted on October 3, 1868, with Myra Bradwell at the helm. Naysayers predicted, naturally, that "Mrs. Judge Bradwell" could never make a go of such an immense undertaking. But within ten years the *Chicago Legal News* was the most successful legal publication in America.

Her first step was to make the paper essential to judges, lawyers, and legislators. To this end, she took advantage of the long lapse of time between the Illinois legislature's passage of new laws and their official publication by the state. As soon as a new law was passed, Bradwell obtained a copy and published it. She also reported important judicial opinions and news from the legal community. The paper became an indispensable tool to every legal practitioner in Illinois.

Bradwell wisely presented the paper as a publication solely devoted to disseminating legal news—yet it also gave her an extremely powerful forum for expressing her own views. The paper's influence was tremendous. Bradwell used it to advocate the cause of women's rights and her other agendas, but her style was sufficiently intelligent, moderate, and well reasoned to draw widespread accolades even from those who disagreed with much of the editorial content.

Bradwell also published editorials on topics as diverse as shabby maintenance of the Cook County Courthouse and shameful conditions in the local poorhouse. She avoided an overly heavy tone by the consistent use of humor. Sometimes she wrote verse poking fun at the law; often she published entertaining anecdotes about happenings in court, sometimes to make a point, sometimes for sheer entertainment. The *Chicago Legal News* gained a reputation as an excellent publication—always balanced, useful, and prompt. It drew rave reviews, except from the predictable few who sniffed at the thought of a female undertaking such an independent enterprise. Bradwell soon began reporting federal decisions, and circulation grew. Soon law offices not only in Illinois but also throughout the Midwest and the rest of America subscribed to the paper. For some twenty years, it was the most widely read legal newspaper in the country.

The *Chicago Legal News* company not only published the weekly paper but also developed into a printing and bindery company with clients nationwide. Courts and law firms from other states requested similar information reporting new legal developments in their areas, and Bradwell responded. She also began publishing law books and legal forms. Yet Bradwell felt the absence of a personal goal: her own license to practice.

In 1869, Bradwell took and passed the Chicago bar exam. When she petitioned for a license to practice, however, her application was denied by the Illinois Supreme Court. Bradwell relied on a statute similar to an Iowa law that extended those statutes referring only to men to include women as well. But the court sidestepped the statutory language by denying Bradwell admission on the basis of her status as a married woman. At that time, wives were prohibited from entering into contracts, inheriting property, or obtaining goods and services in their own name.

Bradwell was, predictably, outraged. She submitted a supplemental brief to the court citing recent changes in the law giving married women the right to own and manage property. This time she was denied on the basis of gender alone. Bradwell published both denials in the *Chicago Legal News* and declared the actions of the state supreme court to be in violation of the political rights of Illinois women. She took her case to the United States Supreme Court, where she was represented by the eminent Wisconsin senator and constitutional law expert Matthew H. Carpenter.

Carpenter argued that under the Fourteenth Amendment and Article IV of the United States Constitution, Bradwell was entitled to the same privileges and immunities as any other citizen, and such guarantee included her right to practice law. The court took two years to decide the case, but in 1873, seven of its eight justices ruled against her on the grounds that constitutional privileges and immunities do not include the right to practice law. The U.S. Supreme Court opinion dragged out the same weary justification that had been heard over and over throughout the nineteenth century to deny women equal opportunities. According to the court: "The nature, timidity, and delicacy which belongs to the female sex evidently unfits it for many of the occupations of civil life."

Shortly after her bar license was denied, the Illinois Supreme Court heaped insult upon injury by denying her the right to be a notary public. Yet indomitable Myra Bradwell continued to make news, and to report it.

Myra Bradwell combined her gifts of logic, emotion, and wit to insure that no slur against female attorneys be allowed to pass, especially when it targeted a friend. When Belva Lockwood was denied admission in Maryland by a judge who called her a "wandering woman," Bradwell swiftly claimed the last word, shaming the judge in print for his lack of chivalry and referring to him as a "judicial tyrant." Another judge won the label *fossilized* for similar transgressions. Bradwell also supported Wisconsin attorney Lavinia Goodell when Chief Justice Ryan of the Wisconsin Supreme Court rendered his decision denying her the right to practice law.

In an 1890 article on women in the law, attorney Lelia Robinson added her own commentary to Justice Ryan's opinion: "The decision in this case did Chief Justice Ryan little credit, for he allowed himself to depart from the legal point at issue to discuss the question of 'women's sphere' from a standpoint of domestic economy quite out of *his* proper sphere as a judge on the bench."

The great Chicago fire of 1871 destroyed the offices of the *News*, but as legend has it, twelve-year-old Bessie Bradwell managed to save the subscribers' book. The *Chicago Legal News* never missed an issue. Myra boarded a train with the list of subscribers, and a Milwaukee publisher filled in until the company was rebuilt.

She also waged a significant battle on behalf of a close friend. After Lincoln was assassinated, Mary Todd Lincoln suffered terribly with the unbearable grief of the death of her husband and three of her sons. In 1875, Mary, who had been living in Florida, decided to visit her surviving son, Robert Lincoln, a Chicago attorney. Although prone to compulsive spending, Mary Todd Lincoln had displayed no signs of what could legitimately be called insanity. Yet Robert Lincoln took advantage of the lax laws of the day to file a petition for an insanity hearing. Thanks to the past efforts of Elizabeth Packard and others, charges of insanity had to be heard by a jury before a person could be involuntarily committed to an institution. Yet the hearings were nonetheless subject to scam and manipulation.

Much controversy has surrounded the events that led to Mary Todd Lincoln's confinement in an asylum. Yet it is undisputed that two of the doctors who testified against her had never met her. In the 1870s, a woman's refusal to submit to male authority, including the orders of an adult son, was frequently deemed an indication of insanity. It didn't take long for the all-male jury to pronounce Mary insane, and she was taken to Bellevue Place in Batavia, Illinois.

Myra and James Bradwell were distraught at this treatment of their friend. They had helped Mary get a home on the same Chicago street after President Lincoln was assassinated, and James had served as her attorney on various matters. Myra made immediate plans to visit her friend in the asylum and intervene. But she was outraged to learn that she could neither see nor write to Mary without Robert Lincoln's consent.

Journalism was Myra's weapon of choice, and she did not hesitate to put the wheels of an exposé in motion. *The Bloomington Courier,* a downstate newspaper, published Myra's piece on Mary Lincoln's confinement. A public outcry ensued, pressuring the asylum's head doctor to allow Myra visitation and correspondence rights, and she and Mary began to exchange letters almost daily.

Mary, who had a sister living in Springfield, Illinois, wanted to be released to go live with her. Myra and James Bradwell were determined to aid these efforts. Meanwhile, Robert Lincoln, equally determined to keep his mother confined, enlisted the aid of Dr. Andrew McFarland, who had played such a prominent part in the life and wrongful commitment of Elizabeth Packard. But as competent an attorney as Robert Lincoln may have been, he was no match for Myra Bradwell. Ever the shrewd strategist, she brought along a Mr. Wilke on one of her visits to Mary. Frank Wilke was in fact the editor of *The Chicago Times.* And he wrote a second exposé, which reached an even broader audience.

A short time later, Mary Todd Lincoln was released to live with her sister, and a few months thereafter the Cook County Court declared her sane. Mary spent her remaining years dividing her time between her sister's Springfield home and a residence in France. She made many gifts of gratitude to the Bradwell family for their assistance.

Myra Bradwell never hesitated stating her opinions or championing her beliefs. She sought to actively effect reform of the legal profession and the judicial process, with the goal of elevating standards of professional conduct so that "the disreputable shysters who now disgrace the profession could be driven from it." She strongly believed that all lawyers had a duty of integrity. She vigorously campaigned against such practices as bribery of jurors, a common problem in Chicago during the latter nineteenth century. She castigated lawyers who breached the trust of their clients through fraud or other abuses of power as the "highwaymen" of the profession. She had no patience for attorneys who let alcohol get the best of them, and identified drunkards both by name and embarrassing deed. Not coincidentally, she also helped eliminate the court's power to punish the press for contempt.

But Bradwell is best known for her work in helping to open the legal profession to other women. She reported in 1879 that in thirty of the thirty-seven states, women were still not allowed to practice law. The *Chicago Legal News* consistently reported which law schools would and would not admit women, and urged those who lagged behind the times to change. Those who heeded the call, such as the University of Chicago, drew lavish praise.

Bradwell mentored Alta Hulett and Ada Kepley, who were studying law in Illinois, and assisted them in seeking reversal of the precedent established in her own case. Meanwhile, Bradwell and Hulett drafted and pushed through a statute securing the right of all citizens to freely select any occupation, profession, or employment without regard to sex. In 1873, Alta Hulett became the first woman licensed to practice in Illinois. Bradwell recorded her triumphs in the paper and subsequently eulogized her as a model for others when she died just three and a half years after her admission to practice.

Bradwell next teamed up with Belva Lockwood, who had to overcome endless obstacles before finally gaining admission to the Washington, D.C., bar. The two lawyers became friends after Bradwell invited Lockwood to speak in Chicago. When the Court of Claims denied Lockwood admission, Bradwell reprinted the court's opinion, which was rife with absurdities, and neatly skewered each lapse of logic. The two then traveled to Washington to lobby Congress to pass a statute providing that no qualified woman should be disbarred from practice before any federal court on account of gender.

Myra Bradwell crusaded for over twenty-five years for the right of women to practice law, and these efforts directly resulted in the admission of women to the majority of courts, paving the way for the final holdouts to give in one by one. She also worked for the right of women to work in other fields, believing everyone had the right to enter any occupation or profession she chose. She gloried in such stories as one she published about a woman who had been ruled eligible by the U.S. Secretary of the Treasury to captain a Mississippi steamboat. No doubt she enjoyed quoting the opinion, which emphasized the right of any person to "paddle his or her own canoe."

Myra Bradwell was finally granted a license to practice law in 1890 by the Illinois Supreme Court, acting on its own motion. Though Bradwell continued her publishing and suffrage work rather than practice law herself, both her son and daughter became attorneys.

In an 1890 article profiling female lawyers in the United States, attorney Lelia J. Robinson quoted a western paper that stated, "Through ex-judge James B. Bradwell, the family of which he is head achieved legal distinction. Through Myra, his wife, it attained legal celebrity."

The Bradwell legacy was passed on to the next generation. Daughter Bessie Bradwell Helmer, the valedictorian of her class at Northwestern University Law School, took over the editing of the *Chicago Legal News* when her mother finally retired from the position, only days before her death in 1894.

CLARA SHORTRIDGE FOLTZ

1849 – 1934

I N 1878, THE UNIVERSITY OF CALIFORNIA OPENED THE HASTINGS College of Law with the goal of raising standards for admission to the legal profession in California. The school sought the kind of prestige possessed by eastern universities, and was one of the first to require a three-year course of study for a law degree. But like those of its eastern counterparts, the doors to Hastings were firmly closed to women. Clara Foltz, upon being denied enrollment at Hastings College of Law, was told that "the rustle of the lady's garments would distract the attention of the young gentlemen."

Clara Shortridge Foltz did not take kindly to closed doors. Described as stubborn, passionate, and smart, she had taught school in Illinois from the age of fifteen, then eloped with "a young Pennsylvania Dutchman of wandering disposition and slight promise" to move west.

Foltz, who enjoyed the advantage of an utterly fearless nature, often proudly proclaimed that she was descended from "the heroic stock of Daniel Boone." She moved to San Jose, California, in 1874 with her husband, Jeremiah Foltz, and their five children. Two years later, the couple divorced, and Clara faced the challenge of supporting a large family alone at the age of twenty-seven. Turning to lecturing on suffrage and the equality of the sexes, she not only began to earn a fairly good income but also became active in the community, helping establish its first paid fire department.

The daughter of an Indiana lawyer and minister who campaigned for Abraham Lincoln, Foltz developed an early interest in law and politics. With the encouragement of her parents and her brother, she embarked on a legal career. She later remarked that she did not antic-ipate the hardships and humiliation she would have to endure.

In 1876 there were no female attorneys in California, but Foltz was determined to apprentice. Despite her perseverance, she met with repeated condescension from attorneys who echoed the platitude that a woman's place was in the home. At first her only offers were for teaching jobs, but she finally found a position with attorney C. C. Stephens in San Jose.

California statutes of the day specifically stated that women could not be admitted to the bar. Foltz immediately campaigned to change the words of the statute from "any white male citizen" to "any citizen or person." Foltz had teamed with the aptly named Laura De Force Gordon to achieve passage of the women lawyers' bill. Gordon, a vig-orous speaker and formidable proponent for women's rights, made frequent unsuccessful runs for public office, but built her career as an accomplished journalist. The "women lawyers' bill" drew a storm of opposition during debate on the California senate floor. In later writ-ings Foltz colorfully recalled, "Narrow-gauge statesmen grew red as turkey gobblers mouthing their ignorance against the bill, and staid old grangers who had never seen the inside of a courthouse seemed to have been given the gift of tongues and delivered themselves of maiden speeches pregnant with eloquent nonsense."

Yet a few voices of reason broke through, with one assemblyman citing contributions of women in medicine. And though Foltz's passionate efforts took two long years, they were ultimately successful. At the last minute, she stormed the governor's chambers to convince William Irwin to resurrect the discarded bill, and stood over him as he signed it at the stroke of midnight on the last day of the legislative session.

Foltz established herself as a skillful practitioner from the start of her legal career, but she wanted a formal education to serve her clients with greater confidence. Together, Foltz and Gordon were determined to break down the barriers of Hastings Law School. Foltz applied for admission in 1878, but her application was tabled until the next board meeting, scheduled for early 1879. In the meantime, Foltz and Gordon simply started showing up for classes. They were mercilessly teased by male students. Foltz noted with satisfaction many years later that she never again saw or heard tell of any member of the class other than herself and Laura De Force Gordon.

As soon as the two women began auditing classes, the Hastings board hurriedly met and issued a resolution establishing that women would not be admitted to the school. The two were summarily thrown out of class by a janitor. As an astute writer for the *Stockton Herald* suggested, "Those directors will repent of their rash consideration before those two ladies die." His prophecy more than bore itself out. After Foltz and Gordon were shut out of the classroom, Foltz went to Justice Hastings, founder of the college, who believed the women had the law on their side. He wrote a note telling the janitor to let her in, but his order was subject to approval by the board. The board, predictably, refused to budge. Foltz and Gordon filed suit.

As the trial began, the judge issued a writ of mandamus ordering Hastings to admit Clara Foltz or to show cause why it could not, and he scheduled a hearing to give Hastings this opportunity. At this hearing, Foltz argued that the acts creating the University of California and all its colleges, along with the rules promulgated under those acts, applied to Hastings. Since those provisions did not exclude women, she argued that Hastings did not have the authority to make rules inconsistent with the regulations governing the university as a whole. In response, the board argued that Hastings, being privately funded and governed by a special trust giving the board of directors authority, was not bound by the general university rules. The board unwisely told the court it did not have the power to tell it what to do. Moreover, it dredged up the familiar refrain about a woman's proper sphere, going so far as to claim that a woman's beauty could make an impartial jury impossible if she appeared as counsel for a criminal.

Predictably, the newspapers had a field day, often obscuring reports of courtroom events with detailed, irrelevant accounts of the litigants' appearance. The *San Francisco Chronicle* provided readers with a description of not only the women's clothing but their hair-styles as well. The *Chronicle* headline of February 25, 1879, left no doubt as to press priorities in the case. "Two Lady Lawyers Who Demand Admission to the Hastings Law College—How They Dress." The reporter went on to wax poetic on Foltz and Gordon's comeliness. Foltz was described as having her profuse hair "done in braids which fall backwards from the crown of her head like an alpine glacier lit by setting sun." About Gordon the reporter gushed, "She had curls enough to supply half the thin-haired ladies of San Francisco with respectable switches." It is easy to laugh this off as a quaint nineteenth-century quirk until one recalls the frenzied cover-age of prosecutor Marcia Clark's hairstyle and wardrobe during the 1995 O.J. Simpson murder trial.

The Hastings directors were shocked when the judge found in favor of Clara Foltz and Laura De Force Gordon, and their appeal to the California Supreme Court resulted in the same decision. One jus-tice remarked that Foltz's arguments were among the best he had ever heard. As a last gasp, the Hastings board passed a resolution to exclude anyone already admitted to the California bar from the law school, but the California Supreme Court was one step ahead of them. It had expressly declared in its opinion that those already admitted to practice must be allowed entry to Hastings. Although Foltz and Gordon had by this time become highly skilled lawyers with little practical need of additional training, they returned to Hastings two years after being escorted out by the janitor.

Foltz was later to recall this case as the greatest in her career, which spanned over half a century. She began her practice with a focus on probate and divorce, but since many indigents sought and received her counsel, she branched into criminal defense work. Appalled by the inequities of the criminal justice system, she advocated for penal reform and other changes, directly affecting the passage of several major laws that remain in effect. The most notable dealt with the development of a public defender system. This program became a pet project, and Foltz labored long and hard to write a model bill specifying qualifications, duties, salary, terms, and other details of the office. She wrote articles for legal journals advocating the system and represented the state in the 1893 Congress of Jurisprudence and Law Reform, where she lobbied for her bill. The Foltz defender bill, as it came to be called, was not adopted by California until 1921, but it eventually became law in thirty-two states.

Foltz and Gordon continued working for women's suffrage while maintaining an active law practice. Gordon gained notoriety after winning for her client acquittal in a sensational murder trial. Foltz continued to handle a broad variety of cases, often in the face of continuing rudeness and harassment by opponents. When an opposing attorney once suggested that Foltz should be at home raising her children, she retorted, "A woman had better be in almost any business than raising men such as you." Accustomed to direct attacks by opposing counsel, Foltz learned to weather them gracefully. Once, a San Francisco district attorney stated in his closing argument, "She is a *woman,* she cannot be expected to reason; God almighty decreed her limitations—this young woman will lead you by her sympathetic presentation of this case to violate your oaths and let a guilty man go free." Foltz handily destroyed both his legal position and personal attack with an appeal to the jury's common sense. She won the case and became renowned for her ability to calmly demolish opponents.

Foltz was also involved in other reforms that weren't so sweeping but were nevertheless highly significant. She worked to abolish the use of iron cages that held prisoners in courtrooms in San Francisco. She saw that juvenile and adult prisoners were separated in the city's jails. She drafted and achieved the 1893 passage of an act creating the first California prison parole system and advocated the adoption of indeterminate sentences as a tool for rehabilitation of inmates. Witnessing the many abuses by district attorneys, she strove to improve the prosecution system. In 1910, at the age of sixty-one, she was appointed deputy district attorney in Los Angeles, becoming the first woman to hold this post.

As a leader in the West Coast suffrage movement, Foltz often found it difficult to balance her busy law practice with the demands for her services as a speaker. After years of campaigning, she was gratified to see a suffrage amendment similar to one she had drafted years earlier pass the California legislature in 1911. Yet she continued to work for passage of the Nineteenth Amendment to guarantee all American women the right to vote.

For a time Foltz edited and published *New American Woman* magazine, in which she extensively voiced her views. She encouraged all women to understand basic legal principles and advised those contemplating legal careers. She went so far as to run, at the age of eighty-one, for governor of California in 1930. She managed to make a respectable showing, too, garnering several thousand votes.

Foltz's energy was boundless. She helped gain passage of laws giving women the right to serve as administrators, executors, and notaries public. She maintained a practice in New York City for a time, devoted to assisting immigrant women. Foltz also founded, edited, and published the *San Diego Bee* newspaper from 1887 to 1890. Later in life, Foltz regretted not spending more time with her children, but concluded in the end that the battle had been worthwhile.

Clara Foltz maintained an active law practice until her retirement at the age of eighty. Many credit her as the first woman to really earn a living from the practice of law. She was awarded a posthumous degree of juris doctor by Hastings College of Law in 1990, which was bestowed at the 1991 commencement. Despite her many achievements, this passionate visionary remained a realist. Once, when asked for her thoughts on practicing law, she remarked that she had found it to be "hard, unpoetic, and relentless."

LAURA DE FORCE GORDON

1838 – 1907

LAURA DE FORCE GORDON WAS PRESENTED WITH AN EXAMPLE of female determination early in her life, when her father was disabled by severe rheumatism and Mrs. De Force supported the family of nine children with her needlework.

Laura, born in Pennsylvania, embarked upon a career in public speaking and journalism as a young woman, lecturing throughout the East. She married a doctor, and the couple moved frequently, eventually settling in Lodi, California, in 1870. Laura became a pioneer advocate of women's rights in Nevada and California, as well as the Oregon and Washington Territories. She lectured frequently and helped found the California Woman's Suffrage Society in 1870. She even ran as an Independent Party candidate for state senator in 1871, receiving an impressive number of votes.

In 1873 Gordon began to focus her attention on newspaper work, editing the women's department of Stockton's *Narrow Gauge*. A short time later she was promoted to editor and publisher of the *Stockton Weekly Leader*, drawing much attention for her unusual role. With her knack for the business side of journalism, she turned the weekly publication into a daily. When she later sold the paper, she went on to edit the *Oakland Daily Democrat*. She also served for a time as an officer in the Pacific Coast Press Association, as well as a correspondent to other newspapers.

During the state legislative session of 1877–78, Gordon played what was called a "spirited and brilliant" part in lobbying for a bill drafted by her associate, Clara Shortridge Foltz, to allow women to practice law in California. This bill was passed at the same session in which the legislature recognized the founding of Hastings College of Law.

Along with Foltz, she applied for admission to Hastings College of Law in 1878, and the two began attending classes together. When they were expelled due to their gender, they partnered to successfully bring suit and argued their case to the Fourth District Court in San Francisco, then the California Supreme Court when the Hastings Board of Directors appealed. The high court ruled that Hastings must open its doors to female students. On December 6, 1879, Gordon and Foltz were admitted to the California Bar. Following their victory and subsequent studies, Foltz and Gordon maintained a law office in California for five years. While carrying on a successful practice in her San Francisco office, Gordon, now divorced, still managed to return to her Lodi ranch on the weekend to spend time with her nephew and other family members who had settled in the area. She later moved to Stockton although she continued to run the ranch.

Gordon was known as capable, eloquent in court, and conscientious in her practice. She won her first murder case within two months after being admitted to the bar. Her criminal cases, in particular, packed courtrooms with spectators. One drew special notoriety. The defendant, a man named Sproule, mistakenly shot and killed a young man named Andrews when he mistook him for someone

Sproule believed had seduced his wife. As described by Lelia J. Robinson in an 1890 article for *The Green Bag,* "It was a fearful tragedy, and the excitement was so great that the jail had to be guarded for a week to prevent the lynching of the prisoner." Gordon took on the defense against the advice of distinguished colleagues. As Robinson described it, Gordon "obtained a verdict of not guilty amidst the most deafening cheers of men and hysterical cries of women, half-weeping jurymen joining in the general clamor of rejoicing."

In 1885, Gordon was admitted to practice before the United States Supreme Court. Her successful defense of an Italian man living in California won her an honorary membership in the Royal Italian Literary Society of Rome.

Gordon was constantly active in Democratic campaigns, covering the California mining country in 1888 and 1890 and campaigning in Nebraska in 1892. Likewise, she was true to her dedication to feminist causes. She served as president of the California Woman's Suffrage Society for more than eleven years, campaigned in 1889 for suffrage in the Washington Territory, and twice served as a delegate to the National Woman's Suffrage Association. On several occasions she joined Susan B. Anthony in appeals for the vote.

Although Gordon was childless, she adopted a nephew, who accompanied her on her many travels. In 1901 she retired from the practice of law to devote herself to managing her Lodi ranch, where she lived until her death at the age of sixty-eight.

LYDA BURTON CONLEY

1854? – 1942?

L YDA BURTON CONLEY WAS A WYANDOT INDIAN WHO HAD A
reputation for thriving on trouble. She was to become the first
female Native American attorney in America. Born in the mid-
nineteenth century, Conley first came to public attention in 1904
when an Indian cemetery in which members of her family were
buried was scheduled to be razed to make way for a commercial
development project. When more conventional efforts to stop the
desecration proved fruitless, Conley and her sister, Lena Floating
Voice, placed warning signs around the cemetery boundaries and built
a hut near their parents' graves.

There they held a vigil, armed with loaded guns, in the
eight-by-six-foot abode known as "Fort Conley." The sisters were
determined that their parents' burial ground not be disturbed, no
matter how long they had to stand guard. Word went out that the
first man to turn sod over one of the family graves would either turn

another for the Conley sisters or have some other person perform a like service for himself.

Holding her gun as she manned her post in the shack, Lyda studied for the bar, wrote briefs, and prepared to represent herself—along with the Wyandot tribe—in a suit against the United States. Contractors who tore down signs and fences found them quickly replaced by the sisters. No shots were fired, but sticks and stones flew on at least one occasion. Once or twice, angry opponents dismantled the shack and burned the lumber—only to find it neatly rebuilt within forty-eight hours.

The siege continued far longer than the public expected. Ultimately, the standoff endured for six years. During this time the sisters gained the support of women's groups and others who sympathized with their cause. Although not yet admitted to the bar, Conley filed suit for an injunction in the United States District Court in Topeka, Kansas, to stop the planned desecration of the cemetery and the scheduled construction. When she lost, she prepared for battle before the United States Supreme Court.

Confident of victory, Lyda Conley filed a sixty-nine-page brief and went before the court to argue her case. The Supreme Court ruled against her, but she had garnered enough public support that the project was halted due to strong opposition. In 1912 she achieved what seemed a final victory when Congress passed a bill protecting the cemetery from disturbance and ruled that the land could not be sold. However, the conflict has flared up on several occasions over the years, with ongoing disagreement between the Kansas and Oklahoma branches of the Wyandot tribe. As a result of the endless dispute, culminating in a 1993 attempt by the Oklahoma Wyandots to move the bodies interred in the cemetery and build a casino on the land, the Kansas Wyandots have petitioned Congress for recognition as an independent tribe.

Lyda was finally admitted to the bar in 1910. She received many requests for legal assistance from other Native Americans and tribes across America. She continued to monitor the cemetery and took a few cases, although her strong sense of ethics reportedly limited her choice of clients, and she earned little money. However, she was often rewarded with traditional tokens of appreciation, including beaded moccasins and a bow and arrow set given by a Plains tribe. Conley, like many of her contemporaries, turned to other work to help make ends meet. She taught telegraphy at a business school and worked as a railroad telegraph operator to bolster her income. Like many early female lawyers, her commitment to a cause she believed in was more important to her than financial success.

Both Lyda Burton Conley and Lena Floating Voice were laid to rest in the cemetery they protected with such devotion. Lena's efforts to protect the sacred land have extended beyond her lifetime. Her tombstone is inscribed, "Cursed be the villain that molests these graves."

ESTHER McQUIGG
MORRIS

1814 – 1902

ESTHER McQUIGG WAS BORN IN PERU, ILLINOIS, ONE OF ELEVEN children. Orphaned at the age of eleven, she supported herself by doing housework for others. She started a millinery shop some years later, applying her talents to creating and selling ladies' hats.

Esther's first marriage ended when her husband died, leaving her with a young son. When she tried to settle his estate, she was appalled to find that women had no rights to their husbands' property, or even to their own children. Esther vowed then to devote her life to women's rights.

While still living in Illinois, she married John Morris. The couple settled down for twenty years to raise their sons, then joined the migration west to the Wyoming gold fields. After several moves, they settled in South Pass City, Wyoming, a boisterous gold rush camp where John became a saloon keeper.

Esther Morris was a woman of considerable stature, both professionally and physically. At nearly six-feet-tall and an ardent suffragist, she was known to be blunt of speech and explosive of temper. Yet Esther was equally renowned for her confidence, wit, and compassion. Though she could be formidable when challenged, she had a generally cheerful disposition.

Morris was among the first crusaders for women's suffrage to enjoy the direct results of her own efforts. In August 1869 she hosted a tea party at her home in South Pass City for prominent guests, including two candidates for representative to the first Wyoming territorial legislature. Morris asked both candidates to publicly pledge to introduce and work for the passage of an act conferring the right of suffrage upon women. Both agreed to do so. The Democratic candidate, Col. William H. Bright, was subsequently elected and made good on his promise. The night before the legislature opened, he drafted a historic document giving every woman twenty-one or older the right to vote at any election, as well as the right to hold office. The controversial bill, debated for a week, eventually passed. The governor signed it into law on December 10, 1869, making Wyoming women the first in the world to win full, equal suffrage.

Toasts were raised at many Cheyenne parties that night. At one, a legislator offered this tribute: "To the lovely ladies—once our superiors, now our equals." Congratulatory cables came from as far away as Great Britain and the king of Prussia. Through the efforts of Morris and other supporters of equality, bills granting women equal rights in property and child custody were passed in the same session, including a law giving widows the right to retain guardianship of their children. Historians suggest that the Wyoming legislature's enlightened attitude was motivated by both a respect for the equal efforts of hard-working pioneer women on the harsh frontier and a desire to draw more women to Wyoming, where only a sixth of the population was female.

When Wyoming women gained the right to vote there was some fear that their presence at the polls would upset the established order and cause an upheaval or even outbreaks of violence. In fact, the female presence considerably quieted the often boisterous and brawling events of election day. A respectful decorum prevailed, according to early accounts published in frontier newspapers.

The attendant right of women to serve on juries also caused a protest, many fearing that women would be too tender-hearted to send criminals to harsh punishments. Again, if anything, the opposite was true. It was reported that female-dominated juries did the job so well that there was a measurable exodus of hooligans from Wyoming.

When the suffrage bill passed, South Pass's presiding justice of the peace, a staunch opponent of equal suffrage, resigned with the snide aside that a woman might better fill the office. On Valentine's Day in 1870, Esther McQuigg Morris was named to that post by the county commissioners. Legend has it that Morris's kindness to an expectant mother, the wife of a young legislator, won her appointment to the bench through the bipartisan efforts of the legislator and the governor. In this way, Esther McQuigg Morris became the first female judge in America.

Judge Morris held court from a slab bench in her log cabin. Large crowds often gathered to observe the novel spectacle of a female judge. The office of justice of the peace must have been an immense challenge in this brawling frontier settlement, which included seven saloons, three breweries, and one wholesale liquor dealer to serve a population of 460. The legal climate of South Pass City was far from genteel. Shortly before Morris took the bench, Indian uprisings had led the government to issue firearms to all civilians. Insisting upon an orderly courtroom, she imposed certain rules to maintain decorum— including one requiring that all shooting irons be left outside. Despite her lack of formal legal training, Morris served with distinction and became admired for making rapid, fair decisions. She handed down seventy opinions, on cases ranging from claim jumping to assault, in the eight and a half months she presided, and earned the town's respect when faced with tough dilemmas. The first case brought before her, for example, involved a personal conflict: The former judge now regretted his decision to relinquish the office and tried to regain his post. Wisely, Judge Morris removed herself from the case.

The job of justice of the peace had its lighter side as well. Morris performed weddings, including one for a locally scandalous couple who had openly lived together for two years. One lawyer who had appeared before her commented respectfully, "To pettifoggers she showed no mercy, but her decisions were always just." She regarded her appointment as "a test of a woman's ability to hold public office," and pronounced herself satisfactory.

Most members of the community were impressed with her achievements, but her husband was unfortunately not among them. When he went so far as to make a scene in the courtroom, Judge Morris fined him for contempt, and when he refused to pay, she sent him straight to jail. Esther McQuigg Morris's motto was "Justice first, then after that the law." She often admonished quarreling lawyers to "Behave yourselves, boys."

After leaving office, Morris reflected on her career in an 1871 article in the *Laramie Sentinel*: "I have assisted in drawing a grand and petit jury, deposited a ballot, and helped canvass the voters after the electing, and in performing all those duties I do not know as I have neglected my family any more than in ordinary shopping."

Nevertheless, escalating domestic disputes between John and Esther took their toll. Esther eventually had to turn to the law for her own protection. In mid-1871, she swore out a warrant against her husband for assault and battery. A short time later the couple separated and Esther moved to Laramie, where her oldest son, Ed Slack, edited the local newspaper. In 1873 she was nominated for state representative on the women's ticket. While she withdrew from the nomination, she emphasized that she was in no way resigning from the women's cause.

Morris set an example for other Wyoming women who were to follow, such as Mary G. Bellamy, who became the first woman elected to a state legislature; and Nellie Taylor Ross, the first female governor. In 1962, Thyra Thomas became the first secretary of state elected to that position.

Morris, always dedicated to human rights, worked in the anti-slavery movement as well as suffrage. She also managed to find time to maintain a flower garden throughout her life, even in the rugged soil of South Pass City.

When Wyoming celebrated statehood in July 1890, Morris was honored as a pioneer for women and presented the ceremonial flag to the governor at the event. She in turn presided at a gathering honoring Susan B. Anthony, president of the American Suffrage Association, in Cheyenne, where Morris then lived. In 1892, when Morris was seventy-eight years old, she was elected a delegate to the national Republican convention in Cleveland.

Morris went on to enjoy a serene and content old age. When she died in 1902, her son gave a public eulogy: "Her quest for truth in the world has ended. Her mission in life has been fulfilled. The work she did for the elevation of womankind will be told in the years to come, when the purpose may be better understood."

In 1934, a monument to her memory was erected at South Pass, Wyoming. Today, Morris's log cabin has been restored and a marker placed. Fifty-one years after she sparked the first suffrage laws at her tea party, the Nineteenth Amendment—giving all American women the right to vote—was finally passed. In 1955, the Wyoming legislature was called upon to choose an outstanding citizen for the Wyoming niche in Statuary Hall in the capitol building. Esther McQuigg Morris was memorialized in a nine-foot bronze statue that dubs her the "Mother of Equal Rights." Another statue stands before the Wyoming state capitol in Cheyenne.

LEMMA
BARKELOO

1848? – 1870

LEMMA BARKELOO WAS ADMITTED TO WASHINGTON UNIVERSITY in St. Louis in 1869, to become the first American woman to formally study at a law school. Born in Brooklyn, New York, Barkeloo was studying music and achieving recognition as a performer when she received a substantial inheritance. Impulsively, she decided to become a lawyer. After applying to Harvard and Columbia and being flatly rejected, she turned her sights westward to St. Louis.

Barkeloo was known as a dedicated student who led her class of five, which included one lawyer with fifteen years' experience. Rather than complete law school, however, she opted to study for the bar after one year of formal education, a common practice at the time. After passing the exam, Barkeloo sought the advice of a judge she respected as to how best to begin her own practice. He advised her to return home to open her office so as to have the support of her family.

Nonetheless, Barkeloo ultimately decided to remain in the West. She felt the people there were more generous in their sentiments and would better sustain her practice. Barkeloo's instincts were right; opportunities for professional women did tend to be better in the western states, with their well-established appreciation of pioneers of all types. Four states—Illinois, Iowa, Michigan, and Wisconsin—offered the first law schools open to women and sustained many of the first female practitioners. Barkeloo's adopted home of Missouri also welcomed several of the earliest female attorneys.

Predictably, Barkeloo was assailed with criticism for her choice of career, but she expected slurs and vowed to endure them with patience. Even so, it is unlikely that Barkeloo could have anticipated the duration, extent, or inanity of some of them. A biographical dictionary published years after her death in fact reports her to have died of "overmental exertion."

Lemma Barkeloo was highly praised for her intelligence, self-reliance, and courage. Shortly after establishing her practice, she became the first female attorney of official record to try a case in court. She died, sadly, of typhoid just months after beginning her career.

Judge Wilson A. Primm eulogized her before a meeting of the St. Louis Bar Association: "It must have been a brave soul that could . . . face the prejudices of society, depart from the usual employments of her sex, devote for years the energies of her mind to the mastery of a science, the dry intricate details of which present nothing of amusement or attraction, and finally to enter into an arena in which men, ofttimes rude and ungallant, are the gladiators."

CHARLOTTE E. RAY

---◦◦◦---

1850 – 1911

C HARLOTTE RAY USED A CLEVER RUSE TO GAIN ADMISSION TO Howard University during the brief period when it refused to admit women. Applying as C.E. Ray, she created quite a stir when she showed up for enrollment. She was, however, allowed to stay, and went on to graduate Phi Beta Kappa. She became the first black female attorney in the United States.

Born in New York City in 1850, Ray was the daughter of well-known abolitionist Charles B. Ray. Some records indicate that she was not the first woman to earn a law degree at Howard University, this distinction belonging to Marianne Shadd Cary, a teacher and editor who reportedly earned a degree but never practiced. Ray, in contrast, developed a highly regarded specialty and practiced for several years in Washington, D.C.

Ray's family had been key workers in the underground railroad network that assisted blacks escaping slavery in the South to gain safe passage into the free northern states. Charles Ray, a highly intelligent and accomplished man of African, Indian, and white ancestry, was first editor and then owner of *The Colored American,* and considered one of the distinguished black leaders of his time. He worked inexhaustibly for the underground railroad and served as pastor of the Bethesda Congregational Church in New York.

Charlotte Ray enjoyed an exceptional education; her parents placed a high value on learning, and all seven children of the family received the benefit of formal study. After graduating from the prestigious Miner Institute, which was vilified by segregationists for the fine education it afforded black children, she went on to study and teach at Howard University. Ray first worked as a teacher in the Normal and Preparatory Department of Howard University, then enrolled in its law school. She was later described by a classmate as "an apt scholar." At that time law students were required to prepare and present essays on various topics. A visitor to the school was impressed by what he characterized "a colored woman who read us a thesis on corporations, not copied from the books but from her brain, a clear incisive analysis of one of the most delicate legal questions." In his annual report of 1870, university founder General O.O. Howard noted that a trustee of the law school was amazed to encounter "a colored woman of such intelligence." By all accounts Ray was an outstanding student, who after graduating with honors in February 1872 was admitted to the bar without incident and then to practice in the supreme court of the District of Columbia two months later.

Ray became the first female attorney of any race in Washington, D.C., the first black female attorney in the United States, and the third woman formally admitted to the practice of law in America. Some of her peers considered her to be one of the leading experts on corporate law in the country. Her style was one of quiet determination, and most of her achievements were accomplished with a low-profile approach. Given the general public view of the intellectual abilities of both blacks and women in her time, Ray's intellectual prowess amazed many people.

In May 1872, an article profiling Ray was published in the *Women's Journal*: "In the City of Washington, where a few years ago colored women were bought and sold under sanction of law, a woman of African descent has been admitted to practice at the Bar of the Supreme Court of the District of Columbia. Miss Charlotte E. Ray, who has the honor of being the first lady lawyer in Washington, is a graduate of the law college of Howard University, and is said to be a dusky mulatto, possessing quite an intelligent countenance. She doubtless has a fine mind and deserves success."

Though her practice never reaped significant financial rewards, she came to be regarded as having one of the best academic minds on corporation law in the country. She was also praised for her eloquence in court. Ray was no doubt hampered by double prejudice, but it has been suggested that her gender was a greater factor in her lack of financial success than her race. Several of her black male classmates built lucrative careers in the law.

In *Noted Negro Women,* a book published in 1893, author M.A. Majors wrote of Ray, "Her special endowments make her one of the best lawyers on corporations in this country; her eloquence is commendable for her sex in the courtroom, and her advice is authoritative."

Unfortunately, most women entering the legal profession in the 1870s were treated as a novelty and found it extremely difficult to make a living practicing law. Shortly after Ray opened her office, the panic of 1873 brought about an economic depression that further undermined her practice; she simply did not have enough clients. Eventually, she gave up the law and returned to New York City, where she taught in the Brooklyn public schools for many years, along with two younger sisters. She remained active in women's clubs but did not keep up with the legal community, although she was an ardent suffragist.

Though little is known about her specific activities regarding the suffrage effort, records show that Charlotte Ray attended the National Woman's Suffrage Association's annual conference in New York City in 1876. She was also reported to have been an active member of the National Association of Colored Women.

In the 1880s Ray married a man whose last name was Fraim, but existing records tell little more of him. She moved to Woodside, Long Island, in the 1890s and was mentioned in Myra Bradwell's *Chicago Legal News* in 1897, as well as in Elizabeth Cady Stanton's *History of Woman's Suffrage*.

Though Ray never succeeded economically in the practice of law, her influence as a role model for others is undeniable. The greater Washington area chapter of the Women Lawyers Division of the National Bar Association, a group comprised of black women lawyers in the District of Columbia area, has recognized Ray's contributions and dedicated its annual award presentation in her honor.

Charlotte Ray Fraim was blessed with both intellectual capacity and the support of a loving family, as well as her birth at a time when black Americans were finally enjoying the first opportunities of freedom and civil rights. As stated by writer Dorothy Thomas, who prepared her biographical entry for *Black Women in America*, "In becoming a lawyer Charlotte Ray justified the dreams of many abolitionists, women's suffragists, and free black Americans. She remains an unsung pioneer."

MARY GYSIN
LEONARD

1850? – 1920?

NINETEENTH-CENTURY WOMEN WITH THE GUMPTION TO challenge established legal and social obstacles to gain the right to practice law were seldom shy about bucking other social conventions as well. Many were not only brilliant and determined but downright eccentric. Mary Gysin Leonard became one of the most notorious attorneys among the many colorful women of justice during the frontier days of the Wild West.

Mary Gysin was the first female lawyer in both Oregon and Washington. But her notoriety preceded her legal career. Born in the mid-1800s, she eventually settled in Portland, where she married Daniel Leonard. The union was a stormy one that lasted only two years before ending in divorce. Daniel charged Mary with infidelity and abuse, while she in turn accused him of swindling her. The case drew the fascination of a gossip-hungry public and received sensational coverage in the Portland newspapers. When Daniel Leonard refused to follow a court order requiring him to pay Mary temporary maintenance, she wrote him a letter filled with passionate threats, including the warning, "Don't fool with a woman like me."

A short time later, Daniel was discovered dead from a gunshot wound to the head. Mary Gysin Leonard, along with an alleged paramour, were charged with the murder. Mary effectively won her first case when she achieved her own acquittal. On the money she inherited from Daniel's estate, she apprenticed with a prominent Seattle attorney, passed the bar, and was promptly admitted to Washington territorial and federal practice. She was, however, denied a license to practice in Oregon by the Oregon Supreme Court, solely because she was a woman. She then impelled a senator of her acquaintance to sponsor a bill specifically allowing women to practice law, which passed the Oregon legislature in 1885.

Perhaps because of her past notoriety, the Oregon Supreme Court still balked at Leonard's application, invoking a one-year residency requirement to deny her license. Leonard went before the court and eloquently argued her case to win admission. She promptly moved back to Portland and began to build a career, gaining notoriety both as a skilled attorney and as a hard-driving brawler. With Mary Leonard's return, Portland regained an endless source of grist for its gossip mills.

Mary demanded she be called "Judge" Leonard, although she generally appeared only in the local police courts. In addition to her law practice, she reportedly operated a combination boarding house and bordello in the center of downtown Portland. The landlord of this establishment continually—and unsuccessfully—tried to evict her. Finally he accused her of threatening his life with a pistol.

Again the unrepentant Mary Leonard went on trial, to the great entertainment of the Portland public. Newspaper reports likened the event to a circus. Despite the entreaties of her four lawyers to stick to the case at hand, Leonard took advantage of her spot on the witness stand to give the audience a retrospective of her career and to vent an endless array of grievances. Whether through legal maneuvering or plain weariness of the extravaganza, the judge finally dismissed the charges of carrying a concealed weapon and required her to pay a hundred-dollar bond to keep the peace. Feeling victorious, Mary issued the following statement to the press: "The lady is not young or stylish withal she is comely and attractive, possessed of sparking wit, and her company pleases young attorneys."

Mary Leonard was to need the friendship of young attorneys. She faced three more arrests during her career, one for suborning perjury, one for threatening violence, and another for an embezzlement charge related to her refusal to pay a witness fee. The latter landed her in jail. Her young attorney friends soon secured her release, and she told a reporter that their efforts had saved her life—and possibly the judge's as well.

In addition to her more colorful antics, Mary Gysin Leonard maintained a busy legal career for many years. She continued to litigate to the very limit of her competency—some said beyond—and kept up a lively practice until she was nearly seventy.

MARY CLYENS
LEASE

1850 – 1933

AFFECTIONATELY KNOWN AS "YELLIN' MARY ELLEN," MARY Clyens Lease was a Kansas lawyer who built a reputation as one of the greatest orators of the 1880s. Born Mary Elizabeth Clyens, she was the sixth of eight children of Irish immigrant parents. After her father died at the Andersonville prison during the Civil War, family friends provided for her continued education. Although Mary worked from an early age to help support her family, she persevered in her quest for a good education and received her teaching certificate at the age of fifteen. Three years later she learned that teaching salaries were much higher in the West, so she left Pennsylvania alone for Kansas, where she taught in a Catholic girl's school.

A short time later, Mary Clyens married Charles Lease. A pharmacist by trade, he shared her yearning to homestead on their own land. Despite their determination, however, the young couple found homesteading a harsh life, fraught with both natural perils and the encroaching control of big business. The powerful companies that operated banks, railroads, and grain elevators controlled farm prices in a way viewed by many as greedy and detrimental to farmers.

The Leases persevered for a number of years, during which time they had four children. Finally, when they found they could no longer make ends meet, they moved to Wichita so Charles Lease could return to the pharmacy trade. But the family still faced financial struggle, so Mary took in laundry to help keep the bills paid. She became an active participant in Wichita civic affairs and formed the Hepatica Society, a women's group whose members discussed issues of current interest.

Hungry for learning, Mary would copy pages from books and tack the reading material to the wall to help alleviate the boredom as she bent over her washtubs. A local attorney who learned of this habit was impressed and suggested she turn her studies to the law. One year later, Mary Clyens Lease passed the Kansas bar and began to practice law. She always refused to take a fee for her legal services, believing that lawyers should focus on social justice and help the poor. Lease had also begun lecturing on such topics as Irish nationalism, women's suffrage, and labor reform. As her fiery style drew entranced crowds, her popularity grew. Her first lecture tour, in 1885, raised funds for the Irish National League.

At one point Lease declined a nomination to be the county superintendent of schools in order to pursue her interest in political activities. She worked with other labor groups to cofound *The Colorado Workmen*, an influential labor publication. She also campaigned for the farmer-supported Union Labor Party and edited its *Union Labor Press* during the 1888 campaign. In 1891, she was elected head of one of the largest local assemblies of the Knights of Labor in Kansas.

Described as "tempestuous and controversial," Lease was also said to have "the face of the dreamer and the poet." Tall, intense, and known for her deep, resonant voice, she could mesmerize crowds of 20,000 as she urged farmers to "Raise less corn and more hell"! Naturally, the press ate this up, referring to her as "the Wichita cyclone," "iron-jawed woman of Kansas," "the Kansas pythoness," and "the red dragon." Yet there was no denying that her orations were intelligent, well reasoned, and struck a common chord.

Lease became known as a dynamic and passionate champion of the farmers. When she was thirty-five years old, she became involved with the newly formed Populist Party, having developed an impressive reputation from speaking strongly at Farmers Alliance meetings. She found her true calling in the Populist movement, which was made up of laborers and farmers who felt exploited by big business, and through these activities she gained considerable political power for a woman of her day. Though she was paid little for the 160 speeches she made during the 1890 Populist campaign, she was instrumental in launching the new party on the national scene. She was widely admired for her fearlessness in the face of her opponents, who were backed by the power of big money.

Lease often lambasted what she called the "greedy governing class" that exploited farmers and workers. General James B. Weaver, Populist candidate for president in 1892, referred to her as "our Queen Mary." Lease and many other women formed an important component of both the Populist Party and the Farmers Alliance in the 1890s.

By now big business was taking sufficient notice of Lease to vent considerable wrath on her. Newspapers warned readers to beware of her "brass and venom"; Senator John Ingalls of Kansas advised her to go home and mend her children's stockings. Outraged, Lease actively campaigned against him to end his sixteen-year run in the Senate—and succeeded. Populist governor Lorenzo Dow Lewelling then appointed her president of the State Board of Charities. Though he later tried to remove her for her outspokenness on the need for reform, she was far too influential by then and stayed put.

In 1900 Lease moved to New York City to work as political reporter for the *New York World,* the liberal Pulitzer publication. She remained popular on the lecture circuit, addressing suffrage, birth control, and labor rights and consistently attacked corruption in politics and business. She kept up her law practice as well, representing poor clients and steadfastly refusing fees for her work. It is notable that she never lost a case that she tried before a jury.

In 1895 Lease wrote a book with the ambitious title of *The Problem of Civilization Solved,* in which she summed up her Reformist vision: "We need a Napoleon in the industrial world who, by agitation and education, will lead the people to a realizing sense of their condition and the remedies, and teach them by wise legislation and access to the land that they can attain such majesty and happiness as will fulfill the hopes of humanity and the promise of the ages."

With the advent of the twentieth century, Lease went on to become an active supporter of Theodore Roosevelt's progressivism, serving for a time as president of the National Society for Birth Control. She eventually faced serious financial and domestic problems and divorced her husband for nonsupport in 1902. In her later years, she lived with her children and continued lecturing in the adult education program of New York College.

ELLEN SPENCER
MUSSEY

1850 – 1936

"**L**IKE A DRESDEN DOLL IN STATURE AND BEAUTY, ELEGANTLY dressed, Mrs. Mussey carried the gentility of an Edwardian dressing room into courtrooms and hearing rooms," wrote biographer Dorothy Thomas. But despite Mussey's genteel countenance, she hardly had an easy start in life. Born in Ohio in 1850 into a family of ten children, she was raised in the shadow of her well-known father, a reformed alcoholic, temperance advocate, abolitionist, and penmanship enthusiast, who developed the Spencerian script that became widely accepted as standard in this country during the later nineteenth century.

Mr. Spencer ran his own school on the family farm. When Ellen's mother died, he expected twelve-year-old Ellen to take over both the household chores and the teaching duties her mother had formerly performed. Added to this burden, staggering for a girl so young, was the stress and grief brought on by the death of her father and a younger sister only two years later. Ellen subsequently developed severe health problems.

Her burdens were eased when she went to live with various older siblings and their families over the next few years. She finally made a permanent home with her brother Henry, a prominent suffragist who worked and lived in Washington, D.C. Ellen soon took over the "Ladies Department" of her brother's Spencerian Business College, an institute that trained young women for work in the government.

Elegant young Ellen quickly became popular in Washington social circles. In 1871 she married Ruben Delevan Mussey, a widower with two young daughters. Mussey, one of the first brigadier generals to organize black union troops in the Civil War, later became a lawyer, a teacher at Howard University, and a church leader. Together he and Ellen had two sons.

After Ruben Mussey suffered a bout with malaria in 1876, Ellen began helping him at his law office. A quick and enthusiastic learner, she took to the law immediately. After her husband recovered and returned to his duties, she continued working at his office for the next sixteen years.

Another series of painful losses in the 1880s and '90s included the deaths of Ellen's stepdaughter, a son, a brother, and her own husband. She paused to consider her future and her need to contribute more to her own and her family's support, especially since her surviving son was preparing to enter college. Applying to National University in the District of Columbia to embark on the formal study of law, Mussey was refused admission on the basis of her gender. A law degree was not required for bar admission, however, and a special waiver was granted to qualify her for the Washington bar by oral examination. She passed easily in 1893.

Mussey was subsequently admitted to practice before the court of claims and the United States Supreme Court. She became an expert in commercial and international law, and also helped win passage of legislation improving women's property rights. A committed suffrage advocate, she worked with the National Association of Women's Suffrage, the North American Women's Suffrage Association, and as chairwoman of the National Council of Women served on the Committee on the Legal Status of Women in 1917 and drafted a bill on citizenship rights that became law in 1922. For twenty-five years she maintained a practice focused on probate, commercial, and international law, including service as counsel to the Norwegian and Swedish legations. Tactful and gracious, Mussey was nonetheless tenacious in her beliefs. Men accepted her and respected her as an attorney, and both genders were captivated by her charm.

But Mussey always considered her most important work to be teaching other young women aspiring to legal careers. In the 1890s, women were admitted to practice before all courts of the District of Columbia, including the U.S. Supreme Court, yet four of the five law schools in the district still refused to admit female students. In order to remedy this situation, Mussey, with Emma M. Gillett, another practicing attorney, founded the Washington College of Law on February 1, 1896. The first class began with three female students. Two years later the college was incorporated under the laws of the District of Columbia. It was the first American law school to be founded by women, and Mussey became the first dean, a post she held for fifteen years.

The fledgling school received prestigious support. The board of trustees included Chief Justice Edward F. Bingham of the Supreme Court of the District of Columbia, Mrs. Cecilia F. Sherman, wife of the secretary of the U.S. Treasury, J. Ellen Foster, an attorney and political speaker, Watson J. Newton, a law professor and Emma Gillett's partner, and Justice Charles B. Howry of the United States Court of Claims. Tuition was only fifty dollars a year, in recognition of the fact that female students generally earned less money than men.

Although its charter maintained that the school was established primarily for women, Mussey and Gillett—opposed to discrimination of any kind—admitted male students as well. The first commencement was held in 1899 with six graduates, all women who had been told by Columbian that women did not have the "mentality" for law. Women served as deans for the school's first forty-nine years. Washington College of Law eventually became part of American

University but remained true to its commitment to a diverse student population, free of discrimination.

Determined to gain recognition and prestige, Mussey set high standards for her students. Many graduates became preeminent attorneys who more than fulfilled her hopes. Mussey regularly presented graduates for admission to practice before the U.S. Supreme Court.

Ellen Spencer Mussey was ever active in organizations that supported political, legal, and social rights of women. At various times she served as the chair of the committee on legislation of the D.C. Federation of Women's Clubs, a powerful organization comprised of various civic and literary clubs. She worked toward the 1896 passage of a bill by Congress that gave women equal rights with their husbands over the guardianship of their children.

From 1906 to 1912 Mussey served on the Washington, D.C., Board of Education, where she led many school reforms then considered unique and progressive, including kindergarten, compulsory education, and schools for retarded children. She also helped establish juvenile courts in Washington, D.C., and her concern for the welfare of teachers was reflected in her efforts to help gain passage of the Teachers' Retirement and Pension Bill. Deeply patriotic, she was active in the Daughters of the American Revolution and other such organizations.

Despite health problems in her later years, Mussey kept her hand in the running of Washington College and remained active in women's suffrage and the National Council of Women's Committee on the Legal Status of Women. She served as chair of that organization, and in 1917, along with Maude Wood Park, drafted and helped gain passage of the Cable Act of 1922, which gives women certain rights to retain their citizenship after marriage, regardless of their husband's nationality. She was also an enterprising member of the National Association of Women Lawyers.

Mussey was known for her limitless energy. Some wondered whether she ever slept. During her career she argued and won at least ten cases before the U.S. Supreme Court—the second woman to appear before that court, after Belva Lockwood. Two of these cases established new legal precedent. She has been credited with numerous changes in the District of Columbia laws governing the rights of women and children, including the repeal of a law allowing fathers to will custody of children to others, even when the mother was living. She helped gain women the right to sit on juries, the right to keep their own earnings in a marriage, and the right to manage their own property while married.

Mussey was one of the original incorporators of the American Red Cross, as well as its vice president and general counsel. Founder and first speaker of the Women's Bar Association of the District of Columbia, she was also a member of the Washington Board of Trade and a delegate to the International Council for Women in Sweden in 1911.

Somehow amid all this activity, Mussey found time to be a prolific writer. She authored a novel and numerous articles, including a 1914 essay on children's courts and juvenile justice for *Case and Comment*. Never a rabble-rouser, Mussey got her point across through quiet, lucid prose. In her article for *Case and Comment,* for example, she wrote: "The agricultural department was established with liberal appropriations to guard our agricultural and natural resources, but it took years of education of our national legislators before a federal child bureau to study the welfare of the nation's greatest asset, the child, could be provided for; and even now the crafty statesman is ready, first of all, to economize on the appropriation for sustaining this work of our children, and last upon his own salary and mileage."

Mussey continued to be actively involved in the affairs of Washington College of Law after she stepped down as dean in 1913 for health reasons. She attended each commencement through 1933, when the law school conferred an honorary degree upon Eleanor Roosevelt. At the time, she was eighty-three years old. Despite her early burdens and health problems, Mussey proved far from fragile. Her life was one of tremendous accomplishment until her death just short of the age of eighty-six.

LETTIE
BURLINGAME

1859 – 1890

B Y THE LATE NINETEENTH CENTURY, MORE OPPORTUNITIES HAD begun to open up for women seeking legal education, especially in the Midwest and western parts of the country. When the University of Michigan took an early lead in admitting women, Lettie Burlingame became one of its first female students. During law school she kept a diary, and her entries reflect the strong influence of nineteenth-century mores, even on women who challenge the status quo. She once wrote, for example, "I have determined to make a specialty of equity. It is very interesting to me, and a very nice subject for a lady to pursue." Like many of her sister attorneys throughout history, Burlingame believed that female lawyers had a duty to work on behalf of other women. She helped form a national organization of female attorneys called the Equity Club.

Unlike many of her contemporaries, Burlingame found most of her professors at law school kind and encouraging. She later complained, however, that one of them aroused her indignation by picking out easy questions to ask the female students. After graduating in 1886, she gained admission to the bars of both Michigan and Illinois. She opened her practice in her home city of Joliet, Illinois, in January 1988.

Despite the genteel perspective reflected in her diary, Burlingame was never constrained by a need to be demure in her practice. "I am just wicked enough," she stated in a letter written shortly after embarking on her solo practice, "to prefer courtroom work." In addition to handling a heavy caseload, Burlingame put a great deal of effort into her work for women's suffrage. She composed poetry and lyrics that became popular in the movement, including "Put on the Orange Ribbon," a stirring song often heard at suffrage rallies.

In 1890, writer and attorney Lelia Robinson reported that Burlingame enjoyed "a remarkable degree of success, business coming in much more rapidly than a newly fledged lawyer can ever reasonably expect." By the end of her second year in practice, with more work than she could handle, she invited Rebecca May, a former classmate at Michigan, to consider joining her in a partnership.

Burlingame practiced extensively before the circuit court, mainly handling civil cases but representing a few criminal matters as well. She was respected for her legal acumen, and attorneys from other states sometimes consulted with her. She handled a number of highly significant cases that set precedent in Illinois law. Burlingame assuaged the fears of those who questioned whether a woman's physical and mental strength were sufficient to withstand the rigors of a legal practice when she wrote to Lelia Robinson that while she had always had "the weakest constitution ever given to mortal lips," legal practice agreed with her: "I continually grew stronger, gained fifteen pounds in weight in six months, and now enjoy the best health I ever had." Unfortunately, her good health was not to endure.

Burlingame was among the first women to have a financially successful solo practice. By her own reckoning she was treated with courtesy in court and respected wherever she went—except, ironically, by a few disapproving individuals at her church. She reportedly won every case she took before her sadly premature death, at the age of thirty-one.

TIERA
FARROW

1880 – 1971

AFTER FIFTY YEARS IN THE PROFESSION, TIERA FARROW WAS dubbed the "Dean of Women Lawyers." Based on her vast array of achievements, the label seems justified. Farrow was born in Indiana in the 1880s, the third of ten children. In her autobiography, *Lawyer in Petticoats,* she relates fond tales of her frontier childhood. In 1885, the family moved to Delphos, Kansas, a small, pretty town built around a park square where the children enjoyed summer band concerts. Her father ran the general store that served the farming community, while her mother took care of the growing family. Mrs. Farrow, a teacher before her marriage, was more educated than most women of her day and passed on her thirst for learning to her offspring.

Tiera frequently helped out in her father's store, a gathering place for local men to relax around the potbellied stove where they swapped exciting tales involving cattle rustling, kidnappings, horse thieves, and murder trials. Tiera listened to their stories, mesmerized. Abraham

Lincoln's name always seemed to come up. Tiera idolized Lincoln and dreamed of somehow emulating the great man when she grew up. Yet as time went by, she became aware of both her potential and the limitations placed upon her by virtue of being born a girl.

But Tiera never lost sight of her ambitions. Around the age of ten, she opened a tiny ice cream parlor in an outbuilding next to her father's store. She successfully resolved her first labor dispute when her older sisters demanded to be paid for taking over Tiera's share of the household chores, and she ran her small business successfully for several summers.

When the family moved to a larger community, Tiera became a leader in the church and high school. The outbreak of the Spanish American War stirred her with longing to join the army, but she was obliged to take refuge instead in reading stories of trials in the newspaper, and sneaking into the courtroom after school to listen to the lawyers.

When Farrow graduated from high school, her goals were unclear, although she was certain she would be a lawyer if she were a man, there were no female-attorney models in her world. But technology would provide an outlet for her enterprising spirit. Typewriters, still new, were just beginning to make their appearance in the West. Farrow thought that if she could become a stenographer, she could gain entry into the fascinating world of law and business.

Farrow's parents were astounded by her boldness as she pleaded her case for business school. Yet she convinced them of her sincere ambition and enrolled in business college in Kansas City, Missouri. Farrow found the strange keyboard and the curlicues of shorthand challenging, but her determination drove her. She began her first job on April Fool's Day of 1899, working for a Kansas City grain firm.

Farrow was constantly reminded that she was wasting her time, as the office was no place for a pretty girl who would certainly marry soon. Her illusions about distinguished businessmen were soon shattered as she witnessed the petty competitions and suffered the inequity of being paid less than her male counterparts while often catching the overflow of their unfinished work. Soon she began to hunger for more education.

Farrow's curiosity led her to the growing feminist movement. Her work to improve conditions for women fueled her dissatisfaction with her current position. She felt a passionate urge to help overcome injustices against women, and by now had become aware of the existence of such a thing as female lawyers.

As she gained experience in the world, Farrow became more venturesome. She made a few inquiries to law schools, only to be notified that "young ladies" were not admitted as law students. This, however, only strengthened her determination. When she made the welcome discovery that the newly established Kansas City Law School offered evening classes, she recalled a quote of Lincoln's: "If you are resolutely determined to make a lawyer out of yourself, the thing is more than half done." She applied forthwith.

Farrow was "frantically eager" to be accepted when she appeared for an interview with the registrar. But though the school had no restrictions on gender, and Farrow met all the requirements, the registrar still hesitated. Much of his trepidation was based on the fact that no respectable girl appeared on the streets alone after dark. Farrow assured him she would find a suitable escort, and she was accepted.

Her autobiography describes her first night of classes in 1901, when she entered a "London fog" of cigarette smoke, to the stunned silence of eighty men. One, however, who had become acquainted with her on the daily streetcar ride came forward and greeted her in a friendly manner, for which she was eternally grateful. She soon became one of the gang, later learning that the men had practically come to blows competing to sit next to her.

Nonetheless, Farrow was occasionally ribbed by her classmates. She was, moreover, reminded of her legal status as a man's chattel when she learned such common principles as the "rule of thumb," which allowed a man to beat his wife with any weapon, so long as it was no thicker than his thumb. It became increasingly disturbing to her to observe the extent of the legal oppression of women. She began formulating ideas on how to use her talents to change these injustices. "More and more," she stated in her autobiography, "I began to see existing laws through the eyes of a woman in a man's world." Even

Farrow's generally supportive professors insisted on excusing her from some sessions on criminal law so as not to shock her maidenly modesty.

Yet Farrow perservered. When graduation day came amid a great flood, Tiera hired a rowboat and made a dangerous river crossing to get to the ceremony. There, the twenty-two-year-old graduate was gallantly honored by her classmates as a rose among thorns, standing there in her white dress among the dark-suited men.

Farrow left law school with grandiose ambitions, vowing to see all her clients, male or female, receive justice. She aspired to become a second Abraham Lincoln, to free women from inequity and to help all who were in trouble.

Farrow's ambitions were far more lofty than her opportunities were plentiful. She broke off an informal engagement to one of her classmates when he suggested they open a practice in which he would go to court and she would handle the office work. Yet even though Farrow knew she would likely have to start as a clerk or stenographer in a law office, she was surprised when she couldn't find even a lowly position. At last she was hired by two young attorneys, who paid her less money than her salary at the grain office. But Farrow quickly took to their practice and began to make occasional court appearances. She became the first female attorney to go on record in any case before the Kansas Supreme Court.

In 1907, at the urging of others, Farrow ran for city treasurer and thus became the city's first woman elected to the office, as well as the youngest elected official in its history. She enjoyed her work and won a second term, but decided to take a different direction when it expired.

Farrow had always wanted to travel abroad, especially to see the conditions of women in other countries. Having managed to save an impressive sum of money, she planned a trip with a friend, a singer, who wanted to add to her training abroad.

During the voyage to Europe, the women teamed up with a group of more experienced young adventurers and amended their plans to encompass a more exotic itinerary. As they traveled throughout the Mediterranean and North Africa, Farrow was moved by the sight of veiled women in Algiers who were virtually slaves to their husbands. The trip included a camel ride across the Arabian desert, as well as a jaunt through Europe. Having learned that women everywhere held similar ideas and aspirations, Farrow returned to America considering herself fortunate to have been born in a country where women were far more free than in other regions. She remained determined, however, to help all women achieve equality.

Farrow teamed up with Anna Donahue to open the first firm of female lawyers in Kansas City. The partnership won the first case they tried in a court of record, and the papers reported with much amusement that courtroom demeanor was unusually gallant between opposing attorneys. Small cases trickled in, and the women took them all. Yet business remained lean. The novelty of their practice drew many who sought counsel, but few of these clients had money.

Donahue and Farrow eventually had to either supplement their income or close the office. Farrow took a job as a court reporter in another city, keeping her position secret so as not to let other Kansas City attorneys learn of their financial difficulties. She later stated that it gave her some of her best experience in learning court procedure and practice. Donahue, too, did part-time work. Those who inquired for one of the moonlighting women were simply told she was away on "legal business."

Eventually, however, Donahue opted to move to New York. Farrow, undaunted, decided to build a solo practice. She was discouraged to find that clients of both sexes expected her to charge less because she was a woman. Like many of her counterparts, she found it necessary to accept many fees in the form of canned fruit and needlework, along with generally worthless stocks and bonds.

Farrow's most infamous case began as a fairly routine domestic matter. A Mrs. Schweiger came to Farrow requesting that Farrow try to have a divorce her husband had obtained set aside, so she could be reunited with her husband and child. Not surprisingly, Mrs. Schweiger had little in the way of funds, but Farrow took the case. She explained to her client that they would probably lose their first hearing and would have a better chance upon appeal of the case. But when events progressed as predicted, Farrow's client became severely distraught. In the courthouse corridor after the first hearing, Mrs. Schweiger pulled an automatic revolver from her bag and fatally shot her husband a number of times before shooting herself in the shoulder.

Farrow was later praised by the newspapers as one of the few to remain calm in the ensuing bedlam. Naturally, Mrs. Schweiger was charged with murder, and she begged Tiera Farrow to represent her. Farrow didn't condone what her client had done, but she knew that there could be extenuating circumstances and believed that all defendants were entitled to have their legal rights protected.

The 1916 trial drew widespread attention. Farrow characterized it in her book as a "doubleheader": a woman charged with murder defended by a female attorney, a Kansas City first. A local newspaper described Farrow as "not at all the sort of person one would connect with the wrangling of attorneys and the heated debates usually attendant upon murder trials."

The trial was certainly sensational in its own right. Farrow's client alternately sobbed, cried out, and had to be sedated. Farrow raised an insanity defense and argued passionately but coherently before a courtroom filled with spectators riveted to the proceedings. The real fireworks occurred with closing arguments, in which both sides conducted summations filled with florid oratory.

Farrow wove a tale of love and betrayal around her drab client, invoking Biblical sagas of Ruth and Sarah, plus references to such grand romantics as Antony and Cleopatra. Theories of insanity and passion were eloquently analyzed. As part of her closing, Farrow implored: "After he sipped the honey from this poor woman's life, he left her. . . . If the situation had been reversed, would Mrs. Schweiger have left him—left him in a helpless condition, wrecked physically and mentally? No, a thousand times no! . . . Here, today and now, is being enacted the last scene in one of the greatest local love stories of our time. . . . You have heard witnesses testify to their knowledge of her great love for him and all that she has endured because of that love. Her story has never been written or sung by any poet and perhaps would never have been known but for this tragedy." When

Farrow finished her fervent plea, there was scarcely a dry eye in the courtroom. Her client was convicted of second-degree murder and given a fifteen-year sentence, then paroled in two years because of ill health.

Farrow never seemed to settle into her practice, even as it grew more successful. There were too many requests for public service that she felt duty bound to honor. She was appointed a divorce proctor, to investigate default divorce cases and try and determine the reasons behind the booming divorce docket in Kansas City. This led Farrow to advocate highly progressive ideas for the time, such as a form of no-fault divorce and a separate court of domestic relations.

Farrow also worked actively for suffrage and equal rights. Because women were barred from joining the Kansas City Bar Association, she teamed with other female attorneys to form the Women's Bar Association of Kansas City in 1917. She was also a member of the National Association of Women Lawyers, and with others helped form the Women's Bar Association of Missouri in 1918.

With the advent of World War I, Farrow helped the National Guard Association in their recruiting efforts, organizing a squadron of pretty girls to stage raids on pool halls and dance halls where young men could be convinced to enlist. She then volunteered as an ambulance driver with the National League of Women's Service.

The combined stresses of the war, her demanding practice, and a brief marriage in 1918 that proved to be a mistake led Farrow to a time of soul searching. In need of a hiatus, she again hungered for education and so enrolled in the University of Illinois, where a friend was studying. Farrow pursued sociology and political science and enjoyed the chance to visit Abraham Lincoln's home in Springfield. Having plunged into her adult life so young, she now, in her thirties, enthusiastically made up for lost time. She pledged a sorority, joined the debate team, and befriended many fellow students. When she graduated in sociology, she won a scholarship to Columbia University, thanks to the efforts of the head of the department, who encouraged her to combine her legal experience and new knowledge in a social service career.

After receiving her master's degree from Columbia, she accepted a job to assist in surveying the Connecticut criminal courts for the American Institute of Criminal Law and Criminology. Eventually, however, she returned to Kansas City and the law. There she maintained a successful and varied practice for many years.

In the 1920s, Farrow and her law partner, Louise Byers, began holding law classes for women. The goal was not so much to train them to become lawyers as it was to familiarize them with legal topics that affected their business and personal lives. The enterprise drew great acclaim and thrived until the Depression.

Subsequently, Farrow was appointed judge of the Kansas City Municipal Court. She was the first woman to hold this position, and again found herself in the spotlight. Deeply moved by the human plights of those who came before her, she put her social science studies to good use. She was highly respected for her clear-cut reasoning and fairness, even if her decisions sometimes raised eyebrows. On one occasion she urged police who had rounded up a group of prostitutes to bring their male clients in as well, stating that there should be no double standard.

The Depression hit hard in Kansas City, and for a brief period Farrow faced grave financial hardship. When the New Deal programs began, however, she served as a case worker and legal aide worker. She continued to work with the county and city relief agencies, and found the duties to be varied and rewarding. In 1943, she took a post as legal aide counselor in the city welfare department.

In 1932, Farrow received the surprise of her life when she heard of a student enrolled in Kansas City Law School named Tiera Farrow Lester. When Farrow sought information, all she could learn was that a student by that name was indeed enrolled, and that she had come from a small town in Kansas. Later, when Farrow was invited to speak to the law school's sorority, she learned that when she had graduated in 1903, a story about her in the Kansas City newspapers had reached the grandfather of a baby girl born a few days later in a rural part of the state. Thinking it wonderful that a girl could become an attorney, he suggested the baby be named after the enterprising young woman.

Farrow was thrilled. She met and befriended her namesake, became her professional mentor, and watched with pride as she became a capable government lawyer. In *Lawyers in Petticoats,* Farrow called her "my daughter by remote control."

World War II again brought out Farrow's patriotism. She volunteered for the Red Cross and provided free legal advice to servicemen and their families. This led to many fascinating cases, often involving complicated marital entanglements.

Farrow denied that she made history; she claimed that she was too busy living it. Yet she acknowledged that an unquenchable fire of ambition and desire to be of service always motivated her. She credits her success not to genius but to being a "consistent plugger."

CRYSTAL
EASTMAN

1881 – 1928

B Y THE END OF WORLD WAR I, THERE WAS A HANDFUL OF
female attorneys in New York City, most of whom were graduates of New York University Law School. Many of these women
banded together to work toward labor and civil rights reform.
Crystal Eastman was one of the leaders of this dedicated group.
Born in 1881 in upper New York state to parents who were both
congressionalist ministers, Crystal was highly influenced by her
mother, who was also a public speaker and advocate of women's
rights and believed all her children should be independent and
self-reliant, regardless of their gender.

Eastman devoted nearly all of her life to the fight to improve
freedom and equality for all human beings. By the time she was fifteen she was speaking on women's rights to a study group, but she
never viewed feminism as a struggle against men, and worked closely
with many male colleagues.

Crystal attended public schools in New York, graduated from Vassar College in 1903, then moved to New York City and received a master's degree in sociology from Columbia University the following year. Eastman lived in Greenwich Village among a community of intellectuals and radicals. She began her work in settlement houses of New York City, where she saw for the first time the deplorable working conditions for immigrants. She soon realized that she wanted to dedicate her life to reform, and felt that a legal education would be the best tool for achieving her goals. Enrolling in New York University Law School, she ran a recreation center at night to support her studies.

Eastman graduated from law school in 1907 and passed the bar that same year. She then joined reformer Paul Kellogg in work on the "Pittsburgh Survey," a major project that represented the first American attempt to study the effects of industrialism on urban workers. Eastman plunged into the often gruesome research, compiling detailed studies of over a thousand industrial accidents and writing extensively on unsafe work conditions. Her incisive work in this field has been credited with sparking extensive reforms in factories nationwide. In 1910, she published *Work Accidents and the Law,* a well-written treatise that spurred many changes in workers' compensation laws. Eastman was appointed to the New York State Employers' Liability Commission in 1909 by Governor Charles Evans Hughes. As the only female member of the commission, she served as secretary, and was directly involved in securing the passage of New York's workers' compensation law.

Eastman was renowned for her grace and beauty. Poet Claude McKay once wrote, "She had a way of holding her head like a large bird poised in a listening attitude." She was married to Wallace Benedict between 1911 and 1915. The couple lived for a time in Milwaukee, Wisconsin, where Eastman served on the Political Equality League and as campaign manager for the 1912 efforts toward women's suffrage in Wisconsin. Though the effort was unsuccessful, she became a cofounder of the Congressional Union for Woman's Suffrage in 1913, and served as delegate to the International Woman's Suffrage Alliance meeting in Budapest.

That same year, Eastman helped organize a suffrage parade of five thousand women to march on Washington the day before Woodrow Wilson's inauguration. The event spawned a riot that was eventually quelled by cavalry troops and the Pennsylvania National Guard. Also assisting in keeping the peace were students from Maryland's Agricultural College. Vowing to guard the women, the young men formed a protective wall to march around them.

When World War I broke out, Eastman returned to New York City, where she served as a leader in the women's peace movement. She became executive secretary of the pacifist American Union Against Militarism, as well as chair of the Women's Peace Party in New York City. With her reputation as one of New York's charismatic new thinkers, Eastman personified the "new woman" emerging at the time.

Eastman eventually became one of the leading civil rights attorneys in New York City. She wrote briefs in deportation cases before the United States Supreme Court in defense of victims of the antiradical hysteria that often targeted innocent immigrants for expulsion from the country. She assisted in *Herndon v. Lowry,* a case in which the United States Supreme Court developed the "clear and present danger" test that set boundaries on restrictions against the First Amendment right to freedom of speech.

Eastman also worked on the first of the landmark Scottsboro boys' cases, defended the president of the International Longshoremen and Warehousemen's Union when he was threatened with deportation, and was instrumental in many other important cases that contributed to the development of civil liberties law.

Between 1914 and 1917, Eastman was credited with making the New York City branch of the Woman's Peace Party one of the most militant pacifist groups in the United States. She viewed the European war as imperialist and strongly opposed American support of the war. Eastman believed that mass killing was never justified, and spoke out against the "preparedness" bills that provided for military training of students in high schools. She argued that if a nation prepared for war, it would engage in war. As a pacifist, Eastman felt that her primary purpose was to "establish new values, to create an overpowering sense of the sacredness of life, so that war would be unthinkable."

Not long after her divorce from Wallace Benedict, Eastman married Walter Fuller, an Englishman who had come to America to manage his sister's folk music concert tour. Both were active in the Greenwich Village peace movement. When America entered World War I, she became one of the organizers of the Civil Liberties Bureau, which assisted conscientious objectors. The organization embraced the goal of protecting all civil liberties and eventually evolved into the American Civil Liberties Union. In 1917 she became managing editor and writer for *The Liberator,* a radical journal founded by her brother Max Eastman. She continued writing for labor and feminist causes, and in 1919 became one of the organizers of a feminist congress held in New York City. At the congress Eastman spoke in favor of suffrage, equal employment opportunities, birth control, economic independence, and equal moral standards for men and women.

Eastman was always searching for a model of a truly humane society. She believed that 1920 was the beginning of an entire new era, with much yet to be done. While many believed the passage of the Nineteenth Amendment signaled the end of the battle for equality, Eastman urged a comprehensive feminism, extending beyond mere suffrage. She proposed a new feminist campaign dedicated to removing all legal discrimination against women, encouraging child-rearing practices that would free children from sexist stereotyping, making birth control information available (it was then considered obscene material, unfit for distribution through the mails), and providing endowments to those who chose to be mothers. Eastman's ideas, however, were greatly ahead of their time, and many formerly active women complacently bowed out of the feminist movement once the war was over and suffrage granted.

Eastman once stated her hope that "with the feminist ideal of education accepted in every home and school, and with all special barriers removed in every field of human activity, there is no reason why women should not become almost a human thing." Had she lived to see the developments of the 1960s and '70s, she would no doubt have been gratified by such events as the 1972 Women's Political Caucus, with such leaders as Gloria Steinem and Shirley Chisholm working toward the establishment of Eastman's ideals.

In 1921, Eastman and her husband went to England with their two children. Walter Fuller joined the British Broadcasting Corporation, while Crystal cofounded a London branch of the National Woman's Party. She continued to write for American publications, often describing the efforts of feminist advocate groups in England. In 1927, she returned to America and began working for progressive advances in education and child care. When her husband died suddenly in England, her own health declined rapidly. She died in 1928 at the home of her brother Ford Eastman, when she was only forty-seven years old.

Eastman was known for her sincerity, her enthusiasm, and the joy she brought to her work. As a lecturer, she appealed to the emotions of the crowd as a deeply moving speaker. Her work helped bring about significant progress in industrial reform, suffrage, and pacifism. A tribute in *The Nation,* published August 8, 1928, perhaps summed up Eastman's life best: "She was for thousands a symbol of what the free woman might be."

FLORENCE
ELLINWOOD ALLEN

1884 – 1966

L IKE MANY WOMEN WHO BECAME EARLY LEADERS IN THE LEGAL field, Florence Ellinwood Allen's beginnings fueled both her intellect and her pioneer spirit. Born in 1884 in Salt Lake City, Utah, Allen came of age in a remarkable family. Her father was a classical scholar, a professor, and a lawyer, as well as a mine assayer and mining manager. He became a Utah territorial legislator and served as the first representative for the state of Utah in the United States Congress.

Allen's childhood spanned the years of her father's most active involvement in the mining industry. The family often lived in cabins near the mine sites, and Florence loved the rough mystery of the mines, with their dark caves and caverns. Her father also influenced her strong commitment to justice. As mine superintendent, he established a program of workers' compensation before it was legally required; and as a legislator, he introduced and gained passage of laws that helped workers. He also framed and established a system of free schools in Utah.

The daughters in the Allen family began studying Latin and other classical subjects early in life. Florence loved to read and listen to her mother, a talented pianist who was in one of the first classes at Smith College. Mrs. Allen encouraged all the interests and projects that captured her children's attention. When Florence expressed trepidation about debate and public-speaking classes in school, her mother advised her to simply "make your point and sit down." Florence found this advice extremely helpful throughout her life. Allen's mother also set an example as a community leader. With other women, she established the first free public library in Salt Lake City.

When Florence entered college at Western Reserve University, her eclectic interests and natural leadership blossomed. She was elected president of the freshman class, wrote verse, edited the college magazine, and was involved in dramatics. She kept up with her piano studies, although she knew that she did not want a career in music.

Shortly after Florence graduated, her mother and four younger siblings traveled to Berlin, where Mrs. Allen had been invited to speak at the International Council of Women at the University of Berlin. Florence and her older sister joined them a short time later, embarking on what was considered a bold adventure for two unchaperoned young ladies in those days.

Florence was still unsure of her calling when she was offered a position as assistant to the Berlin correspondent of the *Musical Courier.* The job involved concert reporting and stenographic work. Soon she was offered a second position at the *German Times,* an English newspaper circulating in Berlin's American colony.

When after two years the family was ready to return to America, the *Musical Courier* offered Florence three times her salary to stay, but she declined. The Allen family settled in Cleveland, where Florence was offered a position as music critic by the *Cleveland Plain Dealer.* She accepted the job and simultaneously began teaching at the Laurel School for Girls. Her curriculum included literature, Greek and German, history, and drama. She also took postgraduate classes at Western Reserve University, working toward a master's degree in political science.

The seed of Allen's future was planted when one of her professors suggested she study law. Western Reserve University School of Law was not open to women at that time, so Florence enrolled in Chicago University. Although she was the only woman among a hundred students, she finished the first semester ranked second in her class. Overall, her experiences with professors were positive, and she was often amused by "compliments" from fellow students who told her she had a "masculine mind."

At the end of her first year of law school, Allen was offered a job by Frances Kellor, who was to become a pioneer in labor laws for women and created the codes used by the American Arbitration Association. At that time Kellor was head of the New York League for the Protection of Immigrants. She sought Allen's assistance in passing and enforcing laws to protect immigrants from exploitation by unscrupulous employers and others of a predatory bent. So Allen moved to New York and enrolled in New York University.

By this time there were enough female law students enrolled for the school to have formed a legal sorority, and Allen was invited to become a member. Remaining true to her principles, however, she refused to join unless a Jewish student was asked as well. When the invitation was not forthcoming, Allen declined membership. Money continued to be a struggle, but Allen managed to persevere and graduated second in her class wearing a rented gown hastily altered with pins by her sister.

During the years between 1910 and 1920, Allen devoted much of her energy toward the push for suffrage. Maude Wood Park, a leader in the suffrage movement, became a good friend and tremendous influence. Known for her intellect, patience, courage and persistence, Park teamed with Allen to speak and organize suffrage groups throughout Ohio. Allen used her legal training to find loopholes in the suffrage laws. In one instance she had to take an overnight train back from Montana, where she had been campaigning for Woodrow Wilson, to argue a case before the Ohio Supreme Court on whether municipalities could decide whether women could vote in local elections.

In 1919—before women had won the right to vote—Allen was

appointed the assistant county prosecutor of Cuyahoga County, Ohio, becoming the first woman in United States history to hold such an office. Allen tried many criminal cases and was soon put in charge of the grand jury process, where she not only oversaw 823 indictments during her first year, but also won over many antifemale jurors. By Christmastime, the same jury pool offered her a gift and a speech of praise.

Allen's work for the suffrage movement had given her a chance to push for human rights, gain knowledge of the entire State of Ohio, and win the friendship and support of many people around the state. Her early litigation on suffrage cases had also provided the opportunity to cross swords with some of Ohio's best attorneys, in defense of beliefs to which her heart and soul were dedicated. This background put Allen in a good position when she decided to run for election to the Court of Common Pleas.

It was Allen's custom to simply move forward toward her goals, ignoring prophecies of defeat. She loved the outdoors and hiked and climbed mountains at every opportunity. She once compared campaigning for election to crossing a treacherous stretch known as "the knife edge" on the highest mountain in Maine. During a trip up the mountain, Allen had calmly strolled across the precipice while the guide watched in disbelief.

Ten weeks after ratification of the constitutional amendment enfranchising women, Florence Ellinwood Allen became the first woman elected to a judgeship, in the first general election in which Ohio women had the right to vote. Allen acknowledged the tremendous help she had received from both women and men, including Cleveland mayor Tom Johnson, a strong suffrage supporter who had arranged to have her nominating petitions printed free of charge. All of the Cleveland papers had backed her in the election, and she credited the entire women's movement, along with pioneers like Susan B. Anthony, for paving her way.

Allen had both the wisdom and the integrity to know that she could not sidestep campaign promises if she was to retain the loyalty of her voters. Once elected to the Court of Common Pleas, she immediately started making the changes she had promised. The court was plagued by both a lack of business administration and quirky provisions, such as one that allowed a key witness, often a crime victim, to be held in jail while the person charged with the crime could make bail and go free. She swiftly saw that the witness law was changed. She gained both admiration and the annoyance of local politicians when she refused to grant special favors to those in power.

Though some of her fellow judges were at first shocked to have a woman on the bench, she eventually won both friendship and cooperation through her practicality, humor, and dedicated efficiency. During one and a half years on the Court of Common Pleas, she heard 579 trials. Her legal acumen also impressed her colleagues, as only three of her decisions in these cases were reversed by higher courts.

Allen drew national attention when she presided over a notorious murder trial, known as the "Black Hand Case." The defendant, Frank Motto, was charged with a double murder. Motto was the head of a robbery ring and suspected of many other violent crimes as well. The case drew notoriety both because of Motto's reputation as a well-known gangster and Allen's position as the first woman in United States history to preside in a capital murder case. The case also marked the first time women had served on a jury in such a case. Allen laughed off a letter she received threatening her life and those of the jurors, containing black outlines of a hand, symbolizing death. The police insisted on giving her protection during the trial, though she did not believe at the time it was necessary.

The jury came back with a sentence of first-degree murder, without a recommendation of mercy. Under Ohio law, this meant that Allen had no choice but to enter the death sentence against Motto. This marked the first time in American history a female judge had been required to sentence a man to death. Allen stated that she did not enjoy the prospect but saw it as her duty. In later years she frequently referred to the Motto case when asked whether women were not too sentimental and emotional to serve on a jury. She replied that women and men were not different in this area, and pointed out that when the Motto jury returned with the verdict, the chairman, a woman, read the verdict impassively, while a man in the back row wept.

In 1922, a vacancy opened on the supreme court of Ohio. Allen's friends and supporters suggested she run for the position. The *Cleveland Plain Dealer*, as well as other newspapers and prominent commentators, endorsed her. As Allen described it, "There ensued a campaign such as I have never seen." Allen became the first woman to run for election to a court of last resort in the United States. Women all over the state who were familiar with her suffrage work volunteered to gather signatures for the petition required to qualify her for the election. Male advocates, her parents, and innumerable friends also helped. Allen needed 21,000 signatures to secure the nonpartisan nomination by petition. Her supporters gathered over 42,000.

Her champions seemed to come out of the woodwork, often through odd connections. Allen's grandfather had been a well-known teacher and school administrator, and many who had known and admired him gave their support to Allen as well. In addition to his political career, her father was well known as the first baseball player in Ohio to pitch a curve ball on a college team. His influence also drew a variety of supporters. She won the election to achieve another landmark role.

Allen had always been interested in international law, especially in the development of substantive law between nations. She hoped that law could eventually become an instrument for ending war, by first making war illegal and then establishing international systems of justice to peacefully resolve disputes between nations. In part, her dedication to peace was personal. Two of her brothers had been killed in World War I, and she was deeply troubled by the waste and the loss to all nations of their finest young men. She described war as "draining the lifeblood of civilization." She saw the efforts being made to substitute the law for war as the highest endeavor in which anyone could engage. Shortly after her election to the Ohio Supreme Court, she began to speak frequently on her theories, which she called "the outlawry of war."

Meanwhile, Allen was settling into her new role as a Supreme Court justice. Her initial challenge was to establish a rapport with her fellow justices on the bench. Her first day on the job, after the justices had heard cases argued and had gathered around a big table to consider their decisions, she sensed some uneasiness among the men. She calmly invited them to go ahead and smoke, and several pulled out pipes and cigars. The tension evaporated, and the new court was on its way to a comfortable working relationship.

While Allen was more likely to achieve her goals through humor and grace rather than confrontation, neither was she one to accept unfair treatment. Shortly after her election to the Ohio Supreme Court, one of the judges of the bench tried to establish a new court division to handle all divorce cases, with the intention of placing Allen in that position. She staunchly refused, pointing out that since most of the male judges were married and she was single, they were better qualified to serve in such matters. She issued a statement to this effect to the papers, and the project promptly died.

Allen was fascinated by the complex and varied questions presented to the court during this period of Ohio's rapid industrial growth. During her eleven years on the bench, she wrote a number of highly significant decisions, many pertaining to the rights of workers in the growing industries. In 1928, she was re-elected by a landslide. But by 1934, when her term was about to expire, she did not relish the idea of campaigning yet again. When one of the judges on the United States Court of Appeals for the Sixth Circuit passed away and a vacancy opened, her friends suggested she apply for the seat.

With the support of professional colleagues, distinguished American women with whom she had worked, and her loyal array of friends, she decided to seek the position. The Ohio Senate unanimously confirmed her appointment, notifying her of this on her fiftieth birthday. She found the endorsement of one of her colleagues, Justice J.P. Stephenson, especially significant, since he had at one time flatly opposed the idea of female attorneys and judges. Stephenson even traveled to Washington to support her nomination. "There is," he stated, "no court too big for Judge Allen."

Allen hardly received a warm welcome from her colleagues on the Sixth Circuit bench, however. One of the judges, she was told, was so upset that he took to his bed for two days. Only two of the six formally congratulated her. But Allen was not overly concerned. She remarked that after eleven years on the Ohio Supreme Court she had learned that judges who were at first opposed to women "accepted us when we handled our work steadily and conscientiously." True to her tradition, she kept abreast of the work and kept her docket clean. One judge who had staunchly opposed her appointment was won over when she insisted on serving as usual the day after a bad fall down a staircase required oral surgery and left her with a bandaged face. Allen knew if she took a day off, attorneys who had traveled a great distance at financial hardship during the Depression years would have wasted a trip. When that formerly recalcitrant judge later referred to a case she had written as "a damn fine opinion," she knew she had joined the club.

Allen continued her public-service work, speaking at colleges and universities for a respite from the demands of the bench. One of her favorite topics was the United States Constitution, which she believed was intended as an instrument for freedom. Her book illustrating this concept, *This Constitution of Ours*, was well received and often quoted. "Liberty," she writes in it, "cannot be caged into a charter and handed on ready made to the next generation. Each generation must re-create liberty for its own times. Whether or not we establish freedom rests with ourselves."

While serving on the Sixth Circuit, Allen participated in the landmark Tennessee Valley Authority (TVA) case, which upheld the constitutionality of this federal agency established for flood control, dam building, regulation of interstate commerce, production of power, and other action on the Tennessee River. The TVA case was the first to be heard under a new three-judge rule requiring cases involving injunctions against acts of Congress to be decided by one appellate and two district judges. Since all the other judges on the Sixth Circuit court were disqualified because of conflict of interest or illness, Allen became the chief judge on the case. Not only were the legal issues complex and challenging, but the case gave Allen an opportunity to move with a cousin to Chattanooga, where she enjoyed relaxing daily walks with her cocker spaniels around the woods of Lookout Mountain. She later described the seven-week trial as at once fascinating and grueling.

Allen also chaired the International Bar section on human rights for several sessions. She joined in the International Federation of Women Lawyers, founded by attorney Roslyn Goodrich Bates of Los Angeles, and traveled worldwide in her work with the organization. The group's goals included visiting women in various countries and presenting programs focused on the legal needs of women, children, and the family. The organization grew steadily with Allen's help, eventually gaining a permanent representative at the United Nations.

Allen maintained a lifelong commitment to helping her "sisters in the law," often influencing government officials to appoint women to high positions and eliminate the traditional barriers blocking their advancement. Through the work of the International Federation of Women Lawyers, laws allowing sex discrimination were removed in several nations. Allen wrote and spoke extensively throughout her career on the relationship between legislation and workable treaties, a complex and frequently misunderstood subject.

In her autobiography *To Do Justly*, Allen looked back on her life as a mix of hard work combined with many rich rewards. She enjoyed deep and lasting friendships with both men and women and participated in many occasions that marked the advances of women in what she called the "great profession of the law." In 1948, female graduates of New York University Law School instituted a movement to finance a scholarship fund in the name of Florence Allen. Eleanor Roosevelt supported these efforts and was made the honorary chairman. A room in the university's new law center was dedicated to Florence Allen, and half the money raised by the alumni committee under Judge Dorothy Kenyon was earmarked for the project.

Allen was pleased, both at the personal honor and for its connection with NYU, which was among the first law schools to open its doors to female students. Another supporter of the project was Justice

Learned Hand, who attended the dinner, served on the committee, and sent Allen a congratulatory letter. At the ceremonial event, Allen spoke on peace through justice, always her passion. She stressed the obligation of attorneys to help establish and maintain peace. She enjoyed another honor in 1952, when she received the bust of Susan B. Anthony for placement in the Hall of Fame at NYU.

In March 1957, the National Association of Women Lawyers endorsed Judge Allen as a nominee to fill the next vacancy in the United States Supreme Court. Having made its recommendation to President Eisenhower, it sent a group to Washington to meet with several assistant attorney generals. By this time, unfortunately, Judge Allen's age had become the main obstacle to her appointment.

After serving twenty-five years on the Sixth Circuit Court of Appeals, Allen retired at the age of seventy-five. Retirement did not, however, mean inactivity, and she remained a senior United States circuit judge, taking part in hearing and deciding cases when she wished to do so, according to her senior status. Upon her retirement, Allen was informed that the New York Association of Women Lawyers, together with many friends, planned to present a portrait of her to the court of appeals. At the dinner celebrating the presentation her entire court gathered for this tremendous honor.

Allen was also delighted to learn that many of her family members would be in attendance—a rare treat, as they were scattered widely across the country and seldom able to travel to the honorary functions so important to her. Her sister, Dr. Esther Allen Gaw, Emeritus Dean of Women at Ohio State University, unveiled the portrait. In her speech at the presentation ceremony, Allen summed up the credo she had lived by for many years: "The attainment of justice is the highest human endeavor."

DOROTHY
KENYON

1888 – 1972

D OROTHY KENYON WAS THE FIRST FEMALE ATTORNEY ADMITTED
to the prestigious Association of the Bar of the City of New
York, but she was best known for her devotion to fighting social
injustice. A strong civil libertarian, she served on the board of the
American Civil Liberties Union and chaired various public commissions that helped establish minimum-wage laws. She was also active
with reform of the New York City women's courts, and instrumental
in efforts to establish public housing in the city. A devoted advocate
of women's rights, she became embroiled in controversy when she
sought to shift prosecution of prostitutes to the pimps and johns
exploiting them.

Kenyon's exposure to the seamier side of life sharply contrasted
the experience of her early years. Born in Victorian New York, she
grew up in a well-to-do Manhattan family, enjoying such luxuries as
a summer home in Connecticut and education at Horace Mann High

School. Her father, William Houston Kenyon, was a prominent patent law attorney, and the family enjoyed an affluent existence. Kenyon attended Smith College, where she received her degree in economics and history in 1908. She described herself as a social butterfly during her college years, with a focus on music, athletics, and an active social life.

A major turning point in Kenyon's priorities occurred during a trip to Mexico, where she experienced her first rude awakening to the reality of social injustice. Transformed, she was inspired to study law at New York University. She graduated and was admitted to the New York bar in 1917. Kenyon's brothers, also lawyers, joined their father's firm when they earned their degrees, but Dorothy gravitated toward government work. She conducted research on wartime labor, and assisted in preparations for the 1919 peace conferences held at various sites after World War I.

Kenyon also became active in liberal Democratic politics in New York City. In 1936, she was appointed by Mayor Fiorello La Guardia as the first deputy commissioner of licenses for the city. She gained notoriety—as well as public acclaim—when she refused to close down Minsky's and other burlesque houses. Kenyon commented that she saw no reason to prohibit "the only beauty in the lives of icemen and messenger boys." After three years in the licensing post, she was appointed to the New York City Municipal Court, where she served a brief term as a judge.

Kenyon's 1936 appointment to the commission that licensed burlesque houses—like Mabel Willebrandt's assignment as prosecutor of Prohibition laws—illustrates another persistent stereotype of women as keepers of public morals and "family values." Ironically, many early female attorneys were dedicated to social reform and increased rights for women in these areas. Rather than enforcing moral constraints, they frequently worked for expansion of rights, especially freedom of choice in family planning. This often brought harsh criticism from the very officials who had channeled them into these positions.

Kenyon also worked for suffrage and became a nationally recognized feminist after women were granted the right to vote. In 1950, she wrote an article for *The New York Times Magazine* entitled "The Case for Women Lawyers (By One of Them)." She founded and directed several consumer corporations and served as legal counsel to the Cooperative League of the United States. In 1938, she was named to a committee of jurists by the League of Nations. She studied the legal status of women around the world and later became the United States delegate to the United Nations Commission on the Status of Women from 1946 to 1950. She was a member of the National Board of Directors of the ACLU from 1930 until her death.

Kenyon's devotion to civil rights and social causes inspired the wrath of Senator Joseph McCarthy, who attacked her with accusations of Communist affiliations in 1950. Kenyon replied by calling him "an unmitigated liar, a coward to take shelter in the cloak of congressional immunity." She was the first witness to appear before the Senate Foreign Relations subcommittee when it began its investigations of McCarthy. Self-described as "crazy about the underdog," she refused to compromise her commitments.

Throughout the 1950s and '60s, Kenyon worked for the civil rights movement, lending legal assistance to the NAACP Legal Defense Fund. She participated in efforts to end the Vietnam War and helped organize a women's coalition to divert federal funds from the military to social programs. At the same time, she became active in the new feminist movement. Kenyon's work for women spanned her lifetime. She fought to end discrimination against female workers during the Depression, campaigned for military commissions for female doctors during World War II, and made many other contributions toward winning improved economic and educational opportunities for women.

A champion of reproductive rights, Kenyon toiled as early as the 1920s for the right of women to obtain birth control and led efforts to revise abortion laws beginning in the 1950s. Her efforts helped set the stage for other attorneys, such as Harriet Pilpel and Sarah Weddington, who won landmark cases before the United States Supreme Court expanding reproductive freedom and the right to privacy in reproductive choice.

Kenyon was renowned for her energy, vitality, and good humor. She was a member of Barnhouse, a Martha's Vineyard colony that included artists, reformers, and intellectuals. While many of her efforts had a broad international focus, Kenyon was also active in her own neighborhood. She worked ceaselessly for improvement of the Chelsea section of New York City, and helped to establish the first legal program for the poor on the lower west side of the city when she was eighty years old.

MABEL WALKER
WILLEBRANDT

1889 – 1963

T HE WOMAN WHO WAS TO BECOME ONE OF THE MOST FAMOUS—
and infamous—female attorney of the twentieth century began
life in a sod dugout on the plains of southwestern Kansas in 1889.
This rugged beginning set the stage for her later life, which was to be
diverse, trail blazing, and always at the forefront of the expanding
field of American law.

Mabel Walker Willebrandt's pioneer spirit was inherited directly
from her parents. Her mother, Myrtle, was a school teacher who left
Missouri by stagecoach, bound for the booming Kansas frontier to
join her brother and stake her own claim among other single women,
who made up a significant proportion of Kansas settlers. It was a hard
life, with a seemingly endless assault of blizzards, droughts, and out-
laws. But Myrtle's religious faith and romantic spirit did not waver.
She married David Walker, an infallible optimist and ambitious
dreamer who nevertheless had a practical bent. Both teachers, they

shared an adaptable nature and determination that they would survive and succeed. The couple led a nomadic life, combining farming, teaching, and newspaper work. Shortly after daughter Mabel was born during a spring drought that wiped out the crops of 1889, the family returned to Missouri in a covered wagon and launched a newspaper in the small town of Lucerne. A few years later they loaded the wagon once again and headed for Oklahoma to join the run for the Cherokee strip. They settled in Blackwell, Oklahoma, in a nine-by-twelve-foot tent. Both Walkers went to work as editors on a local newspaper, then moved on to teaching and farming once again.

From this enterprising and confident family, with its emphasis on practical learning, spiritual faith, and character, Mabel was launched into what would prove to be a remarkable life. Her mother imparted a love of nature that was to last a lifetime; her father taught her useful farm chores, during which he and Mabel would talk "man to man" for hours on such topics as crops, local business, and politics. It was a Walker family credo that girls should be raised as independently as boys, and taught to earn a living.

The Walkers moved to Kansas City in 1902. By this time the family had adopted another young girl, and one day Mabel brought a classmate from a troubled home to the Walker house and insisted the family take her in as well.

Mabel and her newest sister, Maude, went to Manual Training High School. Mabel excelled in a course designed for college prep students. She and Maude also worked in a doctor's office after school to help earn money for the family, who were always on a tight budget. After graduating, both girls continued on to Park College and Academy. The strict regimen of the school was difficult for Mabel after many years of freedom in her schedule at home, but it was her intelligence and outspokenness that caused her the most trouble. Mabel, who saw God as a partner, was uncomfortable with the school's religious dogma. She was dismissed for arguing religion with the president of the school. To complicate matters, the school refused to release her records. Finally, Maude wriggled through the transom above the registrar's office door to retrieve Mabel's file.

Mabel traveled on to the rough lumber town of Buckley, Michigan, with her parents. David Walker opened a bank, and Mabel, whose college work had qualified her to take the teacher's exam, began teaching at a country school. Just getting to the school was often an adventure. She was trapped in a blinding blizzard on one occasion, and nearly lost in a forest fire on another. But Mabel settled comfortably into the life of the rural northern Michigan town. She played basketball on a local women's team and frequently enjoyed picnics at a nearby lake. Meanwhile, she began keeping company with the school principal, handsome twenty-one-year-old Arthur F. Willebrandt.

When a bout with pneumonia left Arthur at risk for tuberculosis, he decided to move to Arizona and asked Mabel to join him as his bride. Armed with her mother's idealism and her father's optimism, she settled with Arthur into one of the many small sanitorium towns near Phoenix. The couple set up housekeeping in a one-room wood-and-canvas cabin. She soon found that she loved to explore the new environment, which she referred to as the "challenging and irregular West."

When Arthur was on his way to recovery and no longer needed her full-time care, Mabel enrolled in the Tempe Normal School to become fully certified as a teacher, and frequently enjoyed camping and hiking with her fellow students. Although only twenty years old, she was considered an unusual student, since married women almost never appeared on college campuses in 1910.

It was during this time that Mabel faced a tragedy that was to affect the rest of her life. A tubal pregnancy required surgery that left her unable to bear children. This loss caused her considerable despair, but she rallied to earn her diploma and teaching credentials. She and Arthur continued on to California.

California in 1911 was a bawdy and booming place, rife with political upheaval. The couple settled in Los Angeles, where Mabel quickly found a job as teacher and principal at an elementary school. A short time later, Arthur's mother joined them in their small cottage. Mabel found herself both breadwinner and housekeeper for three people, Arthur still being in precarious health and unable to work. However, he proposed a plan whereby both would study at the College of Law at the University of Southern California. For the first year, Mabel was to work full-time and take part-time night classes, with a reversal in roles the following year. The scheme never panned out, however, and for the next three years Mabel continued to run herself ragged working full-time, keeping house, and studying law in the evenings. By this time USC boasted several female attorneys as professors, and a rare women's department that even included a special room set aside for female students, where they could study, relax, and socialize.

During her last year at law school, her friend and former USC associate James H. Pope asked her to be his assistant in the office of the police court defender, where she would handle cases for women charged with assorted offenses. She thus became the first female public defender in America's history. At the start of the job she was completing her last semester of law school and was still teaching a full schedule as well. But she jumped into this new work with wholehearted enthusiasm.

Arthur managed to graduate from law school and started a clerking job, but Mabel was still largely responsible for the family's income and household upkeep. This burden, combined with her deep disappointment in Arthur's failure to keep his promises, finally took its toll, and in 1916 Mabel left. She never questioned the decision, yet she was always haunted by what she considered to be a personal failure.

At this time, Los Angeles was still a wide-open town, with the country entering an era of zealous reform. Mabel was in charge of defending clients in a new court especially for female offenders that had been established as part of the reformist effort. Volunteer women assisted female defendants largely charged with prostitution or vagrancy in finding a new path upon their release. Mabel Willebrandt soon introduced innovations into the program. She took advantage of a law allowing women charged with prostitution to request a jury trial in which the man soliciting their services would be required to appear, thus lending more balance to a crime that took two to commit. Meanwhile, she had also purchased a small farm and gained renown as a goat breeder. As always, she managed to dovetail her various occupations. On one occasion she contributed a small herd of goats to a new prison farm.

After completeing law school, Willebrandt opened a small private practice with two close friends, John Shepherd and Fred Horowitz. She continued her work with the city courts and taught night classes to Mexican immigrants. At the same time she took classes toward earning her legal master's degree, believing that it would give her an edge in confronting the obstacles she faced as a woman in the field. True to her love for the outdoors, she and her partners often hiked or camped with the Sierra Club in the nearby mountains.

Willebrandt believed that honesty was the paramount virtue required of a good lawyer. She often quoted Abraham Lincoln, who said, "Resolve to be honest at all events; and if in your own judgment you cannot be an honest lawyer, resolve to be honest without being a lawyer." She frequently found her integrity and character tested. In the very first case she tried after establishing her own practice, Willebrandt had to ask the judge to disqualify himself when she realized he had indulged in one of his customary lunchtime chats with opposing counsel, which gave him inappropriate access to information regarding the case. The judge grumbled but did agree to withdraw, and she won great acclaim for her pluck, even more than for her legal victory over six other attorneys.

As Willebrandt's practice grew, eighteen-hour days became the norm. Yet she still went out of her way to work for the underdog, often helping women charged with prostitution during the influx of soldiers to California during World War I. In 1918, she was appointed chair of the legal advisory board for the second-largest selective service district in the city, presiding over thirty other attorneys.

The war also brought personal heartbreak, when her partner and dear friend John Shepherd was killed in battle. But Willebrandt and Fred Horowitz continued their practice, and the office soon became a gathering place for young female attorneys struggling to launch their own careers. Willebrandt was one of the forces behind the 1918 founding of the Women Lawyers Club of Los Angeles County. To help the club, she began corresponding with leading female lawyers around the country, such as Florence Allen, requesting inspiration and helpful advice. The group made great strides in Southern California. They eventually won the support of the toughest antifemale judge in town, who even agreed to appear as a guest speaker.

Willebrandt believed female attorneys had a responsibility to participate in community life and politics in order to help other women. She worked hard for passage of the married women's property bill through the California legislature in 1919. Willebrandt also remained closely tied to her family. When her father's Michigan bank failed amid recession and labor unrest, she bought her parents a chicken ranch in Temple City, California.

Willebrandt professed no interest in running for public office, though she was a dedicated member of the progressive branch of the Republican Party. When she was nominated for the post of assistant United States attorney general, she found herself embroiled in a political tangle that included an uneasy competition with Clara Shortridge Foltz, whom she had always admired. Nonetheless, thanks to her growing reputation and key endorsements, she found herself appointed to the post at the age of thirty-two. Attorney General Harry Daugherty and President Warren G. Harding were both pleased at the appointment. When President Harding remarked that her only shortcoming was her youth, Willebrandt assured him with characteristic wit that she would soon grow out of it.

Willebrandt was wary of entering a position involving prosecution, and she knew the deplorably low salary—a hundred ten dollars a month; only ten more than she had earned as a school principal—would be a hardship. She was also concerned that she was joining a Justice Department recently shaken by corruption and overloading, as cases arising under the Prohibition laws flooded the dockets. Moreover, her new division would oversee some of the most unpopular laws on the books. She would be responsible for the enforcement of federal laws governing Prohibition, federal income and estate taxes, and the prison bureau, among others.

Willebrandt had always thrived on challenge, however, often

quoting her favorite Bible passage, 2 Timothy 1.7: "For God hath not given us the spirit of fear, but of power, and of love, and of a sound mind." Willebrandt was to draw heavily upon all these qualities as she faced the challenge of the 1920s. When Willebrandt accepted the post in 1921, she had a staff of three to assist her. When she left eight years later, it had grown to the largest division, with a staff of one hundred members and hundreds of aides in the field.

Ironically, Willebrandt was neither a prohibitionist nor a teetotaler, but she believed in enforcing the law, even the unpopular Volstead Act. It turned out to be an overwhelming job. Many Americans refused to bow to the new law, and importers, bootleggers, and moonshiners made easy fortunes. The trade in illegal liquor developed into a major industry, and Willebrandt faced the nightmare of trying to enforce a law upon which Americans were so sharply divided. Her division alone was responsible for 40,000 cases per year, 50 percent of which were for Prohibition violations.

Willebrandt soon found herself America's best known and most controversial female attorney. She collected cartoons that depicted her throughout the era. One that appeared in 1928 was all too accurate, showing her as it did with a rag mop, standing on the shore of the Atlantic, trying to turn back the tide of an incoming ocean of illegal liquor. To complicate matters further, Willebrandt was charged with coordinating the efforts of the various agencies involved in Prohibition enforcement, including the Treasury Department, the Coast Guard, and state and local law enforcement agencies.

She persevered, however, with dignity and tireless effort, taking every opportunity to repeat her message that citizens were expected to uphold the law. An eloquent and poetic writer, she frequently published articles in popular women's magazines, pointing out that murder and bribery lurked behind every cocktail served at a dinner party.

Law enforcement at all levels was rife with corruption during the Prohibition years. Many officers were in cahoots with bootleggers. Willebrandt faced constant turmoil as she tried to weed out corrupt officials in her own department, including a number of United States attorneys. After less than six months in the office, however, she broke the infamous "Savannah Four" ring and put the man known as the king of the bootleggers behind bars. Willebrandt also had major responsibility for briefing and presenting Prohibition cases to the United States Supreme Court. This was one part of the job she truly loved, and during her years in the office she submitted 278 cases to the court.

Willebrandt's achievements concerning federal prisons and taxes helped balance the frustrations of the Prohibition work. She spearheaded efforts that led to the establishment of the first federal prison for women, as well as the first federal reformatory for first-time male offenders. She also set up the first work program for federal prisoners. Her longtime dedication to helping women, along with her belief in taking an enlightened approach to young offenders who were not yet hardened criminals, made this work deeply satisfying.

Willebrandt won many accolades when her new prison for women—which included individualized treatment, work training, and cottages with basic amenities—was built at about the same cost as the traditional cell-block jail. Her admirers praised her ability to win over the hostile and inspire the indifferent.

Though dedicated to her job, she found it constantly stressful and exhausting. Willebrandt longed for appointment to a federal judgeship in California. She realized that no woman had yet been appointed to the federal bench, and it was her foremost ambition to be the first. The greatest obstacle to her goal, however, was the deep division of public opinion based on her role in Prohibition. In 1924, an opening occurred on the federal bench in Northern California. But despite many recommendations, opposition to Willebrandt was too strong, and another judge was named to the position. She was frankly disappointed, but as always philosophical. More openings followed on the California federal bench, but she was never to achieve the post she so desired.

Family and friends were treasured by Willebrandt, especially her parents, to whom she poured out her heart in letters during her difficult tenure as assistant attorney general. She insisted on helping her parents financially, as well as her adopted sisters and their children, and was especially generous in assuring that her nieces and nephews received a good education.

Willebrandt still longed for a child of her own, and in 1925 she adopted a two-and-a-half-year-old girl. Parenthood was challenging, with her breakneck schedule and frequent travel requirements, but Willebrandt was determined to rearrange her life in order to accommodate her daughter. She found it especially appropriate that the little girl was named Dorothy, which means "gift of God." Whenever possible, she took her along on work-related jaunts, even to tours of the federal prisons.

Willebrandt worked tirelessly to help advance the careers of other female lawyers, especially through Phi Delta Delta, the women's legal fraternity. She served as its national president for several years and helped set up a scholarship fund, as well as a networking program to alert other women attorneys to opportunities for employment and advancement. She was also active with other professional groups and much in demand as a speaker on women in the law.

In 1930 Willebrandt wrote an article for *The Smart Set,* a popular magazine of the day, entitled "Give Women a Fighting Chance," that contained a great deal of insight on issues that still challenge professional women today. "When we sum up the columns that make 'success' for the boy on the one hand and the girl on the other," she wisely pointed out, "you find the girl has the much longer column to add." She also counseled that in occupations usually reserved for men, women must persevere and maintain a discriminating balance between womanly charm and professional strength and aggressiveness. Her words still resonate today.

Despite Willebrandt's many efforts and achievements, the press felt compelled to constantly assess her appearance and wardrobe. Willebrandt once grumbled, "Why the devil they have to put on that 'girly-girly' tea party description every time they tell anything a professional woman does is more than I can see." Despite her complaints, however, much of what was written about Willebrandt's attire was complimentary. Reporters praised her style as both business-like and feminine.

The year 1928 proved to be the turning point that led to Willebrandt's decision to leave the Justice Department. She traveled, spoke, and campaigned devotedly for Herbert Hoover, but her support proved to be double-edged. Personifying Prohibition to many, she stirred up controversy wherever she went. Finally, she decided that her involvement in the campaign was causing more harm than good to her candidate, and she withdrew. A short time later she resigned from the Justice Department to take a position as Washington counsel for the Aviation Corporation. Upon her departure, President Hoover wrote what was characterized by the *New York World* as "the warmest praise given by this administration to any public servant leaving office." He emphasized her skill and courage in a position he acknowledged as one of the most difficult in government.

Willebrandt, relieved to be out of the relentless turmoil that surrounded her previous post, was fascinated by the new field of aviation law. In addition to her work with the Aviation Corporation, she launched a diverse and challenging private legal practice. She won a number of landmark aviation cases and discovered a passion for air travel.

Willebrandt loved flight, even in the days when commercial air travel was brand-new and such emergencies as unscheduled landings in farmers' fields were common. Her small airborne entourage provided entertainment for an audience of farmers near Chicago during one such unplanned stopover on the way to the American Bar Association convention in Seattle. Willebrandt had little patience with what she called the "caution artists" who delayed flights due to inclement weather or other inconveniences. She worked with Amelia Earhart to promote air travel, and she eventually took flying lessons herself. She also sponsored aviatrix Jacqueline Cochran in a 1934 air race to Australia. Willebrandt's work with the Aviation Corporation fed a new passion as well as provided the financial security that had up till then eluded her.

Willebrandt participated in the drafting and passage of many significant laws, including the McNary-Watres Act, which set guidelines for airline bidding on transportation of the U.S. mail. She had, within a few years, become recognized as one of the leaders in the emerging field of aviation law, was invited to join New York University's American Academy of Air Law, and also served on the editorial board of the new *Air Law Review.* She chaired an ABA committee on aeronautical law from 1938 through 1942, frequently working with the Civil Aeronautics Authority.

Willebrandt also became immersed in the emerging arena of radio law. She entered this burgeoning field in the patent area and soon moved into litigation handling important cases that helped to define and hone the developing laws. She delved into international claims when she represented her friend Carl Lohman, known as "the Reindeer King" of Alaska, in a claim against the Soviet government. Lohman had once proposed marriage to Willebrandt, but she declined and instead introduced him to Laura Volstead, daughter of the sponsor of the Prohibition law. When Lohman and Volstead married, Willebrandt served as matron of honor. Her forays into the Lohmans' subsequent legal problems brought her into other matters involving international law.

Willebrandt firmly believed that the law should be a living, evolving entity. She often quoted Justice Oliver Wendell Holmes, who once said, "The Constitution is like the bark of a living tree—essential to the nation's growth; it should always be construed to permit the expanding life within."

During the 1930s, Willebrandt had begun representing people in the movie industry and made many friends in Hollywood. She became part owner of a 3,600-acre ranch in Escondido, California, and eventually sent her parents to live there. They brought chickens, horses, and cattle to turn it into a real working enterprise. Dorothy loved the ranch and was allowed to spend an entire school year there with her grandparents. Eventually, however, the ranch was sold when Willebrandt and Horowitz dissolved their L.A. partnership. The family then settled onto a 516-acre farm in Pennsylvania.

In her typically practical fashion, Willebrandt set out to find a farm manager to assist her aging parents. She hired a young black man whom she met while driving down the road, because she admired his style of plowing a cornfield. The man and his wife were to remain a part of the extended family for the next twenty-five years.

The Willebrandt family enterprises remained closely inter-twined, as Mabel's father began to help her in the office on a regular basis. She and Dorothy frequently spent weekends riding and hiking around the farm. They often invited guests—including many of Washington's elite—to join them for riding, baseball games, and swimming. A trunk of shirts and overalls was kept handy for those without appropriate country attire.

Willebrandt's mother passed away just before her parents' fiftieth anniversary. At this time her tax expertise was increasingly demanded by her Hollywood clients, so Willebrandt moved back to California in the early 1940s. Having represented MGM and Louis B. Mayer since the 1930s, she now had a considerable array of star clients, including Grace Moore and Jeanette McDonald, who became close friends. Other clients included Clark Gable, Jean Harlow, and Frank Capra. She represented many members of the Screen Directors Guild and went to bat for the Guild in a confrontation with producers in the late 1930s to hammer out labor-related problems.

Willebrandt worked behind the scenes for her Hollywood friends when the red scare began in the late 1940s. When McCarthyism started to focus on Hollywood, the board of the Directors Guild opted to head off the attack by preparing a noncommunist affidavit for sig-nature by members. This controversial proposal put Willebrandt once more in the midst of a hot debate, when the guild asked her to draft the affidavit and she agreed to do so. Willebrandt was sincerely wor-ried about the threat of Communist infiltration, and she often sup-ported some questionable efforts to stop the threat. But she also rallied in defense of those who were falsely accused. When director Frank Capra, an old friend, faced blacklisting, she advised him to fight back hard and fast. He did so, according to her instructions, and rapidly cleared his name.

Though she continued to maintain an active practice until very near the end of her life, Willebrandt focused more attention on her family in her later years. She remained actively involved in her daughter's life, despite Dorothy's occasional rebellion against her mother's well-intentioned if sometimes overbearing attempts to mold her into a lady. Dorothy had always loved the outdoors and country living, and when she married, she and her husband soon moved out of the pleasant apartment Willebrandt had provided and into a rustic cabin. Willebrandt accepted the choice with grace, and mother and daughter remained close, especially as Dorothy's family grew. Willebrandt took a great interest in her three grandsons and often conferred with them as adult to adult, just as her father had done with her as a child.

Willebrandt argued her last case, involving a $22 million estate, at the age of seventy-three, with a broken wrist that put her arm in a large cast. It was just over one year later that she died of lung cancer. For her eulogy, Dorothy chose her mother's favorite Bible verse of 2 Timothy 1.7, and added 2 Timothy 4.7: "I have fought the good fight, I have run the race, I have kept the faith."

CAROL
WEISS KING

1895 – 1952

FOR THREE DECADES CAROL WEISS KING WAS VENERATED AS A formidable lawyer for the underdog. She practiced in her native Manhattan from 1920 until her death in 1952, where she became famous for her skill, generosity, and seemingly inexhaustible energy.

Weiss was born in 1895 to an upper-middle-class, intellectual Jewish family. Her father was a corporate lawyer who represented companies such as Standard Oil. King's own legal career, however, was to take a nearly opposite direction. King graduated from New York University Law School in 1920, in the midst of the mass roundups, beating, and deportation of immigrants suspected to have Communist affiliations. These infamous "Palmer raids" were named after Attorney General A. Mitchell Palmer. With J. Edgar Hoover, head of the new Justice Department division that was to become the FBI, Palmer staged raids in seventy cities. Federal agents without warrants broke into gathering halls and private homes and arrested thousands.

Ironically, many of the people arrested were Czarist Russians who had fled to America to escape the new Communist regime.

Deeply moved by the injustice of these attacks, King joined forces with the firm of Hale, Nelles and Shorr, which had been playing a key role in combating the raids. King's impetus for attending law school came from her commitment to fight for people in causes in which she believed, and to do it in the forums of the powerful: the courts and legislative bodies. The Hale firm also appealed to King because of the diversity of its members and the people it represented. The partners, impressed with the ambitious young woman, could not afford to hire her as an associate but invited her to open an office in their suite, where they were also renting space to Joe Brodsky, another young lawyer dedicated to human rights. This was not what King had planned, as her husband, Gordon, was a writer without a reliable income, and she had hoped to have the security of a steady paycheck. But she liked the spirit of rebellion that permeated the firm, and quickly signed on.

Like many fledgling lawyers, King had virtually no practical training in the day-to-day practice of law. But with the assistance of the partners, as well as the skilled and jovial Joe Brodsky, she soon learned the rudiments. She also learned that it took a lot to shake things up around the chaotic office. On her first day, while attempting to make a cup of tea on a small alcohol stove in her office, she spilled the fluid and started a fire. As flames shot to the ceiling, threatening to engulf the premises, Brodsky stuck his head in the door and calmly asked, "Do you do this every afternoon at 4:00 P.M. sharp?"

King had always been the young rebel in her family. Her mother, a high-spirited woman, nonetheless fit the mold of the docile Victorian wife. Her father was a traditionalist in many ways, although a liberal intellectual committed to citizen participation in government. He often read aloud from his favorite books to his four children. Carol was the youngest, and from her earliest years she flatly refused to follow the conventional expectations of the day.

The Weiss family enjoyed a comfortable Manhattan home as well as a rustic Maine summer retreat. Carol had an excellent education, including high school at the progressive Horace Mann School. It was a time of great social upheaval, in which women's suffrage, labor organization, and immigration were foremost among the political issues of the day.

The same rebellious spirit that would sustain Carol throughout her work for unpopular causes later in life often got her into trouble during her younger years. When she entered college at Barnard in 1912, freshmen were not allowed to use the front stairs. Carol immediately made a bold dash for them, only to be pushed back down by a group of sophomores and suffer a broken front tooth. Soon, however, she settled into campus life and found an outlet for her energy in athletics, excelling in hockey and basketball. She honed her writing skills by working on the *Barnard Bulletin*, eventually becoming editor-in-chief. When she put out an issue on women's suffrage, she was nearly expelled from the conservative institution. Consistently refusing to follow the dictates of fashion, she was frequently reprimanded at Barnard for violating such rules of decorum as appearing without her hat or gloves.

Carol's history courses stirred her interest in the problems of workers, especially working women. She began to volunteer on behalf of the International Ladies' Garment Worker Union, assisting female workers and immigrants. She also worked for the American Association for Labor Legislation, lobbying for occupational safety and health legislation and workers' compensation laws. It was this experience that sparked her ambition to pursue a legal career, as she repeatedly saw the fruits of her hard work shot down by corporate lawyers.

During this era, many law schools had quotas on Jewish students, and a large number still flatly refused to admit women. And so, like many other young women who were to become leading attorneys during the early twentieth century, she enrolled in New York University.

Shortly before entering law school, Carol met Gordon King. She was as little concerned about his traditional Baptist background as he was about her Jewish heritage—or her steadfast refusal to wear gloves.

They soon married, and Carol proceeded through law school with relative ease. She was, however, frustrated by the lack of any courses on civil rights or labor law, as well as the manner in which her professors ignored the headlines of war, revolution, and oppression of civil rights that she, Gordon, and their friends discussed endlessly.

King began making frequent trips to Ellis Island to represent immigrants threatened with deportation and held for hearings. She found her natural assets aiding her in these efforts. Her friendliness helped her gain assistance from the civil servants who got things done in the labyrinthine bureaucracy, and her shrewd intelligence helped her divine the best and fastest way to obtain hearings for her clients. Even her athletic skills served her as she raced from the detention center to the hearing offices.

However, as with other attorneys working with immigrants, King's victories were few and far between, due to the tough laws that stood in the way of a successful defense to deportation. So King set out to change the law, and so began a lifetime of work in the human-rights field.

After handling many administrative hearings for her alien clients, King was anxious to try a full case before a jury. When a client came in with a fairly standard civil case, she argued to the jury and felt it went well—yet she ultimately lost the case. It was King's first significant personal defeat, and it hit her hard. She felt guilty for letting down her client and lost confidence in her ability to litigate. Convinced she was simply not effective in a courtroom, she went on to devote the vast majority of her time to nonlitigation work, teaming up with a trial lawyer who would argue the cases. Although her distrust of her ability was exaggerated, this new direction seemed to make the best use of her talents. Her creative bent was suited to coming up with new ideas and strategies for changes in the law.

During the early 1920s, strike breaking, red baiting, race riots, and attacks on aliens were rampant. The lawsuits that followed led to the birth of modern civil liberties law. The first Supreme Court rulings protecting individual rights against government intrusions were being written by enlightened justices like Oliver Wendell Holmes.

King soon expanded her efforts to focus on constitutional and appellate work, in addition to immigration law. She began bringing in prominent attorneys from outside the office to assist on key cases. With the help of legal luminary Walter Pollack, she presented the then-novel argument that the Fourteenth Amendment's admonition that no state shall deprive any person of life, liberty, or property without due process of law was intended to protect people from violation of their rights by the states. The case went to the U.S. Supreme Court, and while the individual case was lost, the court acknowledged that King's constitutional principle was valid and correct. This was the type of small, mixed victory that was to sustain King and many other civil-rights practitioners during this era of legal development.

Like most professional women of the early twentieth century, King also found herself charting new waters in trying to strike a balance between her personal and professional lives. In many ways, Carol and Gordon were opposites. He spent lunch at the Harvard Club, while Carol marched in picket lines. He dressed in a dinner jacket each evening, while she barely noticed what she wore. Yet they were deeply devoted to one another, often meeting for an hour to talk during breaks in the workday. During one such interlude, they were even chastised by a policeman who thought them inappropriately affectionate in a city park.

The year 1925 proved to be an especially difficult one for King. Her office was shaken when one of the partners was killed and others decided to take different paths, though eventually the remaining lawyers regrouped and King became a partner in the new firm. King also gave birth to a son that year, and managed to structure her schedule so she could walk back and forth between home and office to breast-feed the baby during the day.

As America moved into the Depression, King became more involved in labor law as demonstrations by desperate workers increased. She was also hit with personal tragedy. During the family's annual vacation to the Weiss summer home in Maine, Gordon King came down with pneumonia and suddenly died. Carol was paralyzed with shock and disbelief. Gordon had just begun to achieve success as a writer, especially with his children's books. In addition to her grief, Gordon's death increased the financial pressure. Carol was devastated, but she vowed to succeed without financial help from her family.

Demands on her time, many of which did not pay, had also increased. The fledgling American Civil Liberties Union had begun publishing its *Law and Freedom Bulletin*, with King responsible for overseeing the editing and publication.

To combat her loneliness after Gordon's death, Carol threw herself into an ever more hectic schedule. With other lawyers she launched the International Juridical Association's (IJA) bulletin, whose editorial board included Alger Hiss, Abe Fortas, and other legal and intellectual leaders. The bulletin dealt with cases involving human rights and disseminated information to other attorneys working in the field.

In 1931, King became involved in the Scottsboro boys cases, in which a group of young black men in Alabama had been unjustly charged with rape. The defendants, denied the right to counsel, were quickly tried and convicted before juries from which blacks were systematically excluded. King immersed herself in the case, rounding up other lawyers to assist with the massive effort.

Eventually, King knew she had to ease her workload and make more time for herself and her family. Fortunately, her son, Jonathan, had exhibited an independent spirit from the start. King's respect for each individual extended to children, and she enjoyed spending time with her son and other children in her family—often in rather unorthodox ways. One of her nieces fondly remembers an evening she spent with her Aunt Carol as a teenager. It began quite properly at a play, then ended at a popular speakeasy.

Meanwhile, the Scottsboro boys case dragged on. In 1933, the United States Supreme Court reversed the convictions, though Alabama was to try and convict one of the young men again, even though one of the alleged victims had recanted her testimony. King plugged away on the seemingly endless case until the final victory, in which the Supreme Court ruled that blacks could not be excluded from juries nor denied their right to due process and equal protection of law as guaranteed to all citizens.

King also continued her work in the constant battle to push through fundamental labor laws, many of which are taken for granted today, such as minimum wage law and restrictions on child labor. In late 1936, a group of lawyers who supported Roosevelt's New Deal legislation met to launch a union of attorneys working toward common goals. King, along with an impressive executive committee of judges, politicians, and leading lawyers, joined the new National Lawyers Guild.

King's work representing flamboyant labor leader Harry Bridges was to mark a new era in her life and in the area of free-speech law. The law of the day provided that a person could be deported for being a member of, or affiliated with, the Communist Party. The Immigration and Naturalization Service was trying to deport Bridges, a labor activist, on very scant evidence of long-past connection with the party. The requisite administrative hearing was to be the first step in his defense, and it dragged on for weeks.

Carol and her colleagues were victorious after round one, when the warrant for Bridges's deportation was canceled. But when the law was amended and Bridges again arrested, King had to travel to San Francisco for a second round of hearings, this time taking Jonathan, now fifteen. The *Bridges* case garnered extensive public attention. Folksinger Pete Seeger, with other musicians, even wrote a song about it. The original *Bridges* defense team rallied, and in 1945 the case went all the way to the Supreme Court, where it forged new ground in both immigration and First Amendment law. The same year, Carol King and her lawyer brother were both involved in cases before the United States Supreme Court, and both won. Of the *Bridges* case Justice William O. Douglas wrote: "Freedom of speech and of press is accorded aliens residing in this country." This was a victory for which King had been fighting all her professional life. She was present when Harry Bridges became a naturalized citizen later that year.

As America moved toward the fifties and the cold war, the rights of immigrants and aliens suffered a severe setback. King again found herself fighting a huge burden of deportation orders issued against her clients. By this time, however, she had decided that Congress must be responsible for protecting the foreign born, and began working with the National Lawyers Guild, friendly congressmen who supported her cause, and the IJA to lobby for legislative protections. Meanwhile, she managed to keep up with her large circle of close friends and relatives, and to indulge in her love of art, filling her home and office with an eclectic collection. She also continued to mentor other lawyers, often advising colleagues that when hit with the unexpected to simply "make a noise like a lawyer!"

When the witch hunts leading up to the McCarthy era began in the late forties, labor unions, leftist groups, and civil-rights organizations were quickly targeted. Predictably, King, who had always been leftist in politics but never a member of the Communist Party, was scrutinized by the FBI. The era also brought a flurry of arrests of the foreign born, including many King clients. Yet in the midst of some of the bleakest hours for immigrants, King attended a dinner in her honor given by the American Committee for Protection of Foreign Born to commemorate her twenty-five years of service.

King was exceptionally skilled at finding narrow points of law and technical arguments to win individual cases, while at the same time looking for broader grounds that could win classes of cases and forge new law. An example of this talent was seen in her representation of John Zydoc. Zydoc had been a Communist Party member in his youth but had lived in Detroit for thirty-seven years, worked the same job for seventeen years, raised children as U.S. citizens, sold $50,000 in United States bonds, and donated blood during World War II, never violating the law nor engaging in any subversive or questionable activities. Yet Zydoc was targeted for deportation and held without bail. Zydoc was to give King her first opportunity to present oral argument before the United States Supreme Court in her thirty years of practice.

Despite her earlier trepidation, King had become a skilled litigator. She rose to the challenge and argued passionately, with a focus on Zydoc as an individual. King was seriously ill at the time she made the argument. The government attorneys who opposed her respected her deeply, to the point of arranging for their own driver to take her to the train station after the court appearance. King went into the hospital almost immediately, where she faced two surgeries for cancer. During the next few weeks she met with many friends, family, and professional associates, and learned that she was to be a grandmother. She remained cheerful until her death in early 1952. Sadly, she was to lose the *Zydoc* case when the Supreme Court ruled that John Zydoc could be held without bail.

King is remembered for her brilliant mind and fighting spirit, as well as for her passion for living and for people she cared about. Though she suffered many crushing defeats in her career, she enjoyed great victories. King helped structure building blocks that subsequent lawyers used to win greater rights for workers, the foreign born, and others to whom King was so committed. Her legacy has long survived her tragically timed death. Even the *Zydoc* case, lost in a 5–4 decision, included broad and strongly worded dissents by the minority justices that provided the basis for later civil rights cases.

King is also remembered for her unique style. She frequently referred to herself as a "he-woman with a heart." By her combination of audacity and charm, she repeatedly accomplished remarkable things. On one occasion she convinced her colleague Wendell Wilke, the head of the Republican Party, to partner with her to argue a case in which her client was the head of the Communist Party. King became a role model for activists and attorneys devoted to civil rights. Today, the immigration project of the National Lawyers Guild annually bestows the Carol King award on an outstanding person or team working in the field of immigration law.

MARGARET
CHASE SMITH

1897 – 1995

MARGARET CHASE SMITH GAVE MANY YEARS OF SERVICE TO Congress, first in the House and then in the Senate. She was one of the first women to be elected to the United States Senate and the first to win election to both houses of Congress. Her career spanned thirty-two years and the terms of six different presidents.

At the time Smith broke into the Senate, it was commonly considered the world's most exclusive men's club, and the Maine Republican was referred to alternatively as "the conscience of the Senate" and a "Yankee to be reckoned with."

Smith was acclaimed for both her thorny personality and the red roses she wore on her shoulder each day. She did not hesitate to hand out severe scoldings to those who were less than forthright with her or who displayed a negative attitude. Yet her steely exterior harbored a tender heart. When President Kennedy was assassinated, she came to the Senate chambers early the next morning to lay a single red rose across his old desk.

Smith was born in 1898, the daughter of a waitress and the town barber of Skowhegan, Maine, and the oldest child in a family of six. She started working at the age of twelve, stocking shelves at a dime store. After graduating from high school in 1916, where she made a name for herself on the basketball team, she taught for a few months in a one-room schoolhouse. She then moved on to the more lucrative position of telephone operator, where she earned ten cents per hour. In 1919 she went to work on a local paper as circulation manager. Eventually she became office manager at a wool mill.

In 1930, Chase married Clyde H. Smith, an active participant in local Republican politics who six years later was elected to the U.S. House of Representatives. Margaret served as his secretary, assisting him in researching bills and traveling along on fact-finding tours for his work on the House Labor Committee. When he died in 1940, she was asked to complete his term.

Margaret Chase Smith took to political office immediately. The old style of grassroots campaigning came naturally to her. With a strong foundation of integrity, she never hesitated to cross party lines to support the ideas she believed in, such as aid to education and government-financed medical care. She was re-elected to the house four times on her own.

When she decided to run for the Senate in 1948, she was opposed by the bosses of Maine's Republican Party, yet won handily. When she was sworn in to her first Senate term in 1949, Smith stated, "I consider that women are people, and the record they make is a matter of ability and desire rather than of their sex." She went on to establish a record of service that more than proved her point, often sacrificing personal fulfillment in the interest of her calling.

Once her political career took off, Smith had little time for her personal life, but she enjoyed many years of close and devoted friendship with her chief assistant Bill Lewis, who lived in the same building. Once, when looking back, Smith commented that she wished she had made more time for love in her life.

Smith was considered taciturn, preferring to work behind the scenes on committees to get the business of Congress accomplished.

She seldom spoke on the Senate floor, but when she did, it was for good reason. One of her most famous speeches, though not considered so at the time, was her reaction to Senator Joseph McCarthy's witch hunt for alleged Communists. Smith resented the way McCarthy preyed upon fear in the new atomic age. She believed McCarthy's major interest was in making headlines. Not surprisingly, as he gained power his tactics and ethics plummeted. Smith became increasingly offended by McCarthy's sordid acts and the damage she saw him doing to both Congress and the nation.

Most Republicans in the Senate either supported McCarthy or kept silent. In the spring of 1950, Smith listened to McCarthy smear the good names of a number of people without offering any evidence in support of his charges. At this, Smith became enraged. She had been in the Senate just over one year and hoped someone else with more seniority would stand up to the demagogue. But she watched for a week and saw those she counted on either praising or deferring to McCarthy's smarmy tactics, and knew she would have to be the one to call him to account. Because congressional privilege protected McCarthy from those who could otherwise file suit against him for slander, Smith, always fiercely independent, felt it her duty to put a stop to the damage he was doing.

Smith gathered the support of six fellow Republican senators before presenting her "declaration of conscience," written at her kitchen table, on the Senate floor. She later recalled being extremely nervous before delivering her speech—and with good reason. It took awesome courage to buck the powerful within a senator's own party. She knew it could be political suicide. On the morning she was to present her declaration, she instructed that no copies were to be given to the press until she had been speaking for three minutes. Rumors abounded both on the Senate floor and in the media. When she rose to speak, most of the senators were present—a rare event.

Smith opened by describing how the Senate had become a forum for hate and character assassination, shielded by congressional immunity. As soon as she began to speak, many of her fellow Republican senators began walking out. A number of Democrats followed. Congressmen in both parties feared McCarthy, and many were too timid to give even an audience to someone who dared to level criticism.

Yet Smith continued to speak out. She invoked the duty to uphold the Constitution, which guarantees not only freedom of speech but also trial by jury, not by accusation. She spoke of the right of all Americans to criticize and hold unpopular beliefs, and the right to independent thought. She spoke harshly against those who put party politics before the Constitution and supported McCarthy simply because they considered him an effective weapon against the Democrats. She stated, "I don't want to see the Republican Party ride to political victory on the four horsemen of calumny—fear, ignorance, bigotry, and smear. It will be a more lasting defeat for the American people."

McCarthy listened to the speech with a snide, contemptuous look on his face. Shortly thereafter, he began a campaign of revenge. He had Smith ousted from her seat on the Senate Permanent Investigating Committee and appointed Richard M. Nixon, the new California senator, in her place. He openly threatened to break her "politically, mentally, and financially." Predictably, he called her a friend of Communists.

McCarthy went on to support a challenger he had handpicked to oppose Smith in the next primary election, a candidate with the backing of big money. Yet Margaret Chase Smith knew her constituents, and knew that a lavish campaign would not impress them. She accepted no money and spent little on her efforts toward election, instead traveling to almost every town in the state to meet and talk to the people directly. When the primary election was held, Smith defeated McCarthy's candidate by a margin of five to one.

As McCarthy became increasingly vicious, people began to sicken at his deplorable tactics. Smith's primary victory had shown that McCarthy was not all-powerful, and this was a blow to the illusion of omnipotence he had carefully constructed. Smith's courageous stand against McCarthy established her place in Congress. She became widely admired for both her outspokenness and her independence.

Finally, McCarthy was censured by the Senate, and his reign of political terror ended.

Margaret Chase Smith went on to become the first woman to be placed in nomination for president at the national convention of the Republican Party in 1968. She served in the Senate until the age of seventy-four, in later years traveling the halls of the Capitol on a small yellow cart. She was often critical of modern campaign strategies, with so much riding upon the amount of money a candidate could spend. Smith steadfastly refused to accept contributions from either individuals or special-interest groups.

Throughout her life, Smith was known for her quick wit and a consistent ability to laugh at herself. She was especially amused when a fourth-grade student at Margaret Chase Smith Elementary School in her hometown of Skowhegan asked her how it felt to be named after a school. In 1989, Smith was awarded the President's Medal of Freedom. Democratic senator Stewart Symington of Missouri summed up the opinion of Smith held by many bipartisan admirers when he said, "She represents just about all that is best today in American political life—even if she is a Republican."

EUNICE HUNTON
CARTER

1899 – 1970

EUNICE HUNTON WAS BORN AT THE DAWN OF THE TWENTIETH century, the daughter of highly respected parents prominent in Atlanta's black community. Her father, originally a Canadian, worked as a national executive for the YMCA and he had been instrumental in making YMCA services available to blacks in the South. Eunice's mother, Addie Waites Hunton, was a teacher who had worked with the YWCA in France during World War I and who continued supporting that organization. With parents so committed to community service, it is not surprising that Eunice became a dedicated leader.

The Hunton family, driven from Atlanta by the violence that swept the city after a series of race riots in 1906, relocated to Brooklyn, New York. Eunice attended public schools there, then accompanied her mother to Strasbourg, Germany, where Addie Hunton studied at Kaiser Wilhelm University for two years and Eunice continued her public education, gaining an enlightened perspective and a love of travel that was to last her lifetime.

After returning to New York and completing her studies, Eunice enrolled at Smith College. By 1921, she earned both a bachelor's and a master's degree, with a thesis that addressed reform in state government. She continued her education with courses at Columbia, then went to work for a series of family service agencies. She married Lisle Carter, a dentist originally from Barbados, and bore a son, Lisle Jr.

Carter rapidly gained respect in her career, but she longed for a more active role in improving society. A devout Episcopalian, her faith, combined with the commitment to public service ingrained during her early years, led her to law. She entered Fordham University in 1927. After graduating in 1932, she was admitted to the bar of New York and began a private practice. She remained active in civic organizations and Republican politics. Yet racial tension again launched Carter in a new direction. Harlem was torn by riots in 1935, and Mayor Fiorello LaGuardia needed people who understood conditions in Harlem to assist in city government. Eunice Carter was appointed secretary of the Committee on Conditions in Harlem. Subsequently, she was hired by New York County District Attorney William C. Dodge as an assistant D.A.

Carter's job involved low-level prosecutions in the city's magistrate court, in large part devoted to prosecuting a nonstop stream of prostitutes. She soon noticed a repeating pattern. Most of the defendants were represented by the same lawyers, dealt with the same bondsmen, and told the same stories. A disbarred lawyer named Abe Karp, reputed to have underworld ties, was constantly present. Carter formed a theory that organized crime had begun controlling prostitution in the city. District Attorney Dodge dismissed the idea, but Special Prosecutor Thomas E. Dewey, recently appointed to investigate organized crime and corruption in the city, was impressed. He invited her to join his staff, which was preparing an unprecedented grand jury investigation into organized crime, with a special focus on the Harlem rackets run by notorious gangster Dutch Schultz. Carter was the only woman, as well as the only black, on the staff. Dewey called his crack prosecution team "Twenty Against the Underworld," and later chronicled its triumphs in a book of the same name.

Carter's hunch proved correct. With Dodge's reluctant blessing, a full-scale investigation was launched, revealing a sophisticated operation controlled by major racketeers, later estimated to gross $12 million a year on prostitution alone, even during the height of the Depression. Connections to various underworld kingpins were also made. Dewey ordered a full-scale raid of eighty houses of prostitution, conducted simultaneously by a force of 160 policemen. Many of the city's best-known madams were arrested, including such luminaries as Silver-Tongued Elsie, Jennie the Factory, Cockeyed Florence, Fat Rae, and Sadie the Chink. Carter was instrumental in developing evidence uncovered in the raid that led to the sensational trial and ultimate conviction of renowned mobster Charles "Lucky" Luciano. The operation was the biggest prosecution effort against organized crime in the nation's history. That same year, Dewey became district attorney and promoted Carter to deputy assistant district attorney for the county. As chief of the Special Sessions Bureau, she was responsible for overseeing more than 14,000 cases each year. She held this post for ten years.

In 1945, Carter returned to private practice. Continuing her involvement in Republican politics, she remained closely associated with Dewey and Nelson Rockefeller. She built a successful trial practice and continued her active community service. Working with various women's groups, Carter strongly supported equality for women throughout her life. She was a close friend of educator Mary McLeod Bethune, and the two traveled together to San Francisco in 1945 as joint representatives of the National Council of Negro Women (NCNW) at the founding conference of the United Nations. Carter was a charter member of the NCNW and served the organization in various capacities, including legal advisor. She was the accredited observer for the organization at the UN for nine years. In 1947, Carter was named a consultant to the UN's Economic and Social Council for the International Council of Women. She also served as chair of its Committee of Laws.

An avid traveler, Carter made regular trips to Europe. In 1954, she was invited by the German government to act as adviser to women in public life. In 1955, she attended the UN Conference in Geneva, where she was elected chair of the International Conference of Non-Governmental Organizations. True to her roots, she was also actively involved with the YWCA. She served on the national board, participated in the international divisions, and was especially committed to the Upper Manhattan (formerly Harlem) YWCA branch.

Carter retired from active practice in 1952, but she remained a steadfast supporter of women's equality and continued to volunteer for public service organizations until her death in 1970. Those who knew her described her as strong-willed, charming, and a stimulating conversationalist who was at ease among people from all walks of life.

FANNY
HOLTZMANN

1903 – 1980

FANNY HOLTZMANN WON FAME AS THE LAWYER WHO "STILLED the roar of the MGM Lion," when she represented members of the exiled Russian Romanoff family in a libel suit over the MGM film *Rasputin*. Also called the "Greta Garbo of the Bar," Holtzmann represented many luminaries of the film industry during the 1930s and '40s, as well as authors, playwrights, and politicians.

During most of her life, however, Holtzmann was famous only to those within her circle of clients and friends—and she preferred it this way. Her beauty and sparkling wit inspired romantic involvement with many suitors, including the exiled King George II of Greece, but she never married. Among the proposals she good-naturedly rejected was one from the ninety-year-old George Bernard Shaw.

Holtzmann's petite, delicate appearance belied her formidable intellect and unique ability to shape the law to do her bidding. Playwright Moss Hart once commented that she was "as helpless as the Bethlehem Steel Company." Holtzmann's achievements during her long career are almost too numerous to list. She participated in the drafting of the original United Nations charter, helped hundreds of Jewish refugees escape Hitler shortly before World War II, and had a hand in the creation of the State of Israel. Holtzmann also worked on the rescue of British war orphans and Hong Kong refugees. Some legal scholars consider her the first true expert in American film copyright law.

Holtzmann was born in turn-of-the-century Brooklyn, where her parents had immigrated from Eastern Europe a few years earlier. Family was all-important to Holtzmann. Her grandfather, Rabbi Hirsch Bornfield, known by the Yiddish endearment *Zaida,* was a tremendous influence on the awkward young Fanny, who could not seem to keep her grades at a level acceptable to the rest of her family. Her beloved Zaida came to America at the age of seventy from his native Polish village, and he lived on another twenty-six years to continue as a respected rabbi and popular community sage. He taught young Fanny integrity, persistence, imagination, and flexibility. Her mother, Theresa, a well-educated beauty from a privileged background, often found life difficult with Henry Holtzmann. Fanny's father was a "professional dreamer," a philosopher, journalist, and poet, in addition to his work as a teacher and social worker assisting other Jewish immigrants. The Holtzmanns' mutual jealousy endured through their fifty-year marriage and kept things noisy around the Holtzmann home.

Fanny was the fourth child born into the growing, boisterous family. Although the family faced constant financial difficulty, they eventually became comfortable as Henry's success and political contacts grew. Theodore Roosevelt, who had met and worked with Henry while serving as police commissioner of New York City, became friends with the Holtzmann family and other Jewish intellectuals in the neighborhood.

Fanny Holtzmann's lifetime of remarkable achievement got off to a very slow start. She loved to read but had little patience with subjects that bored her, and while her siblings achieved in academics, dance, music, and social skills, Fanny struggled to even get through Sunday school. But her fascination with the law began early. When her older brother, Jack Holtzmann, became an attorney, she often skipped school to watch him in court and to help out in his office.

When her grandfather moved in with the family during Fanny's early adolescence, the two formed an instant bond. Fanny loved to listen to his tales of the old country, and to accompany him to plays, theater, and concerts. Zaida was blessed with natural courage and stamina, as well as a knack for entertaining everyone around him. Fanny picked up these qualities as the two roamed the streets bargaining with vendors and recruiting new immigrants for Henry's citizenship class.

Zaida often made informal arguments in the municipal courts on behalf of neighborhood immigrants. He frequently passed his hat through the courtroom, even getting contributions from the judge, to raise the rent money to keep a family from being evicted. Zaida even held his own "court" in the family kitchen, under a tradition of old rabbinical law, to settle minor disputes among members of his congregation. During these sessions Fanny brewed tea for participants and observed the proceedings, gleaning valuable tips on how to negotiate settlements.

Fanny dropped out of high school and began taking a business course in the hope of being able to continue her work around the law. After a short stint as a legal secretary, her employer dismissed her because her shorthand and typing were hopeless. He did, however, praise her natural intelligence and suggest she might do better as a lawyer than as a secretary. Fanny's mother had a close friend who was a female attorney in the neighborhood, and with encouragement from her, Zaida, and her parents, Fanny found the courage to face what seemed a formidable challenge: earning the college credits required for entrance to law school. Though Jack jeered at her efforts, he needed a clerk, so he let her work in his office during the day.

With the added help of a supportive principal, Fanny completed her course work and went on to Fordham Law School as a night student, working with a law firm during the day. The only time she could find to study was during the long trolley and subway rides between her home and the Woolworth Building, where both her office and school were housed. This became a habit for life, and whenever she needed to concentrate totally she would board a large moving vehicle.

Fanny Holtzmann's approach to justice was to remain both eccentric and remarkably effective for the duration of her career. One day while in court to file some papers for her brother, she leaped up and made an impassioned plea for Mrs. Scully, a pregnant woman with nine children who was about to be turned out of her apartment into the street. Following Zaida's tradition, she took up a collection among those in the courtroom and saved the family's home. She went on to "adopt" the Scully family, paying a quarter of her salary to them each week. She continued to share the family's friendship and support throughout her life. The Scully children called her Aunt Fanny Claus.

The firm where Fanny worked during law school represented quite a number of show business clients. The partners were impressed by Fanny's creative ideas on how to better serve them. While still a first-year student, she opened a branch office for the firm in the Broadway district. Long accustomed to being surrounded by important people, Fanny had little trepidation about confronting the powerful. One of her first tasks involved successfully negotiating a settlement with William Randolph Hearst. Soon she became a combination of legal liaison, credit counselor, and business manager for numerous performers, including Edmund Goulding, an English actor and writer.

Goulding was dazzled by Fanny's beauty as well as her skills. A stream of gifts began pouring into the office, and he once took her for an airplane ride, a unique thrill in the 1920s. He also brought her to the famous Algonquin round table, where he introduced her to such literary stars as Dorothy Parker, Robert Benchley, and Alexander Wollcott. Goulding and other clients admired Fanny's savvy, fresh innocence, brilliant mind, and unmitigated chutzpah.

Through Goulding and his friends, a steady stream of talented and creative people flocked to the office. Much of the assistance she provided was in the realm of business management, and she was careful to avoid giving legal advice while still a student, although the clients lined up with retainers in hand. On the day she graduated from law school at the age of twenty-one, she closed a $10,000 film deal that made her late to the ceremony as a result.

Fanny passed the bar with the third-highest rating in the State of New York. But she also needed approval by the character committee, a division of the New York Court of Appeals. She applied for early admission but was turned down after board members received a short, nasty letter by an anti-Semite who accused her of practicing without a license. Fanny was crushed but undaunted. She traveled to Albany to appear before the court of appeals, since the full court had final jurisdiction on bar admissions.

She convinced them to call a special session and argued her case eloquently before three judges, including Benjamin Cardozo, the future United States Supreme Court justice. After her impassioned plea she was admitted immediately, with a waiver of the usual clerkship requirement. Cardozo, impressed with Fanny's spirit, befriended and counseled her. At his suggestion, she took courses on copyright and motion picture production at Columbia University to better serve her growing clientele.

Eddie Goulding remained a close friend and important client as his stellar Hollywood career grew. Speculation about whether the two were in love has never been resolved. Fanny professed she never allowed herself to fall for him, as he was a Gentile, a problem drinker, and above all a client.

Holtzmann's beloved grandfather delighted in her steady progress, providing humor and encouragement until his death at the age of ninety-six. In turn, through her connections with the bootlegging industry, Fanny, though herself a lifetime teetotaler, saw that Zaida received regular deliveries of plum brandy and rye whiskey. Meanwhile, Holtzmann's entertainment clientele increased steadily. She took every case to heart, winning admiration and steady referrals from clients such as Fred and Adele Astaire and Clifton Webb. Yet she also felt a responsibility to help the downtrodden and destitute. She once burst into tears at a meeting with President Calvin Coolidge when pleading for a pardon on behalf of a jailed client, whose distraught wife had threatened to kill herself and their baby. Reportedly, Coolidge sighed and granted the pardon. Ted Berkman, Holtzmann's nephew and biographer, remarked in his book *The Lady and the Law*, "She practiced law as if she had invented it." Fanny herself once explained, "I don't follow precedent, I establish it." Although some criticized her for her disregard of professional propriety, her admirers far outnumbered her detractors.

Holtzmann tried to stay in the background, but a "girl lawyer," especially a young and pretty one acquainted with movie stars and presidents, was a novelty in the 1920s. Holtzmann received plenty of attention from the press. On a trip to England, she was "adopted" by an American Bar Association delegation (though at that time women could not join the organization) and included in events such as a reception at Buckingham Palace. Holtzmann began to commute frequently between New York, Hollywood, and England, as her client base in the three areas grew. The English saw her as a prime source of Hollywood information, and Fanny was happy to provide news, although she was always discreet about keeping secrets. As Holtzmann began to spend more time in Hollywood, she became friendly with Louis B. Mayer, who brought her into the extended embrace of the MGM family.

Though she was known to compare her Hollywood clients to circus animals in need of a lion tamer, Holtzmann was devoted to doing her best for them. A few, such as Greta Garbo, became good friends. Studio heads were also impressed with her ability to forge unique solutions to the problems that kept cropping up in the new industry. As she puttered with Mayer in his kitchen, she often advised him on such diverse topics as how to find suitable escorts for female stars (Holtzmann advised contacting the titled Europeans living in Hollywood) or recommending a clause in actors' contracts providing that voices could be dubbed for those unable to make the transition into sound pictures from the silents. Mayer once referred to her as a female Solomon.

Holtzmann's younger brother David, who followed her to law school, became her partner. It was an excellent match, as David had an outstanding grasp on legal logic and more traditional techniques, balancing Fanny's intuitive style.

Holtzmann's greatest asset was her ability to find innovative solutions to impossible problems, often bringing clients together to the advantage of everyone involved. In 1931, when the Depression was hitting worldwide, she saw and was deeply moved by Noel Coward's play *Cavalcade* while on a trip to England. She arranged a complex scheme involving Coward, the nearly defunct Fox Studios, the British Empire Marketing Board, and others to bring Hollywood money from worldwide markets and help England gain both profits and positive public relations. The subsequent movie deal was credited with saving Fox Studios from bankruptcy, and *Cavalcade* became a box office hit that netted an Oscar. Such coups gained Holtzmann the awe and respect of both colleagues and clients. At last, the gushy press accounts of the "dark-eyed lawyer girl" gave way to serious interviews.

In addition to arranging complicated schemes like the *Cavalcade* deal, Fanny also had a knack for changing history with a telephone call or two. She convinced the executives at RKO Studios to take a chance on one of her clients who was moving from New York to Hollywood, suggesting that Fred Astaire be paired with "one of the girl hoofers on your lot, maybe Ginger Rogers." Clients sometimes called her their fairy godmother.

Holtzmann had a special fondness for authors. She advised such literary icons as Rudyard Kipling, P.G. Wodehouse, Louis Bromfield, and Frances Hackett. Additionally, she often helped authors sell their books to filmmakers. Yet despite her growing fame and high-life connections, she continued to live with her parents while in New York and considered the old family headquarters her real home.

Holtzmann was finally forced to give up a good portion of her cherished anonymity when the *Rasputin* case brought her nationwide celebrity. The Russian Princess Irina, niece of the slaughtered czar Nicholas II, was exiled in France when she called upon Fanny to represent her in a matter that had caused her deep embarrassment. The princess was upset over an MGM movie in which a character she recognized as herself was portrayed as the mistress of

Rasputin, a Siberian peasant who had professed to have magical healing powers and managed to insinuate himself into the czar's home. The princess swore she had never met Rasputin and was outraged at the portrayal. Her husband was reportedly Rasputin's killer, adding yet another odd twist to the story. The princess's mother, sister to the czar, knew the actual details of the events and assisted with the libel suit against MGM.

Holtzmann knew she faced a tough case. In the movie, names had been changed and much was fictionalized. Yet a statement at the beginning of the film presented it as history and proclaimed that a few principal characters were still alive. Moreover, key facts in the film indeed paralleled reality.

She first tried to end the matter quietly with friend Louis B. Mayer, and a tentative agreement was reached. MGM's lawyers, however, refused to approve the settlement. So Holtzmann teamed up with Sir Patrick Hastings, a leading English barrister, and filed a libel suit in England, where the movie was scheduled to open after its American run. As the exiled Romanoffs were penniless, their British cousins, including Holtzmann's close friend King George V, paid the legal fees.

The English jury ruled in favor of the plaintiffs, granting an award of approximately $125,000 in damages. The judge also granted an injunction against further showings of the movie. The case was affirmed on appeal, and it became a landmark in defamation law. Suddenly Fanny found herself in high demand among the international press, London society, celebrities, and royals. For a time, she casually kept company with the exiled king of Greece, George II, who would visit her London apartment for dinner and be put to work helping out in the kitchen, sometimes in the company of George Burns and Gracie Allen. At the same time, Holtzmann was pursued by Prince Frederick of Prussia, but she never became serious about any of her royal suitors. She was also courted by publisher Max Schuster of Simon & Schuster fame, who credited her for suggesting he begin publishing paperback books like the ones she had seen in Europe.

In the 1930s, Holtzmann visited the Polish villages from which her family had immigrated. There she met many relatives still living in tiny, remote, old-world towns. She was deeply moved as her grandfather's tales came to life. On one trip, she alleviated a family crisis by providing dowries for young cousins, as well as a much more valuable gift, her company and influence. Eventually, she put up a dowry for every orphan in the area. On her return to America, she urged others to adopt a family in this poor region, where even a pittance could change lives.

When the Nazis began to come to power, Holtzmann had a personal stake in fighting to admit more Jewish refugees to the United States, especially children. She conferred with her friend Supreme Court Justice Felix Frankfurter, and even met with President Roosevelt, plus every other political power she knew, to push for the admission of Jewish refugees. She gathered together powerful politicians and businesspeople to form the Association for the Resettlement of Oppressed People, to bring war refugees of all backgrounds to new settlements in the United States and Mexico.

Although Joseph Kennedy, patriarch of the political family, was an old nemesis from a bitter dispute in Hollywood, Holtzmann won the support of Joseph Kennedy Jr. and his brother Jack. As always, Holtzmann's ingenuity paid off. Many refugees were able to flee on temporary visas purportedly allowing them to visit America for the 1939 World's Fair. Holtzmann worked tirelessly alongside the young Kennedys, and the group often traveled just ahead of the Nazis, at considerable risk. She endured heartbreaking failures, including the loss of many members of her own family. Yet she successfully helped hundreds of others escape the concentration camps.

In 1945, Holtzmann represented the Chinese delegation to the United Nations. At the same time, she worked with Adlai Stevenson and Eleanor Roosevelt, both of whom became friends, on the early United Nations conferencing efforts. Holtzmann also gave tremendous energy to help establish a Jewish homeland—mediating, garnering support, and lobbying to help bring the new state into being. She was later gratified to see some of her European relatives settle there.

Holtzmann took up painting as a mid-life hobby, and discovered an undeniable, if unorthodox, artistic talent. Hallmark bought the rights to several of her works for use on its greeting cards. She also sculpted, and created a bust of Dwight D. Eisenhower that was admired by the subject, also a friend, and was displayed at the Philadelphia Museum of Art.

All the while she continued her unique practice of combining law, business, and friendship, sometimes achieving almost mystical connections. After reading a book called *Anna and the King of Siam*, she saw the possibility of an acting role for her friend Gertrude Lawrence. She gave the book to Oscar Hammerstein, suggesting he produce a musical, which became *The King and I*. When Lawrence died of cancer, Holtzmann and her brother David established the Gertrude Lawrence Foundation for Cancer Research.

Holtzmann met George Bernard Shaw when he was ninety years old and she instantly recognized a carbon copy of her Zaida. The two enjoyed a lively friendship full of argument, humor, vitality, and wit. Her nephew-biographer, Ted Berkman, referred to Shaw and Zaida as her "twin sages."

In the 1950s and '60s, Holtzmann's practice began to shift toward tax, estate, and corporate work. Yet she kept in touch with such former clients and friends as Greta Garbo, Fred Astaire, and Noel Coward and continued to serve a balanced clientele that included the family of the creator of the Popeye comic strip, whom she represented in a copyright dispute, as well as the people in her old neighborhood.

Holtzmann always professed that she had never met a stranger, and throughout her life she delighted in new people, forging friendships at all levels of society and talking with anyone who enjoyed conversation, especially the very old and the very young.

RACHEL
CARSON

1907 – 1964

F EW INDIVIDUALS, AND FEW BOOKS, MAY BE ACCURATELY credited with changing the course of history. Yet in the case of Rachel Carson and her classic work, *Silent Spring,* this description may be honestly applied.

Rachel Carson's devotion was fueled by her love for the natural world. Carson was born in 1907 in Pennsylvania's Allegheny Valley, the youngest of three children of Robert and Maria Carson. Her father sold insurance and real estate, and her mother was a teacher who taught her to love books, music, nature, and new ideas. Carson later remarked that she could remember no time when she wasn't interested in the outdoors. A solitary child, she spent much of her time in the woods. From an early age she planned to be a writer, and had a story published in the *Saint Nicholas* magazine at the age of ten.

Rachel's intellectual ambition, encouraged by her mother, won her a scholarship to Pennsylvania College for Women, later Chatham

College, where she started as an English major. She soon switched to biology, however, after taking a required course taught by Mary Scott Skinker, known to be a brilliant teacher. The steadfast encouragement of Maria Carson and Mary Skinker proved key to Rachel's achievements. These capable women set an early example that a person's potential need not be hampered by her gender.

At first, Carson thought that she had abandoned her literary ambitions when she made the switch to biology. But she soon discovered that her studies inspired her and gave her something to write about. After graduating magna cum laude in 1929, Carson won a scholarship, with Skinker's help, to Johns Hopkins University. Despite a persistent prejudice against women in science, Carson excelled, teaching summer school at the university even before her graduation. She spent breaks at the Marine Biological Laboratory in Woods Hole, Massachusetts, which strengthened her lifelong passion for the sea. Carson also joined the Zoology Department at the University of Maryland.

In the mid 1930s, Carson was hired by the United States Bureau of Fisheries in Washington as a junior aquatic biologist, one of the first two women to be hired by the bureau in a professional capacity. The sudden deaths of her father and married sister had left Carson with additional responsibilities, as she and her mother assumed care of her sister's two young daughters. Yet she found time to write, publishing in the *Baltimore Sunday Sun* and producing her first article for a national magazine titled "Under Sea," in the *Atlantic Monthly*, in 1937. A prominent author and an editor at Simon & Schuster urged her to develop the article into a book, which became *Under the Sea Wind*.

Carson continued to write throughout World War II, preparing conservation bulletins for the government and managing the publications program of the bureau, which had by then become the United States Fish and Wildlife Service. By 1949 she had been promoted to biologist and chief editor. Shirley Briggs, a colleague and close friend, recalled that Carson's zest and humor helped bring a sense of adventure into the otherwise dull bureaucratic routine. Carson especially enjoyed writing and editing a series of twelve illustrated booklets on the national wildlife refuges, entitled *Conservation in Action* and later was credited with setting a new standard for government publications.

Carson continued writing magazine articles on natural-history subjects to supplement her income and provide an additional creative outlet. She also worked for a period of years on her second book, *The Sea Around Us,* which was serialized in *The New Yorker* and published in 1951. The book became a best-seller and earned Carson, always a private person, considerable notoriety. She was highly amused by one letter, which read, "I assume from the author's knowledge that he must be a man." The book won widespread acclaim, including the John Burroughs Medal, the National Book Award, and the *New York Times* poll as outstanding book of the year.

The book also brought Carson some long-awaited financial security, including a Guggenheim Foundation fellowship that allowed her to resign from her government post and turn to full-time writing in 1952. She was now, as well, able to achieve her dream of a cottage by the sea. In 1953 she built her home in West Southport, Maine, on land overlooking Sheepscot Bay. Family tragedy again brought change, when in 1957 one of her nieces died, and Carson adopted her five-year-old son, Roger Christie. He inspired her to begin writing for children. At the same time, she was preparing to embark upon the most important project of her career.

Carson had been aware of the dangers of DDT and other persistent poisons ever since their use in the private sector began after World War II, but little interest was shown when she proposed articles on the subject to magazines. By 1958, however, she felt compelled to bring these hazards to public attention. Carson refused to accept the devastation of the natural world as an inevitable cost of progress. She put aside her other work and began gathering scientific evidence on the damage wrought by widespread use of DDT and synthetic pesticides. The result was *Silent Spring,* a book that altered the course of law and industry and that sparked an international environmental movement throughout the world.

Before writing *Silent Spring,* Carson had spent fourteen years in the Fish and Wildlife Service for the United States government. It was through this work she discovered the chinks in existing federal environmental regulations and learned of the manipulation of data to obscure the hazards to people and all living things from irresponsible use of pesticides. Carson decided to focus on pesticides in her new book, after receiving a letter from a friend, who implored her to use her position in the Fish and Wildlife Service to help stop government spraying of DDT that was decimating wildlife near her home. Heeding a call begun by John Muir a century before, Carson spoke out for reform—first in her book, and later in congressional hearings, where she testified on behalf of new legislation to protect the environment.

Carson knew that her task would not be easy. As one biographer stated, she had to find a way to "make hydrocarbons compelling." She also knew—and intended—that she would spark an uproar. Therefore, she had to begin with an unshakable foundation to support her theories. And Carson turned out to be the perfect person for this job. Her background was in marine biology, and she had already written several well-received books about the ocean. Her lyrical style and passionate dedication, combined with scientific expertise, gave the book both credibility and readability.

Carson also had to debunk the persistent myth, espoused by the chemical industry, that pesticides were the panacea for famine and plague throughout the world. Instead, she created a scenario of the crisis that could occur if the use of toxins continued unchecked. She eerily predicted events that were later realized in ecological disasters such as the chemical spill at Bhopal, India, in 1985, in which the release of methylisocyanate into a residential neighborhood left 2,000 people dead and 200,000 injured, with tens of thousands more permanently disabled.

Carson knew from the beginning that *Silent Spring* would be explosive in both positive and negative ways. As she suspected, there was a desperate attack by the chemical industry to discredit the book. Chemical companies withdrew advertising from magazines that favorably reviewed the book. It was called a "Communist plot" to ruin

American agriculture, industry, and the economy. Waving the flag of "progress," scientists employed by the chemical companies assaulted her research. Carson was lambasted with sexist epithets, called a spinster, labeled irrational and hysterical, and characterized as an extremist who cared more about birds than starving children.

Yet Carson was not an extremist. She favored selective use of pesticides when necessary to control crop damage in a reasonable manner. What she opposed was the common practice of spraying entire towns and counties with deadly poisons. She wanted both the government and the industry to control such random misuse of chemicals, and to study their effects on both humans and the natural world more carefully before they were introduced into the environment.

Silent Spring, originally serialized in *The New Yorker*, began to make waves even before the full text was published. When the first installment came out, Congressman John Lindsay of New York read portions into the Congressional Record. Jacqueline Kennedy met with Carson and others concerned with the threat of pesticides. President Kennedy directed his science advisor, Dr. Jerome Weisner, to establish a commission to study the problem of pesticides and their long-term dangers, and to prepare a report on the use and regulations of pesticides in the United States. Weisner's report was released in May 1963. It acknowledged the impact of *Silent Spring* and adopted many of its recommendations. The night after the report broke, Eric Sevareid stated on the CBS news that Carson had accomplished her dual aims of alerting the public and building a fire under the government.

Carson was called to testify before the President's Science Advisory Committee. The Senate Committee on Environmental Hazards convened almost immediately, before which Carson testified recommending legislation to protect individuals from poison and provide legal redress when this right was violated. She also advocated restricting sales and use of pesticides, a change in the registration and approval procedures, and government support for research into new methods of pest control that would eliminate or minimize the use of toxic chemicals. Two days later, she testified before the Senate Committee on Commerce, specifically recommending that an independent agency be established at the executive level that would be free from political or industry influence. Her testimony laid the groundwork for the Environmental Protection Agency.

The book truly shook the world in a way not seen since the publication of *Uncle Tom's Cabin,* also written by an American woman. Within a few years after *Silent Spring* was published in 1962, it had been translated into every language of the industrial world, and every country in which it was widely read had begun holding hearings on environmental legislation. The repercussions of the book are almost beyond calculation. The entire environmental movement, previously existing only in the hearts and minds of a few individuals and fragmented groups, sprang into existence as a major global movement. Even today, *Silent Spring* is considered the most vital and controversial book ever written on the environment.

By the end of 1962, the same year in which the book was published, over forty bills had been introduced in the various state legislatures to regulate pesticide use. Moreover, when held up to scientific scrutiny, the book passed with flying colors. Prominent scientists positively reviewed and supported the work, in contrast to industry scientists with their obvious bias. The book paved the way for environmental legislation throughout Europe, as well as in Brazil, Japan, and Israel. In January 1963, Carson was presented with the Albert Schweitzer medal of the Animal Welfare League. She was also named Conservationist of the Year by the National Wildlife Federation, awarded the Audubon Society medal, and honored with many other awards. In 1970, the Environmental Protection Agency opened its doors with the mission of developing and enforcing environmental regulations, and the first Earth Day was celebrated.

Carson once said that she "felt bound by a solemn obligation" to do all she could to save the natural world. Out of her love of nature and of humanity, along with her belief in the right of both to a healthy environment, one woman and one book spawned hundreds of new laws to protect the earth, dozens of environmental reform groups, and perhaps most incredibly, a complete shifting of the attitude of the public and its values. These people, acting individually or through such groups as the Conservation Law Foundation, the Environmental Defense Fund, and the Natural Resources Defense Council, now lobby for legislation, help draft bills and regulations, participate in environmental impact studies, file lawsuits when laws and regulations are not followed or enforced, clean up waste sites, educate children to respect the natural world, and perform innumerable other acts on behalf of the environment.

A prime example of Carson's direct effect on the law is seen in the Environment Defense Fund, which was formed in 1967 with the specific goal of building a body of case law to establish citizens' rights to a clean environment. One of its early efforts was to achieve the banning of DDT, which the EPA prohibited from further use in 1972.

This worldwide shift was begun by one woman who loved nothing better than to watch the migration of the monarch butterflies along the coast of her home in Maine. Because of her efforts, the environment has become a political priority. Carson has become one of the nation's most important role models, demonstrating how an individual—working alone, through grassroots organizations, or through law and government—can literally alter the course of history.

Sadly, before her book was even finished, Carson was already suffering from the illness that would claim her life. Her last years were spent testifying before Congress, receiving honors for her work, and completing a journey to California to see the redwoods, a lifelong dream. She spent many of her later days watching the creatures in the tide pools near her cottage with endless fascination.

Carson had a unique and rare ability to combine scientific and literary genius to produce a work that reflected both her spiritual connection to nature and her devotion to careful scientific research. As one reviewer wrote of *Silent Spring,* "A few thousand words from her, and the world took a new direction."

GLADYS TOWLES ROOT

1905 – 1982

GLADYS TOWLES ROOT WAS ONE OF AMERICA'S MOST successful criminal defense attorneys, as well as one of the most flamboyant personalities ever to appear in an American courtroom. Her boundless energy and legal brilliance became legendary, as she forged her place as a true original in American law. According to biographer Cy Rice in *Defender of the Damned*, she was like "a technicolor pinwheel in perpetual motion in Cinemascope."

Root won more sex-crime cases than any lawyer in U.S. history. She began accepting these unpopular challenges as a matter of principle when other attorneys refused to represent such clients, and she built a career that was both rewarding and lucrative.

Root was perhaps better known, however, for her eccentric personal style. She stood five feet, eleven inches tall, with a regal bearing and a natural sense of showmanship. Many found her overwhelming, but her sense of justice and compassion were undeniable. It was often said that her legal mind was as brilliant as her costumes. At various times Root was compared to Mae West, Perry Mason, Richard Barnum, and the goddess Juno. Tourists even came to watch her courtroom performances. Her star quality was undeniable, and best of all, the dramas in which she participated were real. It was often said that Root acted, and was treated, like royalty. The crowds who came to watch her fell silent and stepped respectfully aside when she passed.

More important, however, was the fact that Root was a highly respected member of the California bar who averaged some seventy-five court appearances per month. She defended people of all races and social strata, often charging no fees. She frequently spent her weekends traveling to distant jails and formidable prisons to visit her clients. Her courtroom presentations were dramatic but dignified, and juries occasionally broke into spontaneous applause at her eloquent summations.

Root went to great lengths for her clients, often using unorthodox methods to win their acquittal. She employed investigators, researchers, psychiatrists, and scientists in order to cover all possible bases, in an era when such efforts were rare. She immersed herself in the study of subjects as complex as medicine, ink analysis, and forensic chemistry to prepare for cross-examination of her opponents' experts. Never hesitant to bring out the lurid details of a case, she often went to shocking and controversial lengths, bombarding the reputation of prosecution witnesses, including the alleged victims.

Root was born in 1905, on the same day California became a state. She grew up on a wheat ranch, now covered by the sprawl of downtown Los Angeles. Her mother, Clara Dexter Towles, had worked as secretary to the speaker of the house of the Kansas state legislature before the family moved to California. Her father, Charles Towles, had hoped to be a lawyer, but financial pressures interrupted his education and he instead made a comfortable living working for the Singer Sewing Machine Company. Root grew up in a protected, upper-class home, far from the seamier worlds that would captivate her in the future. Yet her mother instilled in her a philosophy of compassion and a belief that good deeds are rewarded in the long run.

From grade school on, Gladys loved dramatics. She staged shows in the family barn and was a member of the Community Players of Hollywood for a time. Her love of color and mischief also surfaced early. One Fourth of July she painted her father's car red, white, and blue. Although mortified, her father admitted that he couldn't fault her patriotism.

Gladys always yearned to stand out and loved creating a sensation. Both her role as a fashion nonconformist, and her skill as an advocate, appeared early on. In grade school, she argued with the teacher over why she had to wear the school uniform when the teacher was not forced to do so herself. As an adolescent, she created her own unique outfits for special occasions, often just hours before she was due to arrive. Sometimes the results were unexpectedly spectacular. On one occasion, a hand-knit angora swimsuit she wore to a beach party stretched its way to transparency on her first dip; on another, she pilfered a silk slip from her older sister and meticulously pinned fresh leaves over it to create a gown for a spring dance. Unfortunately, after hours of dancing in the heat, the leaves sensed a premature autumn and began dropping to the floor.

Fortunately, Gladys's foresight, as well as her skills in fashion design, improved. Her mother encouraged her dramatic talents and hoped she would become an actress, but her father favored law. He suggested during her freshman year in college that she should be on "life's real stage—the courtroom." In a sense, she satisfied the ambitions of both parents.

In 1930, Gladys graduated from the University of Southern California law school. Newly married to Frank Root, she was filled with enthusiasm and ambition. She opened a tiny office in Los Angeles's financial district, just blocks away from skid row.

Root anxiously awaited her first client. Finally, a Filipino man wandered in, explaining that he had ducked into the building to escape the heat and think things over. During his ponderings, he had come to the realization that he needed a divorce, and saw that there was an attorney in the building. Gladys eagerly prepared the papers. Two days later, however, the same man sent a telegram to her from the city jail. She hurried downtown to meet with him, her father's lucky derby perched atop her head. Nearly denied admission to the jail, she was finally allowed to see her client—only to discover that her first case was to defend a murder charge. The man explained he had caught his wife *in flagrante delicto* with a paramour and he killed her. When he asked Root if she had ever lost a case, she could truthfully tell him she had not.

After she left to prepare her defense, the enthusiastic defendant told the other inmates about his great new lawyer. The other unfortunates were intrigued, especially when they learned she cared little about the client's ability to pay fees. Prophetic cries of "Get me Gladys!" rang throughout the jail. Within a month, fifteen defendants had signed on. At first she received little money, but she never worried about starving, as she was frequently paid in chickens, ducks, or geese.

As her mother predicted, Root's generosity paid off in the long run. At one point her office was handling some 1,600 cases a year, more criminal cases than any other private American firm. Clients scorned by other lawyers, particularly those charged with morals offenses, flocked to her door. The misfits, the friendless, and the fundless sought her out, and few were turned away.

Root managed to save her first client from the electric chair, garnering a charge of manslaughter with a short sentence instead. The following year, she won what she later considered the most important case of her career. Another Filipino man came to her to obtain the legal right to marry his Caucasian girlfriend. Root not only researched the law but delved into genetics, racial definitions, and the legislative history of the statute prohibiting such marriages. She quickly formed an argument based on improper classification of the Filipino race, and the law was declared unconstitutional. She received an outpouring of gratitude from California's sizable Filipino population.

It wasn't long before lines of clients began to form outside the door of Root's office—few of whom were able to pay. Her father suggested politics as a means of drawing clients with more cash. Non-partisan Gladys asked him which side she should support, and he suggested

Republicans because they had more money. So Gladys joined a local Junior Republican Club, and she was soon elected president.

With her typical style, Root staged a daring fund-raiser. Organizing a reception in honor of President Hoover, she emptied the treasury to print stylish invitations and sent out dozens—including one to the president, who was not otherwise scheduled to appear. Tickets to the event quickly sold out, more invitations were printed, and the money flowed in.

Finally, she panicked. She sought the assistance of party bigwigs who had urged the young Republicans to do something to enliven the party. But no help was forthcoming. She had also failed to plan her wardrobe, and as guests began to fill the Hollywood Knickerbocker Hotel, Gladys and her mother hastily fashioned an evening dress by draping and pinning two Belgian lace tablecloths around her frame. The attendees waited, growing more restless. Gladys reluctantly rose to address the crowd, just as a telegraph boy dashed in with a message from the president, thanking her for the great honor and extending polite regrets. Speeches and accolades followed. Gladys did not learn until two years later that her mother had arranged for a friend in Washington to send the bogus telegram.

Root's career in politics was short lived. The club sent her to serve as a delegate to a political meeting in Washington, insisting that she wrestle a crate of oranges across the country by train and bus to distribute to other female delegates. Ten minutes into the first session, she stood to speak, only to be told by the moderator that junior delegates were to be seen and not heard. Enraged at being denied a voice, Root stormed back to the hotel and out of politics forever. She gave the oranges to the manager of the hotel, compliments of the Junior Republican Club of Southern California, with instructions that he may serve them to anyone he chose—preferably Democrats.

Times remained lean for Root, and she frequently knitted dresses as she interviewed clients. But news of her skills and aggressive approach in court spread, and her practice among the downtrodden grew rapidly. One derelict even penned a poem in her honor: "Root de toot. Root de toot. Here's to Gladys Towles Root. Her dresses are purple, her hats wide. She'll get you one instead of five."

As Root's finances gradually improved, her wardrobe became more spectacular. Before long she was one of the most visible and talked-about people in Los Angeles, as much for her formidable legal skills as her exotic fashion sense. Even those who referred to her as the "lady in purple" or the "peacock from another planet" respected her talent and success. Root never dressed in conventional courtroom attire, even when addressing the United States Supreme Court. In her single appearance before the nation's highest tribunal, she refused to don the traditional black robe. She was described by local newspapers as wearing "a tight-fitting bronze taffeta dress hemmed with brown velvet, bronze ankle-strap shoes, a topaz ring the size of a silver dollar, and a pin with a stone weighing 190 carats at her bust. Over the dress was a monkey fur cape, all white. Her huge hat was of the same material as the dress and her hair was dyed to match the topaz." The Justices' eyebrows were raised, but Root was allowed to proceed in her own customary attire. Root once explained that these were her working clothes, and if she dressed like the average person she wouldn't be able to do her best.

Judges seldom questioned Root's choice of courtroom dress, with the exception of her Supreme Court rebellion. On the rare occasions she was admonished to remove her hat or make another alteration, she generally followed the court's directives. On one occasion when a judge asked her to remove her hat, she obeyed, only to expose rows of rainbow-colored pin curls. The judge quickly ordered her to put the hat back on. Another time, when she wore an especially low-cut dress to court, the judge hastily called a recess, "to allow any person whose body is overly exposed to make certain alterations that will eliminate a nudity which now prevails." Rather than changing her outfit, Root returned after the recess with attractive lace covering her décolletage, and the trial proceeded. Ever resourceful, she had simply gathered toilet paper from the ladies' room and used her manicure scissors to fashion it into a scalloped lacy design.

Soon Root was making some seventy-five courtroom appearances each month, a pace she maintained throughout her half-century career, including during two pregnancies. She chose a different costume for each appearance, favoring suede, velvet, sequins, ermine tails, and black chantilly lace. Her outfits were either skin tight or draped with dozens of yards of fabric. Her hair, long and naturally blond, was dyed every imaginable shade, sometimes several at once. Root's eccentric style was based on more than pure whim. Having studied the psychological effect of colors, she believed the hue of an inmate's surroundings affected his attitude—a theory that has found scientific support in more recent years. One of the first questions she asked a new client was about his or her favorite color, and she made a point of wearing that shade to boost morale and ease the client's worries. Some had specific requests. One desperado asked for metallic silver with a red rose. Root, of course, obliged, and argued his case in a gown of silver lamé.

Root's unique taste extended to the decoration of her home and office. Her Hancock Park mansion featured a mirrored foyer, sequined doorknobs, and draped satin and velvets. She eventually built a fourteen-room office suite in downtown Los Angeles, with an exterior of black marble trimmed in gold, a purple glass door bearing her name, and an interior predominated by all shades of purple. The elegant office building was so close to skid row that some compared it to a new suit worn over dirty underwear.

On one occasion, Root was spotted strolling down Wilshire Boulevard with her hair dyed pink to match two lambs she led on a leash. Upon questioning, she cheerfully characterized herself as "a little nuts" and "a screwball." Yet many regarded her as an uninhibited, brilliant woman imbued with a sense of drama that could not be suppressed. She neither drank nor smoked, and her only vice was chocolate. She celebrated courtroom victories by asking her maid to produce one of the five-pound boxes of the candy, which she kept stashed for such occasions.

Root was an early advocate of psychiatric treatment, as opposed to punishment, for offenders with identifiable disorders. She pointed out that when such people were incarcerated they were usually released in a more dangerous condition later. She often requested psychiatric examination of the accusing witnesses as well, to weed out those trying to frame the defendant.

Root also helped overturn archaic laws prohibiting "unnatural" forms of consensual lovemaking. She defended many individuals charged with violating these laws, often married couples. She also opposed laws against prostitution, as well as against homosexual relationships between consenting adults. She believed that such laws did nothing to stop behavior that had persisted for centuries; police time, she believed, would be better spent prosecuting true criminals.

Root, a staunch proponent of racial equality, represented many black and Hispanic clients, and had no tolerance for bigotry. On one occasion she coldly turned away a group of neighbors from her exclusive suburb who were circulating a petition trying to prevent Nat "King" Cole from moving into the area because of his race. After a brief lecture on civil rights law, she sent them packing.

Even a lawyer as sharp as Gladys Towles Root could occasionally be taken in by a client. In one case she won an acquittal for a blind defendant by convincing the judge that he would have been unable to commit the crime as charged in his sightless condition. At the end of the case the defendant graciously thanked the judge, remarking that the moment he looked at him, he knew he had an honest face. Another time, after successfully defending a compulsive Cadillac thief, she was called to jail to defend him again after a lapse in good behavior. Root discovered, to her great amusement, that she would have to decline due to a rather serious conflict of interest: It was her own Cadillac the thief had swiped.

Gladys's marriage to Frank Root ended after eleven years, and a few years later she married John C. "Jay" Geiger. Jay Geiger was the West Coast representative of a fashion magazine, and likely the only man in California who could equal Gladys in showmanship. The couple were considered by friends to be the perfect match. For special occasions they coordinated their outfits, sometimes even serving food and drinks in that color scheme. On one particularly memorable occasion, Gladys appeared in a sheath of multicolored sequins ending in pink ostrich plumes, with Jay at her side attired in a pink satin tuxedo. The couple loved to entertain, and their parties always had a twist. Gladys once called upon her dressmaker to create a suit and evening gown for a pair of pigs. On another, a skunk wearing a cape and jeweled collar was escorted by her uniformed chauffeur into the party promptly at 11:00 P.M. Their lavish Christmas parties became legendary, and at one point it was rumored that invitations could be scalped for a hundred dollars each.

Jay and Gladys enjoyed a uniquely joyful marriage. They delighted each other—and the children—with a constant parade of pets, not only dogs and cats but peacocks, monkeys, and rabbits. A green parrot named Pablo that sang opera often accompanied them on social occasions, perched atop a shoulder. Pablo usually displayed impeccable manners, but one evening at a prestigious Los Angeles restaurant he suddenly dashed to a neighboring booth and viciously bit the neck of a man who was dining. When the patron leaped up, outraged and bleeding, he turned out to be a local judge who had found one of Gladys's clients guilty the previous day.

Root created a sensation wherever she went. On a rare pleasure trip aboard a Norwegian ship bound for Panama over the Christmas holidays, she embarked with several trunks. Some of these held her wardrobe, of course, but the others were teeming with presents for the captain and crew, along with enough decorations to bedeck the entire ship. As the crew performed traditional Norwegian dances on deck, Root danced with the captain, resplendent in a red knit dress covered with white ermine tails. Thereafter, whenever the ship docked at the Long Beach port, Root sent a car to fetch the captain and officers to her home for dinner.

Jay Geiger served as Gladys's office manager for many years. He suffered through a long, agonizing illness that was heart wrenching for both, but he never lost his love of life. At one point when he rallied, he took up gourmet cooking and became a master chef until his health failed again.

Root's influence in changing the treatment of disturbed offenders was widespread. Even in the mid-twentieth century, it was not uncommon for judges to offer a defendant convicted of a sex crime the alternatives of prison or castration. Root vehemently opposed this practice, and was once cited for contempt after violently arguing with a judge on behalf of her nineteen-year-old client, who had been given a favorable prognosis for psychiatric therapy. In the end, she obtained a writ restraining the judge from further advocacy of castration as a sentencing alternative.

Root was outspoken on many issues. Though she deeply loved her own children and grandchildren, she became indignant when children lied on the witness stand. She was deeply saddened by children who lacked integrity and honesty, knowing that their futures were not promising. She blamed parents of vindictive children and felt that adults who did not give children adequate attention allowed the children access to warped influences. Root had seen many lives destroyed by false accusations, even when the defendant was ultimately acquitted.

Root also spoke frequently on the causes of criminal behavior, and she advocated the prevention of sex crimes through early education of children and safety training by police in schools.

Reflecting some thirty-five years after beginning her practice, Root urged that law schools should teach ethics and humanity before money. She recalled that when she was studying law, it was ingrained that attorneys were agents of the public, in the service of assisting human rights. Though her salary eventually settled in the six figures, Root always believed that winning her cause was more rewarding. Throughout her career, she continued to represent indigent and unpopular clients. In a notorious case of the mid-sixties, she represented one of the alleged participants in the kidnapping of Frank Sinatra Jr., although the case later brought on accusations that she had induced the defendant to give false testimony at trial.

In a system all too anxious to criticize female attorneys who appeared quiet and feminine as passive; and those with aggressive approaches as mannish, Root found her own route to success. Despite her flamboyance, she was never cast in the role of court jester. Devoted to the cause of equal justice for all, her dedication to her clients led to individual victories as well as significant developments in the law. She won many cases others had written off as lost causes and gave hundreds of down-and-out defendants their first encounter with real justice.

Root's career spanned a period of over fifty years. For her entire life, she seemed to thrive on histrionics and controversy. The federal government won a judgment against her in tax court in 1969, but Root appealed it all the way to consideration by the U.S. Supreme Court. In 1980, just two years before her death, she represented thirteen defendants charged in a pyramid scheme.

Root's final moments of life were spent in an appropriate summation of her calling. Attired all in gold, she was arguing on behalf of two brothers charged with a deviant sex crime when she collapsed and died of a heart attack in a Pomona, California courtroom. As the *Orange County Register* noted, her dramatic exit seemed somehow right, exactly the way she would want her life finally to end.

ROSA
PARKS

1913 –

O N DECEMBER 1, 1955, A SIMPLE ACT OF COURAGE CHANGED
the course of American history. At that time, the Jim Crow laws
of Montgomery, Alabama, required a black person to stand and offer
a seat to any white person who boarded a bus—even when blacks
were sitting in their own segregated area at the back of the vehicle.
Rosa Parks was on her way home from her job in a tailor shop one
evening when a white man boarded the bus. The driver ordered her
to stand up and give him her seat. Parks refused and was arrested. As
she explains in her book, *Quiet Strength,* it was not her goal to start a
movement; she was just tired of social injustice. Parks was known as
quiet and reserved. Yet within four days of her arrest and subsequent
release, she had become a symbol of courage to the black community
of Montgomery and others who supported equality. Her quiet act of
rebellion set the course of the modern civil rights movement.

Rosa Louise McCauly was born in Tuskegee, Alabama. She began
her education at a rural schoolhouse in Palm Level, Alabama, then

attended Miss White's School for Girls, a private institution in Montgomery. She spent tenth and eleventh grades at Alabama State Teachers College for Negroes. Always close to her family, she left the school before graduating when her grandmother and mother became ill and needed her care. In 1932, she married Raymond Parks, a self-educated man with extensive knowledge of domestic affairs and current events. Though he worked as a barber, he left many people with the impression that he had a college degree. With his encouragement, Rosa received her high school diploma in 1934.

Ray Parks became involved in the Scottsboro boys' cases in the 1930s, working to help free a group of young black men who were unjustly accused of rape. Ray and Rosa Parks both volunteered for the local NAACP, where she eventually became the youth leader of the Montgomery branch. Parks's mother had benefited from the NAACP's work to secure equal salaries for black and white schoolteachers in the 1940s.

Parks was preparing for a NAACP youth conference at the time of her arrest in 1955. Working as a tailor's assistant at the Fair Department Store, she earned seventy-five cents an hour. She was also working as a part-time seamstress for white activist Virginia Durr, and the two often discussed the deplorable persistence of segregation in the South. Parks introduced Durr to the NAACP, and Durr encouraged and assisted Parks in her work for justice and equality.

Montgomery citizens, both black and white, were outraged that this well-respected, soft-spoken woman was arrested and jailed simply because she would not bow to the Jim Crow laws. A boycott of the city bus line was quickly organized by black citizens and their white supporters. It lasted 381 days, and 42,000 people dedicated to ending segregation found other transportation or walked. Rev. Martin Luther King Jr. was appointed spokesman for the boycott. He gained national attention for his message emphasizing the importance of nonviolent approaches to change. Other protests against segregated buses, restaurants, and recreational facilities spread throughout the country, as national news covered the boycott in Montgomery. Thousands who believed in equal rights supported the effort. On December 21, 1956, the United States Supreme Court declared the bus segregation laws unconstitutional.

Ray and Rosa Parks moved to Detroit in 1957, where Rosa continued to work for civil rights, traveling, speaking, and participating in peaceful demonstrations. For twenty-two years, she worked for Congressman John Conyers of Michigan. Ray also continued actively working for civil rights until his death in 1977. Ten years later, Rosa and her friend Elaine Steele founded the Ray and Rosa Parks Institute for Self-Development, set up to motivate and direct young people to develop their highest potential. The institute teaches black history, offering courses in communications, economic skills, health, and political awareness. It also provides scholarships to talented students.

Although now over eighty years old, Rosa Parks still speaks at schools and gatherings throughout the country. She has been recognized as a symbol of freedom, courage, quiet dignity, and determination throughout the world. Parks credits much of her strength to the strong religious faith that has sustained her since her childhood. Her grandfather in particular influenced her devotion to freedom. He taught her that love, not fear, must be her guide.

Parks saw an opportunity to make a difference that day in 1955, when she was ordered by the bus driver to give up her seat. "I had no idea history was being made," she said. Parks speaks with pride of the way that the building fear and bitterness turned to power when people finally united to organize and protest. It was a great sacrifice for many to forgo bus transportation, but people persevered. One day after the boycott ended, when the United States Supreme Court decision was handed down declaring the laws unconstitutional, Rosa Parks rode a nonsegregated bus for the first time.

Parks is sometimes uncomfortable with the credit she has received for beginning the modern civil-rights movement. She was, she emphasizes, "just one of many who fought for freedom." Parks has explained that it would have compromised her dignity if she had buckled one more time to the Jim Crow laws, or if she had reacted violently. For her, it was a matter of self-respect.

Parks is pained by the prevalence of crime and hopelessness

among many young black people today. In August 1994, when she was eighty-one years old, she was struck and robbed by a young black man who invaded her home. She speaks of the incident with regret, but as she states in *Quiet Strength,* "Despite the crime and violence in our society, we should not let fear overwhelm us. We must remain strong. We must not give up hope, we can overcome." She urges people to unite in their efforts, as in the Montgomery boycott, an event whose unity set a model rarely achieved since.

Parks knows the importance of role models for young people and speaks of those who were so important in building her character and dignity. She recalls the courage and inner strength of her husband, Ray, who was devoted to civil rights and changing racial conditions; her mother, who taught her pride even under racist conditions; and her strong and loving grandparents, in particular her grandfather Sylvester Edwards, a former slave, who had been cruelly mistreated by an overseer and taught her mother and Rosa never to accept mistreatment. Martin Luther King Jr. also set a profound example in day-to-day living.

Today, Parks tries to use her negative memories of racism and segregation to continue her efforts toward justice, freedom, and equality. She says she is inspired by the children with whom she works, emphasizing that if the changes begun by the civil rights pioneers are to continue, young people must be the ones to keep the dream alive. In learning history, Parks believes young people are reminded that their ancestors suffered, struggled, and died to bring them the degree of freedom they now enjoy. She urges others to be role models and to set an example of love, respect, values, work, cooperation, nonviolence, and community service.

In 1969, Detroit renamed a street in honor of Parks. She has received numerous awards and honorary degrees, including the Martin Luther King Jr. Nonviolent Peace Prize awarded in 1980; the same year, *Ebony* readers chose her as the living black woman who had done the most to advance the cause of black America.

CECELIA
GOETZ

1917 –

CECELIA GOETZ WAS ONE OF MANY ATTORNEYS WHO EARNED her law degree during the mid-twentieth century only to encounter strong opposition when she tried to break through the barriers designed to limit female attorneys to the few fields deemed appropriate. Goetz received her legal education at New York University, where she served as editor-in-chief of the law review during her third year. After graduating at the top of her class in 1940, she aspired to work as a trial attorney for the government. But when she tried to gain such a role, even in departments known to be headed by liberals, the prejudice against females as government litigators rose up as a solid wall. It was suggested that she was "much too attractive to be a good lawyer."

Yet Goetz persevered. Eventually, after working at other agencies she secured a position with the Department of Justice. When she applied to be a prosecutor in the Nuremberg trials of Nazi war criminals after World War II, however, she was turned down because of her gender. Despite the fact that female secretaries, nurses, and clerks were serving in the American Zone of Occupation, she was told that there were no facilities to house her during the trials. Goetz, however, was not to be denied the work she so passionately desired, and she pressed her case. Impressed with her record, General Telford Taylor, chief United States prosecutor at Nuremberg, signed a "waiver of disability" form in order to add her to his staff—the acknowledged "disability" being Goetz's gender.

Goetz's efforts paid off. As associate counsel and the only woman on the Krupp trial team, she played a major role in the prosecution of Alfred Krupp and various Krupp officials. She presented first the aggressive war count, and when that was dismissed, the slave labor count upon which all the defendants but one were convicted. She made quite a splash with the international media when she addressed the Krupp tribunal. A 1948 article in the *New York Sun* noted she gave a "striking performance" in her opening statement. Goetz especially impressed the British delegation, whose members swarmed to congratulate her.

After Nuremberg, Goetz's career took a different direction that led her to break ground in other fields of law. She was named assistant chief counsel to the Office of Price Stabilization in 1952 (the first woman to be named to a high legal post within that agency), then returned to New York University to earn an L.L.M. degree in taxation in 1957. Goetz practiced at several New York firms before joining Herzfeld & Rubin, where she became a partner in 1964. In the meantime, she married Jack I. Spiegel in 1958 and raised two sons. She was appointed special master for the New York Supreme Court in 1977. The following year, she became a United States bankruptcy judge.

Goetz was the first female judge appointed to the United States Bankruptcy Court within the Second Circuit. Yet she often downplayed her accomplishments. As she told the *National Law Journal* in an interview four years later, "Once you put on a robe, the male-female distinction disappears, at least as far as the people who appear before you are concerned. They don't see you as either male or female." Goetz believes that the role of judge overrides that of the individual. Although she has acknowledged her belief that women sometimes bring special qualities to the bench, she sees little difference between a good male judge and a good female judge. "All judges," she told the *National Law Journal*, "must have patience, a willingness to listen, compassion, and above all integrity. I'm afraid there's nothing very startling in any of that."

As a member of the Association of the Bar of the City of New York, Goetz served on the Federal Legislation Committee, the Committee on Bankruptcy and Corporate Reorganization, and the Trade Regulation Committee. She has also been active in the New York County Lawyers Association for many years, serving on the Legal Aid Committee, the Civil Court Committee, the Women's Rights Committee, the Elder Law Committee, and the Federal Courts Committee. In 1985, Goetz was reappointed to the bankruptcy bench for a fourteen-year term. She retired in the mid-1990s, returning to private practice of counsel to Herzfeld & Rubin. Subsequently, she left that post to join the panels of mediators maintained by the bankruptcy court for the Southern District of New York and for the district court for the Eastern District of New York. In 1994, she was admitted to practice in Florida, more than a half century after her first bar admission in New York.

Goetz has received numerous awards for her service and achievements. In 1991, she was honored by New York University Law School with the Judge Edward Weinfeld Award. She received the William Nelson Cromwell Association Award from the New York County Lawyers Association in 1994.

SOIA
MENTSCHIKOFF

1915 – 1986

UNIVERSITY OF CHICAGO LAW PROFESSOR FRANK ZEMING once referred to Soia Mentschikoff as "the first woman everything." The label fit her well. Mentschikoff's achievements are truly remarkable, especially given the period in which they were accomplished. In the early 1940s, while she was still in her twenties, she became one of the first female partners of a Wall Street law firm. In 1947, she was the first woman invited to teach law at Harvard, three years before Harvard finally admitted female law students. She went on to become the first woman on the law school faculty at the University of Chicago, and the first woman elected president of the Association of American Law Schools. In 1974, she was named dean of the University of Miami Law School, yet another first.

Mentschikoff's greatest contribution, however, may have been her principal role as one of the drafters of the Uniform Commercial Code. The code helped to streamline the flow of interstate commerce by modernizing and standardizing the laws regarding the sale of goods.

Yet Mentschikoff became uneasy when held up as a role model. Her modesty is evident in a remark she once made to an interviewer, comparing her life to the song "Doin' What Comes Naturally."

Mentschikoff came from a line of strong individualists. Her grandmother dared to smoke publicly in nineteenth-century Russia. Her mother was even more headstrong, vehemently refusing to accept the traditional arranged marriage. Her paternal grandfather was a Russian immigrant and silver miner. Mentschikoff's father was born in America but traveled back to Russia as a young man, where he met and married her mother. The young couple came to California, but when their first child died in infancy, the young mother insisted that any other children should be born in the homeland. Thus Soia and her brother were born in Moscow, where Soia entered the world in 1915. The family fled just before the Revolution, among the last Americans to escape.

Soia's remarkable intelligence became apparent early in her life. She began considering a legal career when she was twelve, after reading about Clarence Darrow and the Scopes Monkey Trial. After skipping several grades of public school, she entered Hunter College, part of the New York City college system, at the age of fifteen. It was the height of the Depression, and Mentschikoff frequently saw men selling apples, people standing in bread lines, and families digging bunkers in the hills of Central Park for shelter. The young student was fascinated to see how people pulled together for survival and change.

In college, Mentschikoff studied English and political science, and her natural flair for leadership began to emerge. She ran for two offices her second year and was elected both president of the sophomore class and president of the student self-government association. About this time she also read the biography of William M. "Boss" Tweed, who had controlled New York City politics for many years. His philosophy of recognizing the voting public as a set of groups with distinct needs gave her insight into human social structure, a concept she was to apply often later in her life.

Mentschikoff began law school at the age of nineteen, one of twelve women in a class of 250 students at Columbia University. She regularly attended the "at home" gatherings for students hosted by Professor Karl Llewelyn, who was already famous as both a renowned academic and a successful attorney. She became his assistant her second year. The two could sit for hours debating fine points of law.

Mentschikoff graduated in 1937, determined to forge a career as a litigator. At the time it was still considered very unusual for a woman to work in the courtroom, but Mentschikoff's mind was set. When she began interviewing for jobs, she sought out the top partner at a Wall Street firm. John W. Davis of Davis, Polk and Wardwell had the reputation as a great litigator, as well as being a former presidential candidate. Davis tried to steer Mentschikoff into other areas of law more traditionally considered within the proper realm of females, but she held fast to her goal. When he asked her to meet with another attorney at the firm, she assumed he was still trying to guide her away from litigation, so she went to another Wall Street firm, where she was promptly hired as a litigator. She later learned that Davis had requested she see the head of the litigation department.

Mentschikoff stayed with the firm of Scandritt, Tuttle and Charlaire for four years, developing a specialty in labor law. In 1941 she left to become general counsel for a corporation that was experiencing labor difficulties. After six months on this job, she returned to Wall Street to join another firm, Spence, Hutchkiss, Parker & Duryee, as a labor relations expert. She was named partner after only three years.

Mentschikoff considered herself a humanist rather than a feminist. She believed that when a woman is first rate, barriers can be surmounted. She rejected affirmative action of any kind, believing instead in personal achievement as opposed to group advantages. In fact, Mentschikoff once stated that she considers affirmative action for women insulting, suggesting that women are not as good as men.

Mentschikoff acknowledged that World War II gave women an advantage in the job market. She later recalled her practice in New York City during the 1940s as the most exciting time in her career. It was then that she reconnected with her former professor Karl Llewelyn. She joined the team working to draft the Uniform

Commercial Code (UCC). Throughout the 1940s and '50s, the effort continued to formulate the code that would revise and standardize state business laws. It took nearly a decade to put together a first draft, with many people contributing to the enormous endeavor. Mentschikoff ultimately became one of the principal drafters. Yet she always called it "Karl's code" and acknowledged the thousands who contributed to the massive undertaking.

In 1946, Karl Llewelyn and Soia Mentschikoff married. The fact that he was much older than Soia and already renowned as a legal genius mattered little to either. The two enjoyed many years of shared professional and personal rewards.

By the end of the 1940s, recognition of Mentschikoff's own fine legal intellect was becoming established. Her work on the UCC netted her an invitation to teach at Harvard University. Ironically, her entire tenure at Harvard was completed by 1949, one year before the first female students were allowed to enroll. But Mentschikoff had found a new calling as a professor. She kept her classes lively and entertaining and became a very popular instructor.

Despite her rejection of feminist dogma, Soia Mentschikoff gracefully broke through some persistent barriers on behalf of other women. When male friends on the Harvard faculty wanted her to join them for lunch in the male-only faculty dining hall, the headwaiter refused to seat her. She was nonplussed, but her colleagues became quietly indignant and insisted she be seated. The dining room was open to women thereafter.

Mentschikoff continued working with her husband on the UCC while teaching at Harvard. When a draft was finally completed in 1949, she began traveling throughout the nation to gather input on how the code could be improved, and lobbying the states to set the stage for its passage. She spoke to people involved in commerce, banking, business, law, and politics. An enthusiastic advocate for the code, she had a natural talent for explaining the huge and complex collection of laws in a manner that made it clear to others. The code underwent revisions all through the 1950s and into the '60s. It was finally adopted by every state except Louisiana.

At a conference on the UCC at the University of Chicago in 1950, both Karl and Soia were asked to join the faculty by Edward Levi, then head of the law school. At this time Chicago was renowned for its progressive, intellectual, and academically free atmosphere, and for this reason, Karl was anxious to commit immediately. Soia, after some reluctance over leaving New York, also agreed, becoming the first female to join the law school faculty at yet another university, as one of only a handful of female law professors scattered throughout the country.

Mentschikoff and Llewelyn both thrived at the University of Chicago. They bought a huge old house, to which they welcomed her parents. Soia's two nieces also joined them every summer. The girls eventually became permanent members of the household when their parents divorced and their mother suffered health problems. Additionally, faculty, friends, and students constantly filled the home. Sunday evenings were reserved for student gatherings featuring cider, doughnuts, and good conversation. The fifties saw some of Mentschikoff's busiest years. She did much of her work at home, filling the dining room table with papers and books, so she could spend time with her nieces. Her boundless energy helped her juggle her busy home life, teaching duties, work on the UCC, and innumerable other activities.

The early sixties brought difficult changes for Mentschikoff. Karl Llewelyn died suddenly in 1962, and a short time later Edward Levi left his position as head of the law school to become provost of the university. Mentschikoff later reflected that the only two geniuses she had ever known were Llewelyn and Levi.

After Levi's departure, the law school began to change. A rigid, doctrinaire atmosphere replaced the progressive philosophy. Meanwhile, Mentschikoff's schedule continued to become more demanding. She attended international delegations, served on the education commission of the American Bar Association, was appointed counsel for the National Endowment for the Humanities, served on a commission dealing with the rights of American Indians, and participated in many other activities. Her contributions to the profession and to the public seem endless. In 1974, she became the first female president of the Association of American Law Schools. She served as ABA delegate to the association the same year.

Mentschikoff had also begun teaching one semester a year at the University of Miami Law School during the late 1960s. By 1973, she had become disenchanted with the changes at the University of Chicago. When Dr. Henry Stafford of Miami offered her the opportunity to move to south Florida to become dean of the law school, she saw the opportunity as a wonderful challenge.

Miami was not recognized as one of the top law schools in America, and Mentschikoff was anxious to put her stamp on the place. She insisted on full autonomy, limited enrollment, a larger faculty, and a new library. At the same time, a new building for classes and offices was being constructed. Mentschikoff spent so much time at the construction site, eagerly overseeing the progress, that the workers presented her with a hard hat of her own. She won their respect by intervening to make sure the work stayed on schedule, using her persuasive skills to deal with such matters as delays in deliveries of supplies. She likewise persuaded lawyers of national prominence to join the faculty and attend symposia at the school.

Predictably, some at the university growled about the changes she instituted, dubbing her "the czarina." But Mentschikoff cared little about detractors, as she transformed Miami into an excellent law school.

Mentschikoff established a home in Coral Gables and tried to retire several times before finally leaving the post of dean in 1982. She has referred to law as the last of the universal disciplines. After a career spanning nearly fifty years, Mentschikoff planned to relax, yet her varied endeavors kept her retirement busy and active. In addition to traveling and writing, she continued to be involved with the University of Miami Law School.

FLORYNCE
KENNEDY

1916 –

D URING THE 1960S AND '70S, LECTURER, LAWYER, AND WRITER Florynce Kennedy became one of the most popular speakers on college campuses—and one of the best-known black women in America. Throughout her life Kennedy followed her own conscience, unconcerned about the opinions of others, and was once quoted in an Australian paper following a tour of that nation as saying, "I don't give a damn what people think. I say what the hell's on my mind, and that's that."

Kennedy's vast confidence and keen devotion to causes she believes in have kept her on the warpath for most of her life. Born in 1916 and raised in Kansas City, Missouri, Florynce was the second of five daughters born to an educated mother and a loving father who worked as a waiter, a porter on a train, and at one point owned a taxi business. She characterized the family as "pooristocrats" in the black community. Some of Florynce's fearlessness was likely inherited from her father. She recalls that when she was very small, the Ku Klux Klan came to the Kennedy home and told the family to get out of the neighborhood. Her father met them at the front porch with his shotgun, and the hooded cowards never returned.

Kennedy attributes her early success and confidence to her parents, who gave her and her sisters a secure knowledge of their own self-worth. "By the time the bigots got around to telling us we were nobody," she once remarked in an interview, "we already knew we were somebody."

Florynce's father, Wiley Kennedy, often worked nights but always brought home treats for his daughters and taught them early never to accept mistreatment or abuse from another person. The Kennedy parents did not believe in hitting their children and made it clear to school authorities that no one was to strike the Kennedy girls. Flo believes that this strongly affected her attitude toward authority. Respect was something to be earned, not automatically bestowed.

Florynce's mother gave her security, hope, and taught her resourcefulness. Zella Kennedy spent hours straightening the girls' hair and dressing them in beautiful clothing that she sewed herself. The sisters did well in school and stuck together in support of each other. Kennedy also recalls that her mother neither accepted nor resented their poverty, but laughed a lot and did remarkable things with what the family did have. The Kennedy children were always made to feel special, and received Christmas presents even in years where this meant the bills would have to wait. Zella Kennedy was determined that the family would never go on welfare. At one especially low point, she tried to convince the welfare department to give her a loan, but they told her she could not pay it back. And so she went to work instead.

Kennedy's commitment to political causes did not come early in life. As a teenager, the sisters were popular and resourceful, often borrowing their father's taxi to search out good times. They frequently threw parties despite their scant resources, and enjoyed going to public dances during the days when the Kansas City music scene was at its height.

Kennedy's solid upbringing and the values it instilled were to be tested severely in the coming years. On a trip to Chicago with her sister, the girls were refused service at a bus-stop coffee shop. They were dragged backward off of their stools, and in the process Florynce aggravated a childhood back injury. As a result, she had to lie flat on her back in a body cast for several weeks, and eventually required surgery to fuse vertebrae. She later successfully sued the bus company and luncheonette.

After high school Florynce and her two oldest sisters opened a hat shop. It was not lucrative but it paid the rent, and they enjoyed working in an area where jazz musicians often passed by. The sisters themselves, musically talented, sang on the radio with their own show for a time.

In the late 1930s, the family moved to a better Kansas City neighborhood, where Florynce made friends with "big shot" lawyers, including the head of the local chapter of the NAACP. Her first significant political action occurred when she helped organize a boycott of the local Coca-Cola plant, which refused to hire black truck drivers.

Eventually, however, after the death of her mother and the marriage of her sister, Kennedy moved to New York to share her sister's apartment while her new brother-in-law was stationed in Virginia. She went to work at the Veteran's Administration, then took the civil service exam to become a clerk with the United States Treasury. She began classes at Columbia and returned to her interest in law—not because of any tremendous passion for righting society's wrongs, but because the lawyers she knew were better off than most other people. She also knew that she did not want to be a mother, a nurse, or a teacher.

As Kennedy continued to work, moving on to the Museum of Natural History and Gimbel's department store, she completed her degree and applied to law school at Columbia. At first she was refused admission because she was a woman. So Kennedy pointed out to the administrators that while schools could still get away with sex discrimination, racial bias was now illegal—and in her case, the true rationale for excluding her could be either race or gender. The tactic succeeded, and Kennedy began class as one of eight women, the token black. This event taught her the value of using what she later dubbed the "testicular approach"—applying the right pressure to the appropriate sensitive area—in this case, the school's fear of increasingly common race discrimination suits.

Though she continued to work part-time in the law school library, she managed to graduate in three years, albeit low in the class rank. Kennedy freely admitted she really didn't have a "legal head," lacking the mathematical objectivity law school tried to instill. She was also disgusted by the values taught at the established law school. She saw repeated use of the law to "maintain the bullshit" and blame the victim, rather than putting it to work as an instrument of change and justice. She saw law school as an attempt to teach students to put aside their humanity.

Kennedy nonetheless credited an excellent sociology professor at Columbia with influencing her understanding of the world, and it was at this time her political view began to take a leftward turn. There was no revolutionary sensation; it was simply a matter of common sense. Even when writing her 1976 autobiography, *Color Me Flo: My Hard Life and Good Times,* Kennedy stated she was not sure she was so political because she wanted to do good for others as because she wanted to live the best life possible and not be bored to death.

Kennedy graduated from law school in 1951 and clerked before she opened her own office in 1954. She began doing matrimonial work, as well as some assigned, unpaid criminal cases to gain experience. Times were so lean she had to moonlight at Bloomingdale's over Christmas to pay the rent. She also went through a major health crisis that nearly killed her and ultimately required the removal of three feet of intestines.

In the late 1950s, Kennedy acquired a law partner and a husband, "both of whom ultimately proved disastrous," she recalls in her autobiography. Her husband, Charlie Dye, a Welsh science fiction writer ten years her junior, was a heavy drinker with a bad temper who customarily worked as a security guard. But he was also a wonderful storyteller with a great sense of humor, and he shared Florynce's love of jazz. He stood by her when her partner ran away with most of the firm's money. As always, Florynce refused to panic. Charlie helped out in the office, and again she survived. The couple went through a series of breakups and reunions before Charlie died a few years later.

Kennedy gradually expanded her practice. She represented Billie Holiday (who called Flo "the hip kitty from Kansas City") late in the singer's life, and handled Charlie Parker's estate after his death. She saw the corruption and exploitation of these artists by the music industry, and became incensed when she learned how little they received for their talents and sacrifices, while others reaped huge profits. Kennedy was innovative in finding new ways to use legal tools to collect money owed to the artists' estates by publishers and record companies.

But these efforts also left her disenchanted with the law and made her doubt her ability to continue to work within the system to accomplish social change. The assassination of John F. Kennedy also deeply affected her. By the late 1960s, she had begun spending less time on law and more time on her political activities. With other activists, Kennedy set up the Media Workshop to address racism in the media and in advertising. The organization found that picketing was an effective way to quickly gain the attention of the upper echelon. This led to another Kennedy credo: "When you want to get to the suites, start in the streets."

Kennedy's career as a speaker got its unwitting start at a 1967 antiwar convention in Montreal. When activist Bobby Seale was not allowed to speak, Kennedy became enraged. She stormed the platform and started, as she put it, "yelling and hollering." As a result, she was invited to speak in Washington and paid two hundred fifty dollars, plus expenses.

As the sixties progressed into the seventies, Kennedy's popularity as a speaker increased. Her colorful language earned her the nickname "Foulmouthed Flo." She became involved with the National Organization for Women early in its inception, but eventually left to found the Feminist Party in 1971, whose first major action was to support the presidential candidacy of Shirley Chisholm.

Kennedy is a woman of many contrasts. Her speaking style commands respect, yet her natural warmth comes through as well. In addition to being outspoken, she is shrewd enough to know when to refrain from comment in order to get the upper hand. Once, as a fledgling attorney, she let opposing counsel repeatedly call her "young lady" throughout the trial, because she saw the jury becoming as irritated as she was. Not surprisingly, she won the case. Kennedy also developed a finely honed sense of humor and irony. She once noted that in the two most antifeminist institutions in society, namely the church and courts of law, men wear dresses.

Kennedy has dedicated her lifetime to agitating against oppression and racism, which she describes as spanning from coast to coast and border to border. Likewise, she urges others to do so, and to come together to challenge oppression. She states that she is not out to change the world, only her pro-rata share, and believes we all can do the same. "If you want to know where your apathy is," she has often said, "you're probably sitting on it." She blames widespread apathy on what she refers to as the four I's: Ignorance (*I didn't know*); Innocence (*I'm not to blame*); Impotence (*One person cannot make a difference*); and Incompetence (*The government knows and will do whatever is best*). She criticizes the "zombie-ism" prevalent in society. Anyone, she believes, can use three major powers available to all citizens: body power (the physical presence with which we act and show numbers); dollar power; and voting power.

Self-described as "a loudmouth middle-aged colored lady with a fused spine and three feet of intestines missing and a lot of people think I'm crazy," Kennedy believes in living a life with "taste and brains." Yet she seldom wonders why she is not like others, instead finding it a mystery that more people are not like her.

It is not difficult to see why Kennedy enjoys her activities so much. Many of the protests she has organized have been colorful, to say the least. The Media Workshop held annual "Hollywood Toilet Bowl" festivals to protest treatment of women by the media, presenting awards to companies that failed to hire women or to serve them with respect as members of the audience. At a 1973 "Pee-in" at

Harvard Yard, organized to protest the lack of facilities for women on campus, Kennedy pointed out that bathrooms have always been a handy way to make those who are unwelcome feel inferior, citing the long history of racially segregated facilities throughout the South.

She has often stated her frustration with America's "jockocracy," or preoccupation with balls. She laments that on any night a television viewer can get the full scoop on every sports team in America, while many important political issues are avoided.

Although Kennedy has continued to practice law occasionally, in order to participate in such actions as a suit to divest the Catholic Church of its tax-free status based upon its political activities against abortion legislative reform, her disenchantment with the legal system remains. She describes what she calls the whorehouse theory of law, comparing the legal profession to a bordello, serving those preferred customers able to afford the luxuries of justice.

In celebration of her seventieth birthday, Kennedy was "roasted" by friends and admirers at Playboy's Empire Club in New York City. The event drew guests from a broad spectrum, including Phil Donahue, civil rights lawyer William Kunstler, and activist-comedian Dick Gregory. Kennedy was honored for her work as a lawyer, writer, civil rights activist, television producer, and leader.

Perhaps Kennedy's most consistent message has been that we all can, and should, do something to fight oppression and better society. Writing for Robin Morgan's anthology, *Sisterhood Is Powerful*, Kennedy states: "We must take our little teaspoons and get to work. We can't wait for shovels." In addition to her autobiography, Kennedy has written several books, including *The Pathology of Oppression* and *Abortion Rap*, one of the first straightforward books on abortion, which she co-authored with Diane Schulder.

RUTH HARVEY
CHARITY

1920? –

RUTH HARVEY CHARITY, WHO BECAME ONE OF THE NATION'S leading black civil rights attorneys and president of the National Association of Black Women Attorneys, traces her interest in civil liberties law to a single episode early in her life. Born in the segregated South, Ruth was walking down a city street with her mother when she saw a white girl about her age sitting at a drug store counter eating an ice cream sundae. When she said she would like to go in and have one too, her mother explained that they couldn't, because they were Negroes. Angered, Ruth asked her mother, "Aren't we Americans too?"

Ruth's mother was a teacher and her father a minister and school principal, so she considered her family middle class and more fortunate than many. Yet as she got older she became increasingly aware of where she could and could not go solely because of her race. She also learned shocking secrets behind the genteel façade of southern society, such as the ugly conspiracy of a local social club, in which the white matrons agreed to set low pay levels for their black domestic servants.

Ruth Harvey resolved early in life to do something about such injustices. She enrolled in Howard Law School, where her interest in civil rights law flourished. Elected president of the Howard chapter of the NAACP, Ruth helped organize the first sit-in at a Washington, D.C., lunch counter in 1944. Although the experience was frightening, she was greatly pleased when the restaurant was desegregated a short time later.

After law school, Ruth returned to her hometown of Danville, Virginia, where she set up a solo practice with the goal of working to end the persistent discrimination against blacks. One of her first cases achieved desegregation of the local library, which maintained a spacious, well-stocked facility for whites and a separate facility, consisting of a poorly supplied cubbyhole, for blacks. Inspired by her success, she continued to conduct sit-ins and file suits, soon gaining desegregation of the city park. She married Ronald K. Charity and raised a child as well.

Charity also continued her work with the NAACP, persisting in the face of discrimination from white lawyers both in and out of court. In an interview with author Karen Berger Morello in the early 1980s, Charity recalled that a court clerk once tried to stop her from handling the record books in the clerk's office. When she told the clerk she was a lawyer and threatened to file suit, the clerk stared at her as though she was "right out of the zoo." But Charity got the books she needed.

Charity built a prosperous practice, including work in criminal defense. She recalls that her gender was sometimes an advantage, as in cases when she could argue on behalf of a young offender as though he were her son, a good kid who needed a little straightening out. Her proudest moment came when she defended 1,300 civil rights marchers after a 1963 arrest. Rev. Martin Luther King Jr. was involved in the case, and the marchers were set free.

Charity participated in Democratic Party politics and served on the Democratic National Committee. She was the first black woman south of the Mason-Dixon line to serve in this capacity. When the National Bar Association, an organization for black attorneys, persisted in refusing to allow female attorneys to hold any office other than secretary, she formed a women's division of the organization, which eventually split off to become the National Association of Black Women Attorneys. Charity served as president of this organization and continued to expand her work in the public-service arena. She founded and became president of the Virginia Association of Black Women Lawyers.

Her lifelong commitment to politics, both at national and local levels, led her to found and serve as president of Black Women for Political Action. She was also assistant to the director of the President's Council on Consumer Affairs, as well as industrial relations analyst for the Wage Stabilization Board. To date, she remains the first and only black woman elected to the Danville, Virginia, city council, a post she held from 1970 to 1974. She was also a charter member of the National Women's Chamber of Commerce.

Charity's dedication to public service has extended to education as well. She served on the board of trustees of Howard University and the Palmer Memorial Institute and continues to lecture and consult for civil rights, political, and education groups.

CONSTANCE BAKER
MOTLEY

1921 –

C ONSTANCE BAKER MOTLEY WAS BORN IN NEW HAVEN, Connecticut, in 1921, where she grew up as one of twelve children in a financially strapped family. Nevertheless, her parents held out high hopes for their children's achievement. They had come to America from the Caribbean island of Nevis, and attended an Episcopal church where the minister offered lectures on black history. Thus Constance gained insight into her cultural background, although New Haven was 98 percent white.

While still in high school in 1938, Constance attended a lecture by local New Haven attorney George Crawford, where he described a civil rights case in which a black man had won the right to attend the University of Missouri Law School. Constance Baker had been exposed to racism when she and her friends were denied admission to skating rinks and segregated beaches. She was convinced that she wanted to be a part of the growing civil rights effort, although she was unsure of the direction she would take. She became involved in local youth civil rights groups, then graduated from high school and took a job varnishing chairs while she pondered her future. Two years later she attended another event organized by George Crawford. Wealthy white philanthropist Clarence W. Blakeslee had requested to meet with black leaders in the area, to learn why a community center he had helped to build in a black neighborhood was not being used by more people. Constance was the only one present who spoke bluntly about the program's flaws. Impressed, Blakeslee asked why Baker wasn't in college. She answered the question with one word: money. She told Blakeslee she had always wanted to be a lawyer, and he agreed to finance her education. So in 1941 she set off for Fisk University in Nashville.

The trip marked Constance Baker's first journey through the segregated South. Although she had faced discrimination before, this marked her first encounter with the ugly Jim Crow laws. The experience was unforgettable. Because of her race, she could not attend the theater, eat in many restaurants, or try on clothing in department stores. She soon transferred back north to New York University.

When she was accepted at Columbia Law School, Clarence Blakeslee helped Baker acquire a lawyerly wardrobe and encouraged her to enroll in public speaking courses during the summer breaks. As she ventured into the professional world, Baker soon learned that bigotry was everywhere. She encountered rude rejections when seeking summer clerk positions. In one case, an appointment she had made by telephone was abruptly canceled when a white male partner stuck his head out of his office door and had a look at her. Motley later wrote, "When I graduated in 1946, you would not have been able to find a single person willing to bet twenty-five cents that I would be successful in the legal profession."

In her third year, however, she was hired to clerk for future Supreme Court Justice Thurgood Marshall, who was then the director of the NAACP Legal Defense Fund. She had dreamed of helping other blacks and now knew she had found her calling. Baker went to work on the civil rights cases that paved the way for the landmark ruling in *Brown v. Board of Education,* in which the United States Supreme Court held that "separate but equal" in education was inherently unequal, and ordered public schools to desegregate. The same year she graduated she married Joel Wilson Motley, a real estate and insurance broker.

Several of the cases leading up to *Brown* were especially close to Baker's heart, as they involved challenges by black law students seeking to enter white schools. In 1949, while representing a group of black teachers who were being paid less than their white counterparts, she and her partner John Lynch became the first black lawyers since Reconstruction to appear in the federal court in Alabama. When word spread through the town that there were two "nigra" lawyers—one even a woman!—the event took on the quality of spectacle. A vast audience spilled into the halls for a glimpse of such a curiosity.

As Baker and her colleagues went on to try cases throughout the South, they faced a constant barrage of prejudice. It was often difficult for the attorneys to find accommodations, since decent hotels were closed to blacks and local families were afraid of reprisal if they hosted attorneys who had come to town to upset the status quo. Motley later commented, "I wonder how many lawyers have had the experience of preparing for trial in a flophouse. That was the only room I could get."

Constance Baker Motley eventually became the NAACP Legal Defense Fund's principal trial attorney. She was a keen, forceful litigator, always exceptionally well prepared. Jack Greenberg, who succeeded Thurgood Marshall as director of the NAACP Legal Defense Fund, called her the "anchorwoman" of his team. She won nine of the ten cases she argued before the United States Supreme Court. Several established desegregation of colleges and professional schools. Throughout the 1960s, she represented Dr. Martin Luther King Jr. During the same era, she won a seat on the New York State Senate and became a borough president of Manhattan, the first black woman to hold either position. She was greatly admired by Lyndon B. Johnson, who called her "the greatest friend blacks had since

Lincoln." He persistently worked toward having her appointed to the federal bench, often against staunch opposition. In 1986, Constance Baker Motley became the first black woman to sit on the United States District Court for the Southern District of New York. She became chief judge of the panel in 1980.

Motley has managed to successfully blend career and family throughout her remarkable life. Her husband has provided steadfast encouragement. Their son, Joel Motley Jr., graduated from Harvard Law School and went on to become a lawyer and investment banker. The family relaxes together at a country home in Chester, Connecticut, and travels to the Caribbean each year.

Motley has written extensively for legal and professional journals, covering a plethora of topics related to equality and human rights. She is optimistic about the expanding opportunities for black lawyers and predicts a bright future for intelligent, dedicated young men and women. She believes that most formal legal barriers that once blocked the progress of minorities have been removed by civil rights litigation, and that most of the remaining problems require political solutions. The momentum for change will come, she feels, from a new breed of lawyers.

SHIRLEY
CHISHOLM

1924 –

I N 1968, SHIRLEY CHISHOLM BECAME THE FIRST BLACK WOMAN
elected to the House of Representatives. During her political
career she worked to further the causes of education, veterans' rights,
and civil rights, and won wide acclaim for her effort. In 1972 she
campaigned for nomination as the Democratic candidate for president. Her achievements and "firsts" seem endless. Yet the role of trailblazer was nothing new to Shirley Chisholm; it was a path she had
followed all her life.

Shirley Aneia St. Hill was born in 1924 in Brooklyn, to parents
who had immigrated from the West Indies island of Barbados to
escape the famines of the 1920s. She was the oldest of four daughters
born to a baker's helper and his wife, a talented seamstress who took
in sewing. From an early age, Shirley was curious, independent, determined, and mouthy. Her outspokenness was locally renowned by the
time she was three.

The St. Hill family constantly struggled to earn enough money to make ends meet. While the three girls were still toddlers, their mother took them back to Barbados by steamship, where they were to live temporarily with their grandmother while their mother stayed in America to work full-time. The family planned to save to buy a home of their own in New York. Shirley's grandmother, Emilie Seale, was a tall woman with an air of unmistakable authority. She had a tremendous influence on young Shirley. While the separation from their mother was painful, the St. Hill girls quickly adjusted to life with the large extended family living on the island. Their grandmother was strict, but Shirley, though obedient, remained independent. She attended school in a local church, in which seven classes were held in one room.

Hard times continued for Shirley's parents in the United States. Another daughter was born, and though they struggled on for several more years toward their dream of owning their own home, the family soon saw that it was not to be. Shirley's mother returned to Barbados in 1933 to bring back the older daughters when Shirley was almost ten. The reunion was joyful but required a painful separation from their grandmother, who had imbued Shirley with strength, dignity, and love.

The toughest change, however, was from the quiet Barbados village to the noisy city and new school. Because she had not received training in American history or geography in Barbados, Shirley was enrolled with younger students. Yet she was three years ahead of her classmates in other subjects. When Shirley became bored and began acting up, her teacher fortunately recognized the cause of the problem and arranged for a tutor to help the restless student catch up to her correct grade level. Shirley quickly went on to jump ahead a grade.

Shirley gained an early interest in world affairs from her father, who loved to read newspapers, often going through two or three a day and discussing current events with the family. While Shirley was well informed, she never experienced racism until her parents moved to a new neighborhood in the Bedford-Stuyvesant area of Brooklyn. More racial mixing in this area made for increased tension between the groups. But Shirley found the greater problem to be sexism. Her high grades were brushed aside as insignificant because she was "just a girl." Shirley noticed that her history lessons were short on accounts of great women. Yet from her father she learned a great deal about black history, including the contributions of many women, and she loved to read biographies from the local library. She was especially struck by the story of Harriet Tubman, famous for her heroic efforts with the underground railroad, and with suffrage leader Susan B. Anthony. Both leaders had often compared the roles of blacks to those of women in the United States in the early nineteenth century.

Shirley also began taking responsibility for caring for her three younger siblings at this time, watching out for them for a part of each day while her mother worked outside the home. This gave her an early insight into the importance of day care, an issue that was to become a primary target of her political efforts.

Shirley's academic excellence in public high school won her offers of scholarships to Vassar and Oberlin Colleges, but family finances made going away to study nearly impossible. So in 1942, she enrolled in Brooklyn College to study sociology. At the same time, she began to attend local political functions. When she graduated, Shirley taught in Harlem and began studying for a master's degree in education at Columbia University, taking night classes. It was there that she met Conrad Chisholm, also a native of the West Indies. But Shirley was determined to complete her education, so they waited to marry until 1949.

For six years, Chisholm worked as director of a private nursery school in Brooklyn. Then she took a position with the New York City division of day care. During this time the Chisholms tried to start their own family, but after Shirley suffered two miscarriages she decided to devote her life to all children, rather than having a family of her own.

As the civil rights movement gained momentum in the early 1960s, Chisholm became familiar with such leaders as Martin Luther King Jr. and Malcolm X. In particular, she admired Malcolm X and his emphasis on self-help within black communities. She joined with other blacks to form the Unity Democratic Club in Brooklyn, an organization that quickly became one of the most powerful political clubs in the area.

In 1964, Chisholm decided to run for the New York State Assembly, over the objection of many of the men in the club. Yet she campaigned hard and won the election, to follow the lead of Bessie Buchanan of Harlem, who had been the first black New York State assemblywoman. At the time of Chisholm's election to the New York State Assembly in 1964, she was the only woman and one of only eight black representatives.

Shirley Chisholm was determined to take an active role in her political career. She introduced the first bill to extend unemployment insurance to domestic workers, and it was duly enacted into law. She joined a committee on education, where she worked to increase state funding of day care services and of public schools. After she was re-elected, she introduced another bill to create a program called SEEK, which provided state college scholarships for promising black and Hispanic students.

In 1968 Chisholm decided to run for Congress in the newly created district where she lived with a campaign slogan of "Fighting Shirley Chisholm—unbought and unbossed." After winning the primary, she faced a tough race against James Furmer, who had gained national prominence for his civil rights activism. Her opponent tried to capitalize on gender issues, and his approach backfired. Chisholm won by a two-to-one margin to become the first black woman in the United States House of Representatives.

As usual, she jumped into her new role with great enthusiasm, serving on the Veterans Committee and working long hours in her Brooklyn office to directly serve the people of her district. When she was in Washington, D.C., she turned her efforts toward helping the local poor.

After she was re-elected to the seat, Chisholm was assigned to the committee she most wanted to join, Education and Labor. By this time she had gained considerable political savvy. She decided to target her reform efforts by using the existing laws rather than introducing bills to establish new ones. She invoked antidiscrimination laws to help people get housing, day care, jobs, and to acquire money for organizations in Brooklyn. During her fourteen years in the House, she was an outspoken advocate for civil rights, women's equality, and other progressive issues. She was an early member of the National Organization for Women, one of the founders of the National Women's Political Caucus, and spokesperson for the National Abortion Rights Action League.

When Chisholm spoke on the campus at a southern college early in 1970, a white male student suggested she run for president. At this time she dismissed the idea as impossible, but the thought stayed with her as the 1972 election year approached. Chisholm felt that the time was ripe for change. She received much encouragement, especially from college and black women's groups. Yet almost all of the politicians she approached, regardless of their race or sex, advised her against such an undertaking. Undaunted, Chisholm announced her Democratic candidacy in January 1972, stressing that although she took pride in her race and gender, she was not the candidate of black America or of the women's movement, but the "candidate of the people."

Chisholm was only the second woman to make a serious run on a major party ticket for the office of presidency, Margaret Chase Smith having been the first, in 1968. Chisholm used her platform to speak out on issues important to her, including her devotion to children, women, minorities, the end of the Vietnam War, and tax and welfare reform. She also supported freedom of reproductive choice and the rights of gays.

Chisholm campaigned with little money and was troubled by the bickering between special-interest groups, who repeatedly tried to claim her as their own. Meanwhile, she still had to fulfill her responsibilities as a congresswoman. Chisholm campaigned on her own qualifications as a grassroots politician who had overcome barriers at every step and "made it within the system in spite of the system." She made no secret of her desire to shake things up, and won enough votes in each state to keep her campaign rolling. When she won 5 percent of the vote in California, she became entitled to Secret Service protection.

During the campaign, supporters wore buttons that read Ms. CHIS FOR PRES. The choice of terminology was not without significance. "Ms." was a new term in the early seventies, and Chisholm became instrumental in bringing about changes for women, especially in the area of job opportunities. Chisholm always maintained that she had suffered more discrimination because of her gender than her race.

In her 1972 bid for the Democratic presidential nomination, Chisholm lacked money, organization, and serious consideration from her male opponents or the media. Yet she managed to keep her campaign alive until the Democratic National Convention, where she won over 150 votes on the first ballot.

Chisholm never had any real expectations of winning the office of president, but she wanted to give those she viewed as the neglected Americans a real choice in their vote. She later spoke of her satisfaction in knowing she had made an impact. Many blacks registered to vote for the first time in order to cast their vote for her. She inspired many other women and minorities, paving the way for others who now felt they had a serious shot at gaining political power.

After the 1972 campaign, Chisholm returned to her work in Congress. She pushed hard for the passage of various anti-poverty programs and worked in support of the Equal Rights Amendment. She was crushed when President Nixon vetoed a minimum wage bill that had passed both houses of Congress after she had put in enormous effort to win its enactment. She started voicing an intent to retire from politics in 1973, but her constituents, and her determination, kept her in office. Chisholm managed to find time to write two autobiographies, *Unbought and Unbossed* and *The Good Fight*, which describes her run for the presidency. In 1976 she became the first black and the first woman to serve in the House leadership position of secretary to the Democratic Caucus.

After her marriage to Conrad Chisholm ended in 1977, Chisholm married Arthur Hardwick, an architectural designer. When he was seriously injured in an automobile accident in 1988, she took stock of her future and decided she wanted more time for her personal life.

Chisholm left Congress in 1982 after serving seven terms for a total of twenty-five years in politics. She retired from the House of Representatives in 1983 and has limited her political activities to campaigning for other candidates since that time. Besides teaching courses on politics, race, and women at Mount Holyoke College, Chisholm served as first chairwoman of the National Political Congress of Black Women. She continues to speak on political issues and to encourage other women to enter politics. "I don't believe there are really going to be real changes in America," Chisholm once said, "until women are in decision- and policy-making positions in this nation."

SANDRA DAY
O'CONNOR

1930 –

L ITERALLY OVERNIGHT, SANDRA DAY O'CONNOR WAS SWEPT
from obscurity to become one of the most famous women in
the world, certainly the best-known female lawyer in America.
Although she was a loyal Republican, generally considered conservative in her views, people of various political persuasions were
pleased when she was nominated for one of the top legal jobs in the
nation. While each new appointment draws attention, O'Connor
was the first Supreme Court justice to become a media superstar.
And all because she was a woman.

The quiet southwesterner from the Arizona Court of Appeals
suddenly found herself thrust into the limelight and badgered for
interviews, autographs, and speaking engagements; every opinion
she had ever written was analyzed by an army of legal pundits. It is
no wonder, then, that she claimed that the most difficult part of her

first year on the court was all the attention and publicity her new job engendered.

Sandra Day was born in 1930, the eldest of three children on a 300-square mile cattle ranch in southeastern Arizona. The Lazy B ranch was founded by her grandfather in 1880. The comfortable old ranch house where Sandra grew up had neither electricity nor running water. By the age of ten, she had learned to drive the ranch truck and tractor and to fix windmills and fences. Yet despite their rugged life, education was very important to O'Connor's parents. So Sandra was sent to El Paso to live with her grandmother during the school years in the interests of a better quality of schooling. She loved the ranch life and often became homesick, anxious for the summer to return.

Sandra's tomboy side was balanced by her love of reading and her academic talents. She graduated from high school at the age of sixteen. Because her father had wanted to attend Stanford but hadn't had the opportunity, that university was her one and only choice. O'Connor later credited Harry Rathbun, a Stanford professor, as a key mentor who helped shape her life. Rathbun held seminars where he discussed personal ethics and goals, urging each student to discover how he or she could make a difference in the world. O'Connor, who described him as brilliant, kind, inspiring, and almost saintly, once remarked that she decided to attend law school because Rathbun demonstrated so clearly that the law could be an instrument for social good. It took only five years for Sandra to complete both her undergraduate and legal studies at Stanford. In law school she was ranked in the top three of her class and won a prestigious spot on the editorial board of the *Stanford Law Review*. It was there she met and began dating John O'Connor, whom she married shortly after her graduation in 1952.

O'Connor was not absolutely certain that she wanted to be a lawyer, but knew she wanted a career of some kind, and John supported her ambition. He still had one year of law school to complete when she graduated with honors. O'Connor's stellar academic record would have provided any man with an impressive array of choices, but she had no offers from any San Francisco or Los Angeles firms. The only job she was offered was a position as a legal secretary. Finally, she was hired as deputy county attorney for San Mateo, California.

O'Connor loved the work. When John graduated, he landed a job with the army's Judge Advocate General Corps. This required a move to Frankfurt, West Germany, and Sandra accompanied him as a civilian lawyer for the Quartermaster Corps. Three years later, the O'Connors returned to America and settled in Phoenix.

Sandra opened a private practice with one partner, but as three sons were born, she put her career on hold to stay home with her children. She continued to volunteer at a school for disadvantaged black and Hispanic students, however, and was elected president of the Junior League of Phoenix. During her five years off from the practice of law, O'Connor remained active in volunteer community activities that kept her in touch with the legal community. She wrote and graded bar exams, organized a lawyer referral service for the county bar association, acted as juvenile court referee, and sometimes served as a bankruptcy trustee. During this time she learned that women were the backbone of church and civil organizations serving the elderly and handicapped, as well as the primary movers in education.

When her youngest son started school, O'Connor returned to law as an assistant attorney general. Meanwhile, her affiliation with Republican Party politics intensified. In 1969 she was appointed as a state senator for Arizona, and was subsequently re-elected twice to serve for a total of six years. She was elected majority leader in 1972.

O'Connor's energy, her attention to detail, and her constant hard work gained her the admiration of her colleagues. She was known to be tough when the occasion called for it, as well as tactful in dealing with delicate matters. She rejected blind loyalty to the party platform and voted according to what she considered right for each issue. She made it hard for people to pin her down or categorize her.

Eventually, O'Connor began to miss the constant change and challenge offered by the practice of law, so she left the legislature in 1974. The following year, she was elected as a trial judge in Phoenix. O'Connor could be tough on the bench, especially against violent criminals, but most considered her decisions to be fair. The job was often difficult. O'Connor reportedly cried in chambers once after sending the mother of two young children to prison. Yet she supported the death penalty and wasn't afraid to impose it against murderers.

In 1979 O'Connor was named to the Arizona Court of Appeals. Her decisions on the appellate bench reflected careful research, and a direct, clear writing style. When U.S. Supreme Court Justice Potter Stewart announced his intention to retire in 1981, O'Connor's name promptly appeared on lists of candidates prepared by both Attorney General William French Smith and White House Counsel Fred Fielding. President Reagan had promised to appoint a woman to the next opening on the bench. Justice William Renquist was especially supportive. The two were friends who graduated from the same law school class at Stanford and worked together on the law review. O'Connor was also acquainted with Chief Justice Warren E. Burger.

The appointment of Supreme Court justices is one of the president's most powerful tools. It can have ramifications that continue for decades, long after the president's term. Yet Reagan had little hesitation about O'Connor's appointment. Justice Department lawyers began investigating and interviewing O'Connor. All were impressed and enjoyed visits to her Arizona home, where she served them lunch. O'Connor, gracious and intelligent, was exactly the type of justice the president wanted: female, conservative, and Republican. She sailed through Senate confirmation hearings, gracefully sidestepping awkward questions about some of her past stances on various issues.

As O'Connor began her new job the first Monday of October 1981, she faced a task many would consider daunting. In addition to a handful of cases that are appealed to the United States Supreme Court as a matter of right, the court must sift through nearly five thousand cases per year that come before it as discretionary appeals. From these the court chooses those most legally significant, a number fewer than two hundred. The justices hear argument by attorneys from 10:00 A.M. to 2:00 P.M. Monday through Thursday, and then vote on Friday. This process is one of the few in government that remains totally secret, with only the justices present.

As O'Connor began participating in the voting process, she was categorized in the camp of the leading conservatives, Justices Burger and Rehnquist. She voted with Renquist on 123 of her 139 votes during her first term, earning the two the nickname "the Arizona twins." Yet O'Connor remained ready to assert her independence when her views differed from those of her colleagues. Unlike many justices who view the first term as a form of apprenticeship, O'Connor took an active role in the process as soon as she joined the court. She did not hesitate to question attorneys during argument and wrote articulate, forceful opinions. Her strong position on states' rights established her as a member of the conservative coalition, but her views varied on other issues.

O'Connor has been labeled priggish and ribbed for her reserved demeanor. At a Washington party, not long after her appointment to the high court, a pro football player advised her to "loosen up, Sandy baby." Yet O'Connor has never been overly concerned with the opinions of others, and this independence was seen early in her tenure. Not long after her appointment, she opposed Justices Burger and Rehnquist in her vote on a sex discrimination case that involved a man who was denied admission to a state nursing school. O'Connor found the exclusion to be a violation of the Fourteenth Amendment. In a footnote to the opinion she wrote, she referred to the 1873 case that denied Myra Bradwell's admission to the bar.

A great deal of speculation arose as to how O'Connor would vote when abortion cases came before the court, since she had never taken a clear stand on whether women had a constitutional right to such a choice. A partial answer came in June 1983. *Roe v. Wade* was reaffirmed in a 6-3 decision, striking down a battery of state-imposed restrictions on a woman's right to choose, but O'Connor sided with the minority. While other legal issues were the focus of the case, O'Connor finally made her stance clear in writing the dissent. She supported laws requiring a twenty-four-hour waiting period, as well as those requiring that second-trimester abortions be performed in a hospital. She reiterated her opinion that states have an interest in protecting potential human life throughout pregnancy. Naturally, the decision drew praise from President Reagan and others opposed to abortion, but sharp criticism from many who supported abortion rights and felt that the decision was insensitive to the poor. Some debate remained as to whether O'Connor's opinion reflected more about abortion or about her notoriously strong stance on states' rights.

On other issues, O'Connor frequently provides the swing vote. Since she was sworn in as a member of the nation's highest court on September 25, 1981, O'Connor has been touted as the leader of the "new center" of the court. In her years on the bench, she has emerged as a thoughtful and distinctive voice. Some have suggested that the diversity of her professional experience prior to this position has given her a broader frame of reference than most of the justices have.

O'Connor has provided a strong model for many women through her strength, stamina, and efficiency. She has managed to maintain a life outside the court, adapting to accommodate both the demands of her job and her personal requirements. Fitness has always been important to her, and soon after her appointment to the Supreme Court she organized an exercise class for the Court's female employees, including herself, in the previously all-male gym. She enjoys playing doubles tennis with her husband, who practices with a Washington, D.C., law firm. She is renowned for her gourmet cooking, with a special affection for Tex-Mex food. Friends from the Southwest often bring fresh tortillas when they come to visit.

O'Connor has often acknowledged the special challenges for women in the legal profession. As she observed in a 1985 speech, "Women's equality under the law does not effortlessly translate into equal partnership in the legal profession." She has also noted that opportunities are still greater for women in the public rather than the private sector. And she acknowledges that most women still bear the primary responsibility for child rearing and household duties. In a 1990 interview, O'Connor recalled that it was never easy to combine the responsibilities of career and family, but she stated that it was worth it because she loved both her work and her family and wouldn't have traded either. While she admitted that some corners had to be cut, she feels her sons learned to take personal responsibility.

Today, with four justices generally considered to be conservative and four who usually take the liberal stance, O'Connor often finds herself in the position of tie breaker. O'Connor cast the deciding vote in eleven 1995 cases. During the same term she wrote thirteen concurring opinions, more than any of the other justices. Her role in history is still being forged.

RUTH BADER
GINSBURG

1933 –

T HE SECOND WOMAN TO ASCEND TO THE HIGHEST COURT IN
America had even less success in landing her first job after law
school than her sister on the bench, Sandra Day O'Connor. Ruth
Bader Ginsburg began her legal education at Harvard, where she
served on the law review, then transferred to Columbia. When she
graduated in 1959 she was tied for first place in the class. But not
one firm to which she applied was forthcoming with any job offer.
She clerked for a federal district judge, aware that any man with her
background and grades could have chosen from a smorgasbord of
firms or high-court clerkships.

Ginsburg credits the efforts of one of her professors in helping
her finally land a clerkship. He had to persuade the federal district
judge that she could manage her family life without cutting short the
hours needed for work.

The path that brought Ruth Bader Ginsburg to the United States Supreme Court was a long and arduous one. Ruth Bader was born in 1933 in Brooklyn, New York, where her father worked as a furrier and a haberdasher. Ruth was the second daughter of Nathan and Celia Bader. Her older sister contracted meningitis and died at the age of eight. Ruth's mother, who had not been able to attend college herself, placed a high value on education and achievement. At Madison High School in Brooklyn, Ruth earned top grades and served as editor of the student newspaper. She also twirled the baton and served as treasurer of the "Go-Getters Club." Yet her high school years were difficult. Celia Bader fought cancer for four years, and died the day before Ruth graduated from high school.

Perhaps because of the tragedies encountered in her youth, Ruth developed a stoic countenance, never letting her emotions interfere with her logical outlook. She entered Cornell University in 1950, where she met Martin D. Ginsburg, whom she married shortly before graduation. Ginsburg recalled her college days in the fifties in a 1993 interview with the *ABA Journal*, remarking that "the thing to do was be a party girl," and "the most important degree for you to get was an MRS." Classmates remember "Kiki" Bader as popular and vivacious, a façade she kept up by doing her studying in the more obscure libraries around the Cornell campus so as to avoid being tagged a grind.

Ginsburg's entry into the legal field was actually more romantic than pragmatic. According to a 1993 *People* magazine article, when Ruth and Martin began discussing marriage, they decided they would like to work in the same field. Law was chosen by process of elimination. Ruth's family was skeptical and recommended teaching instead, but once her mind was made up, Ruth was determined.

Martin enrolled at Harvard Law School in 1954, and Ruth followed him two years later. Ginsburg recalls that she did not find it particularly difficult to go to law school as a married woman with a child, thanks in large part to her husband's egalitarian philosophy and culinary skills. There were, however, other challenges. While Martin was in the army, Ruth worked in a Social Security office, where she was taken on only temporarily and only at the lowest grade because she was three months pregnant. At a reception during her first year of law school at Harvard, the dean asked each of the nine women why they had chosen to attend law school, "occupying seats that could be taken by men." Ginsburg never forgot that remark. Then Martin was diagnosed with cancer during her second year, while he was still a student as well. Fortunately, prompt treatment cured the disease, and Ruth gathered notes from his classmates so he could graduate on schedule.

In 1958, while still a student at Harvard, Ginsburg was not allowed to enter the old periodical room at the Lamont Library because she was a woman, and she was obligated to send a male colleague in to get the information she needed. This solution was typical of Ginsburg. Never one to make a scene when a confrontation was avoidable, she preferred to quietly work her way around the problems she encountered.

During law school, Ruth acquired a steely determination and left her previous concerns with image and popularity behind. One classmate dubbed her "Ruthless Ruthie" for her dedication to her work. Shortly after her nomination, upon learning that a law school classmate had recalled nicknaming her "Bitch," Ginsburg quipped, "Better bitch than mouse."

When Martin landed a job in New York, Ruth transferred to Columbia University for her last year of law school. She graduated tied for first in her class and served on the editorial board of the law reviews at both Harvard and Columbia. Despite these stellar credentials, each law firm to which Ginsburg applied for a job passed her over. She later remarked, "To be a woman, a Jew, and a mother to boot—that combination was a bit much." She finally clerked for U.S. district judge Edmond L. Palmieri, then returned to Columbia in 1961 to join a project studying civil procedures in courts around the world. Her activities included two long stays in Sweden, where she was impressed by the quality of child care available to faculty and students at the University of Lund.

In 1963 Ginsburg joined the faculty of Rutgers Law School where she wore oversize dresses to conceal her second pregnancy for as long as possible. Ginsburg's entry into the field of women's rights did not occur until the late sixties. The ACLU's New Jersey affiliate, receiving increasing complaints of sex discrimination, began referring the cases to Ginsburg. As she became more involved in the work, Ginsburg found it fascinating and hoped she could help to effect significant change. In 1972, she joined the faculty of Columbia Law School, where she became the first woman awarded tenure. She taught civil procedure, conflicts of law, and constitutional law for several years. During the same era, she served as general counsel to the ACLU and organized the ACLU's Women's Rights Project.

As a ligitator in the 1970s, Ginsburg chose her cases carefully, taking those that would allow the Supreme Court to see with clarity the unjust consequences of widely accepted laws and practices. She shrewdly selected those in which a positive outcome for women would benefit both sexes, the goal being to establish equal protection for both genders, not special privileges for women. In one such case, a widowed father was unable to receive Social Security benefits for child care, because the law provided benefits only to widowed women. In another, Ginsburg represented a female Air Force officer who was seeking a housing allowance and family medical benefits, which were available only to male officers. Ginsburg brought the effects of discrimination into sharp focus before the court, demonstrating the harm of such laws to men as well as women. Her determined efforts brought down barrier after barrier that blocked both genders from equal opportunity. At each appearance before the court, she paid quiet tribute to the memory of her mother by wearing her pin and earrings.

One of Ginsburg's most important contributions to the development of women's rights law was her work in cases that established that the Fourteenth Amendment guarantee of equal protection of laws applies to sex discrimination. While a strong supporter of a woman's right to choose abortion, Ginsburg criticized *Roe v. Wade* for its failure to incorporate a women's equality perspective along with a privacy rationale, and for moving too far too soon.

Dean Herma Hill Kay of the University of California School of

Law at Berkeley has credited Ginsburg for creating the intellectual foundations for the present doctrine regarding sex discrimination. Ginsburg's work before the Supreme Court was innovative in that it frequently attacked laws that appeared to benefit women, such as those that exempted women from jury service but that actually served to undermine equality.

Ginsburg's low-key, precise courtroom manner won her the attention and respect of judges from the beginning, and was as effective outside the courtroom as in it. An active member of the American Law Institute, Ginsburg presented a six-page memorandum arguing for the organization to move its dinners from the men-only Century Club in Manhattan until the club policies were changed. The dinners were duly relocated.

Ginsburg left her position at Columbia in 1980 when she was appointed to the bench of the U.S. Court of Appeals for the District of Columbia Circuit. In 1993, President Bill Clinton appointed her to the United States Supreme Court.

Justice Ginsburg is admired by both liberals and conservatives as fair, levelheaded, and simply a very fine judge. "She is so clearly qualified to be a Supreme Court justice, and she has attained that stature with such studied professionalism," wrote a journalist in a 1993 *Mirabella* magazine article, "that the radical nature of her accomplishments can easily be obscured."

The *New Republic* heaped praise on President Clinton for choosing a judge who was highly regarded by a broad spectrum of citizens. The article described Ginsburg as "a civil libertarian and a scholar who combines intellectual independence with personal integrity. But her most important quality . . . is this: she appears to have a constitutional philosophy."

At the same time, Ginsburg's judicial moderation has been criticized by both the far left and the far right. But Ginsburg answers only to her own ideals. "A judge steps out of the proper judicial role most conspicuously and dangerously," she has said, "when he or she flinches from a decision that is legally right because the decision is not the one the home crowd wants."

Ginsburg has counseled law students to engage in a dialogue with, not a diatribe against, those they wish to convince. "The effective judge will strive to persuade," she told New York University law students in 1993, "and not to pontificate." Much of her success has been based not upon the ability to wage a war or win a fight, but rather the skill to reason with others in a logical, give-and-take manner. Over her thirty-year career she has maintained her conviction that the law can help to change the world, and that lawyers working within the system can make a real difference.

Nonetheless, Ginsburg is not hesitant to point out the absurdities that presented obstacles in her past. In a 1993 interview with the *American Bar Association Journal* she stated, "In the days when I clerked from 1959 to 1961, the U.S. attorney would hire no women in the criminal division, because that was considered inappropriate work for a woman. Never mind that women were representing criminal defendants in the defense side of legal aid, where they were paid very little. There were all those irrationalities."

Like O'Connor, Ginsburg found the spotlight to be one of the most difficult aspects of her appointment to the United States Supreme Court. While she feels that diversity is important in the makeup of the Supreme Court, she rejects the idea of such notions as a "Jewish seat" on the court. Ginsburg does feel that the presence of two women on the court may affect the way that the other members view the real-life issues behind the law. As she remarked to the *ABA Journal*, "I do think that being the second woman is wonderful, because it is a sign that being a woman in a place of importance is no longer extraordinary. It will become more and more natural."

Ginsburg has steadfastly rejected the idea alternately espoused by traditionalists and feminists alike that the law should grant special treatment to women. She has been a strong supporter of laws such as the Family Medical Leave Act which established leaves and benefits for new parents of either sex. Her view has come under attack by certain feminist legal scholars who believe the law should emphasize women's differences from men. She has been saddened by such criticism but defends her position. At the University of Chicago symposium on feminist legal theories held in 1988, she spoke against the "discordant tendency to regard one's feminism as the only true feminism, to denigrate rather than to appreciate the contributions of others."

Ginsburg is, in a way, a rare breed of pathfinder. Never one to display a revolutionary temperament, she is instead known for her fairness and sense of balance. Yet there is no denying the tremendous impact Ginsburg has had in shaping the law. When President Clinton offered praise for her work on behalf of women's rights, he stated, "Many admirers of her work say she is to the women's movement what former Supreme Court justice Thurgood Marshall was to the movement for the rights of African-Americans."

Some view Ginsburg as stern and austere, but those who know her often speak of her warmth. Law professor Deborah Jones Merritt of the University of Illinois clerked for Ginsburg while she sat on the court of appeals, and for Sandra Day O'Connor on the U.S. Supreme Court. (Five Ginsburg clerks later worked with O'Connor.) According to Merritt in a 1993 *ABA Journal* interview, Ginsburg is passionately committed to her family and friends, and views her clerks as another family. Merritt recalls Ginsburg's willingness to perform marriage ceremonies for former clerks, and her fondness for Merritt's own young son.

By all accounts Ginsburg has managed to harmonize her busy career and attention to her family with astonishing grace. Her son, James, told *People* magazine that the family was almost always home for dinner, and that his mother always checked to see that he was doing his homework: "She was always there when I wanted her to be—and even when I didn't." Ginsburg's daughter, Jane, is now a tenured law professor at Columbia, she and Ruth being one of only four mother-and-daughter teams to attend Harvard Law School. Martin Ginsburg, a highly respected tax attorney, still does the cooking and is locally renowned as a talented chef. The Ginsburgs live in a co-op in the Watergate complex in Washington, D.C. Both hold fast to their ideals. On one occasion they gave up golf membership at a club that appeared to discriminate against minorities.

Those who have known Ginsburg for many years have often

commented on both her big heart and her soaring intellect. Her lack of effusiveness often obscures such qualities from the public eye. Yet her natural reserve is undoubtedly an element of her success. She is known to have deep and abiding passions, particularly for opera. Ginsburg was hoping to be an extra at the Washington Opera in 1993 until her Supreme Court nomination bestowed on her a starring role of a different kind. According to the *New York Times,* Ginsburg also loves to read mysteries, watch old movies, ride horseback, and water-ski. A friend once remarked that Ginsburg plays golf as she decides cases: aiming left, swinging right, and hitting down the middle.

GLORIA
STEINEM

---ᐳ◦◦◦ᐸ---

1934 –

PERHAPS MORE THAN ANYONE ASSOCIATED WITH THE MODERN
movement for women's rights, Gloria Steinem captured the
attention of mainstream America—both women and men—and
made people reconsider the way they thought about the roles and
rights of women. The voice of modern feminism, with Steinem at its
helm, identified inequities, exposed abuse, and demanded change.
And the change that resulted has truly been vast, with sweeping
reforms in both public attitudes and the law.

Steinem emerged as a woman who was intelligent, articulate, and
determined—but also attractive and unapologetically fond of male
companionship. Mainstream women who had been turned off by the
man-hating media image of feminists suddenly found someone with
whom they could identify. By her words, her appearance, and her personality, Steinem demonstrated that commitment to equality for
women was not incompatible with any kind of life. As stated by her

biographer Carolyn G. Heilbrun, Steinem "became simultaneously the epitome of female beauty and the quintessence of female revolution. Her life offers testimony to the power of contradictory behavior." Steinem herself summed it up well, and echoed the feelings of many women when, in response to the inane question, "How can you be a feminist in a miniskirt?" she simply replied, "Women should wear what they damn well please."

Steinem's unique, difficult upbringing left her well equipped for her future role. Her paternal grandmother had been an early suffragist, and a delegate to the International Council on Women held in Switzerland in 1908. Because she died when her granddaughter was five, Steinem did not learn about this until her own career as a feminist and writer was well established.

Steinem's parents came from different religious backgrounds, her father Jewish and her mother Presbyterian. The couple made an interesting mix in other ways as well. Leo Steinem was a spendthrift who adored and was a playmate to his children. Leo was a dreamer and lover of show business, and the family remained in Toledo, Ohio, until Leo began a summer resort in Michigan. To earn money in the interim, the family traveled in a house trailer to Florida or California, with Leo selling antiques along the way. Gloria's mother, Ruth, had been a teacher and reporter before her marriage, sometimes writing under a male byline at the request of her publisher. She gave up her much-loved career in journalism to move to Michigan and work with Leo to keep the resort afloat. Ruth was frugal by nature and constantly worried about money. Leo, on the other hand, frequently invested in impractical business schemes.

Due to the family's nomadic lifestyle, Gloria did not regularly attend elementary school, sometimes missing entire years. Their mother's teaching certificate warded off the truant officers, who never seemed to examine it closely enough to notice that it was limited to college calculus.

Yet Steinem's early years provided her with a unique education. Born in 1934, Gloria was a voracious reader from early childhood, as well as a cheerful, adaptable child. She enjoyed summers at the family resort running wild around the lake, spending entire weeks in a swimsuit. These itinerant years accustomed her to a gypsy lifestyle, which she was to continue as a freelance writer, speaker, and political leader. Her father provided an example of the type of man she would always admire—loving, humorous, respectful, and a true friend to his daughters. He also instilled in Gloria his own delight in freedom, insecurity, and dreams.

Steinem's mother affected her in a different way. Though the relationship between Ruth Steinem and her children was undoubtedly loving, Gloria faced the most difficult time of her life when her parents divorced, and she and her mother were living in a poor working class neighborhood in Toledo. Ruth had begun to suffer bouts of depression when her husband's life precluded her own journalistic career, including a major nervous breakdown before Gloria was born.

At the age of ten, Gloria found the parental roles reversed. She became primarily responsible for her mother's care, with her father in California and her sister away at college. The next seven years were grim indeed, yet Steinem persevered through the deterioration of her mother's health and the deepening of their poverty. It was during this period that she learned to protect herself, guard the privacy of what was going on at home, and put her talents to work. She continued taking dancing lessons, both as a means of escape and a way to earn money. Her dance class often performed at places like a local Eagles' Lodge, where chicken wire protected the bandstand from bottles heaved by unruly patrons.

These tough years also made Steinem take a hard look at the traditional role of women in her blue-collar neighborhood. She was determined not to follow the path of her contemporaries into this narrow world, in which the failure to marry young was seen as the ultimate shame. These years also shaped her commitment to reproductive rights, as she saw many of her classmates become pregnant, then marry a boy who dropped out of school and began to work in one of the local factories.

Gloria escaped her dismal surroundings with the help of books, the radio, and her vivid imagination. A favorite fantasy revolved around a dream of rescuing the unfortunate, a unique perspective at a time when most girls imagined themselves being saved by the proverbial knight in shining armor. Yet Gloria's experience as her mother's caretaker was to affect her outlook throughout her lifetime.

When Gloria graduated from high school, she and her sister convinced her father to return to care for Ruth for a year so Gloria could go to Washington, D.C. Through the sale of the family home and assistance with her mother's care, first by her sister then in a mental hospital, Gloria found her way to Smith College. Smith had the reputation as a choice college for young women. Gloria saw college as a shelter and escape from the constant anxiety she had suffered at home.

Smith also provided Steinem with a glimpse into a completely different world. She majored in government. Her classes gave her a new perspective on the conservative, male-oriented approach that dominated academia. Because of her mother's experiences, she also volunteered at a mental hospital, where she became more sensitive to people in truly wretched circumstances, as well as to the callousness of the wealthy toward such people. Steinem also learned to apply the skills she had learned in blue-collar Toledo. She taught her preppie classmates how to iron clothing in exchange for tutoring in French. This small but important gem of wisdom remained with her. She often counseled others not to worry about their background——whether it was odd or ordinary, it could be put to valuable use. Gloria spent her junior year abroad in Paris and Geneva, which opened her eyes to the appreciation of other cultures. She considered law school, but eventually concluded that she could have at least as much influence from outside the profession by trying to connect law to social justice.

Steinem also had her first serious boyfriend her senior year at Smith. Blair Chotzinoff was an aspiring documentary filmmaker who was funny, kind, and courted Gloria with such romantic gestures as sky writing her name above the campus while working weekends as a National Guard pilot. It was truly a storybook romance, 1950s style, culminating with the couple announcing their engagement. However, while Gloria truly loved the young man, she found herself fleeing from marriage rather than seeking it out like her classmates. She broke the engagement and set out for to India on a post-graduate fellowship after graduating magna cum laude in 1956.

While Steinem was in London awaiting her visa to India, another key event occurred which would shape her destiny as a crusader for women's rights. Steinem had always been careful about birth control during her relationship with Blair, but when they broke their engagement she threw away her diaphragm. The couple had one last, careless encounter before she left the country, and soon thereafter she found herself pregnant. Abortion was legal in England, but only if two doctors would certify it was for the well-being of the woman. Gloria ultimately located a compassionate male doctor willing to take the risk, and who arranged an appointment with a female surgeon willing to perform the procedure. In exchange, the doctor made Gloria promise she would do what she really wanted to do with her life.

This experience moved Steinem deeply in several ways. She felt for the first time that she was taking responsibility for difficult decisions rather than reacting to what happened to her. She also knew how lucky she was to find safe, caring professionals to perform the abortion, when many women were dying at the hands of back-alley butchers. But the procedure was outrageously expensive, and wiped out over half of her savings to fund her travels in India. Steinem was nonetheless determined to continue.

India proved to be a watershed experience. Steinem quickly became immersed in the culture, wearing the traditional sari and taking a series of odd writing jobs to replenish her funds. She also became sensitive to the lack of birth control and its effect on the lives of women in India.

Steinem joined the followers of Gandhi on a walk through a riot-torn area of South India to urge peace between the warring castes and to campaign against the caste system. Along with Devaki Jain, an Indian economist who was to become a lifelong friend, she studied Gandhi's tactics of nonviolent protest. Steinem shared Gandhi's belief in the inherent goodness of human beings. The trip also gave her the first evidence of her talents in writing and advocacy.

Yet when she returned to America in 1958, she found it difficult to find a market for these skills. Steinem headed for New York, drawn by the freedom, excitement, and diversity it promised. But opportunities for women were limited, even in the nation's most cosmopolitan city. Falling through the cracks of the job market, she found that she was overqualified as a secretary or a clerk, but unwelcome in upper-echelon jobs. Eventually, she moved to Cambridge, Massachusetts, to work with a nonprofit educational foundation, encouraging students to attend international youth festivals, even though they were communist-sponsored.

Steinem was determined to return to New York and begin her career as a freelance journalist. After working for a political satire magazine, she connected with editors at *Esquire* and others in the magazine trade and began writing steadily, producing brief pieces for various publications. She began a relationship with *Esquire* art director Robert Benton, who was to remain a lifelong friend and whom she credits with setting her on her professional path.

As the 1960s progressed, Steinem's career brought her increasing success and visibility. A *Newsday* profile published in 1965 touted her as "the world's most beautiful byline." Yet along with the popular articles she wrote for slick magazines, profiling well-known writers, people in the arts, and the New York lifestyle, Steinem also continued her involvement with civil rights, migrant farm workers, and the Vietnam War. The two worlds rarely dovetailed, but occasionally she wrote exposés. Later, she continued this on television by trading a social or political topic for a celebrity interview. Steinem made her first leap toward fame when she went undercover to pose as a Playboy bunny in 1963. She wrote an article on the grueling, thankless reality behind the supposed glamour of the bunny's life, and was sued by Playboy.

One thing Steinem was not doing during this time was getting rich, although many assumed the contrary. The practical skills she had learned in blue collar Toledo served her well. She acquired sample and second-hand garments and shared a one-room apartment with artist Barbara Nessim.

In 1968, Steinem finally landed her first assignments as a political writer, when *New York* magazine was founded by a former *Esquire* colleague. She also volunteered at the 1968 Democratic convention for peace candidate George McGovern, and was disillusioned by the violence as well as the way the media portrayed it. Meanwhile, Steinem had become deeply involved in working with Cesar Chavez, Marian Moses, and others who were determined to stop the exploitation of migrant farmworkers. She used her journalistic contacts to draw the attention of major national magazines to the plight of the workers, the violence of the growers, and the national boycotts being organized. Cesar Chavez expressed his amazement at what Steinem was able to accomplish on her own.

Steinem experienced a personal turning point when she reported on a hearing on abortion law repeal for her column in *New York* magazine. She later claimed this event catalyzed her feminism, as she connected with other women who had endured illegal abortions and shared their feelings of isolation, danger and stigma.

Steinem began writing about women's rights, but quickly found that the media was skittish. Many editors wanted to run anti-feminist articles alongside hers to show "both sides"——when they did not reject her proposals outright. Women's magazines told her they'd already published their token feminist article for the year, while male colleagues warned her not to let herself be identified with "those crazies." But Steinem was determined to write of her own experience and that of other women marginalized by the media.

When Steinem wrote an article profiling black activist Dorothy Pitman-Hughes and her pioneer storefront child-care center in 1970, the two became friends. Steinem was terrified of public speaking, but she teamed up with Pitman to begin addressing groups. Steinem and Pitman both saw a deep connection between women's rights and civil rights, between the sexual caste system and the racial one, and believed it was important for women to address them together.

When Dorothy Pitman-Hughes decided she no longer wanted to travel after having a baby, Steinem teamed with the outspoken black attorney Florynce Kennedy. The two were a big hit, always in great demand on the lecture circuit. Kennedy's outrageous, colorful style balanced well with Steinem's low-key approach. Steinem consistently remained calm and unflappable, as Kennedy injected humor, neatly flaying ignorant harassers with her wit. When one man accused the two of being lesbians, Kennedy quipped, "Are you my alternative?"

Eventually, however, Kennedy moved on to different projects and Steinem teamed with Margaret Sloan, a gifted speaker who had marched with Dr. Martin Luther King Jr. Years later, all the speakers who teamed with Steinem commented on her remarkable energy and commitment. Despite the breakneck schedule they followed, Gloria would frequently stay after a meeting had ended to help local groups organize grass roots projects.

Steinem was soon deluged by requests for information and guidance. Assignments for articles about the feminist movement gradually came her way. Ironically, when she wrote an essay on feminism for *Time* in 1970, she learned she was paid less than male journalists writing similar pieces.

In the late 1960s, Steinem was befriended by attorney Brenda Feigen. Feigen had listened to Dean Irwin Griswold of Harvard Law School tell her incoming class of 1966 that the women were taking the place of male breadwinners. Steinem later became the first woman asked to address the Harvard Law Review banquet. Feigen was arranging the 1970 congressional hearings on the Equal Rights Amendment and asked Gloria to testify.

Feigen thrived on conflict, while Steinem, despite her eagerness to write and speak on controversial topics, hated direct confrontation. Together, the two founded the Women's Action Alliance to help women around the nation who were seeking information on how to change their daily lives, but didn't have time to join an organization. The overwhelming response led to the idea of a newsletter. Feigen suggested a magazine that would appeal to a wide variety of readers. Thus the concept of *Ms.* magazine was born.

As plans to launch *Ms.* simmered, Steinem worried about the magazine's ability to gain sufficient advertising support, but many talented writers were anxious for an outlet for their feminist articles.

Clay Felker, her old colleague at *New York* magazine, offered generous assistance in launching the first issue. The magazine premiered in spring 1972, and immediately struck a common chord among readers across the country. The premier issue sold out in eight days and drew 20,000 letters. Though deeply committed to *Ms.* magazine, Steinem vowed to stay a maximum of two years.

At about the same time, Steinem, seeing the desperate need for political clout and unity among women committed to the feminist effort, helped found the National Women's Political Caucus. Steinem and Feigen joined with such leaders as Bella Abzug, Shirley Chisholm, Betty Friedan, and Patsy Mink to form a unified political voice in support of women's issues and feminist candidates.

Steinem also recognized a need for economic support of the women's rights groups. She helped establish the *Ms.* Foundation for women, the first multi-racial, multi-issue national women's fund. Meanwhile, she was elected to serve as spokesperson at the 1972 Democratic convention by the National Women's Political Caucus. She also continued to help forge a direction for the fledgling *Ms.* Most of all, Steinem wanted the magazine to reach mainstream working women.

As she suspected, gaining advertising was difficult. Yet Steinem and the other editors persevered. As *Ms.* writers such as Alice Walker began to become well-known, *Ms.* started reaching mainstream women with legal and political ideas that exposed such problems as domestic violence, early sexual abuse, and sexual harassment in the work place. Committed to providing a forum for divergent views, *Ms.* reported the horrible abuse and exploitation that went on in the pornography industry, while exploring the dangers of censorship in the suppression of healthy sexuality and erotica.

Naturally, both Steinem and the magazine drew fire. Often, the same article would offend more conservative readers and angered those who thought it should have gone further, including some who castigated Steinem as a sellout to the mainstream. But Steinem trusted her wisdom and absorbed the hurt inflicted by such accusations. Despite the criticism that her vitality, success, and beauty attracted, plus her emotional and physical exhaustion, she kept up her relentless schedule and found time to enjoy a personal life.

In 1975 Steinem began a relationship with Stan Pottinger, then the head of the Civil Rights Division of the Justice Department. Like all the men who had been important in her life, he was caring, supportive, politically compatible, and smart. Pottinger was also no stranger to the efforts toward equal rights for women. On first joining the Justice Department, he had been astonished to learn that his colleagues perceived no problems in women's rights. In response, Pottinger created a task force to work on changing the government's attitude, and he called on Steinem to assist in this effort. She in turn arranged for Brenda Feigen and future Supreme Court Justice Ruth Bader Ginsburg to join him in a meeting.

When Pottinger contemplated hiring her as a consultant in the Justice Department, it became clear that the FBI had been watching her and others in the feminist movement, compiling extensive files. Through the Freedom of Information Act, *Ms.* magazine acquired reports on J. Edgar Hoover's routine surveillance of the "women's liberation movement" from 1969 through the Watergate years and published a cover story on the vast sums of tax dollars wasted on this undertaking.

By the mid 1970s Steinem had become a political icon. Though she missed having a real home and a full personal life, she could not turn away from her commitments. With author Robin Morgan, she wrote an exposé on the horror of female genital mutilation, and has continued to work with individuals and international groups trying to outlaw and eradicate the practice. She testified at platform committee hearings in preparation for the 1976 Democratic convention, met with the National Women's Political Caucus, and worked on the Democratic Women's Agenda '76. At the convention, she was gratified to see real effects of the women's rights movement and the progress gained since the 1972 convention. Women were now recognized as a political force to be taken seriously, and the media were far better informed about issues crucial to female equality.

Steinem's close friend Bella Abzug wrote legislation to create the National Women's Conference, with huge conferences in each state to elect its delegates and outline the issues to be voted on. It was to be a kind of constitutional convention for women, and a landmark effort marking the first time federal funds had been allotted to such an undertaking. Steinem was named to the commission as well. Her role was largely to unify various groups and help in the election of delegates to the conference from various states. At the conference, she was asked by the many different groups of women of color to serve as their scribe and coordinator as they fashioned a plank. She was instrumental in including Native American land and fishing rights for the first time.

The National Women's Conference and the plan it produced ultimately had tremendous influence in reshaping both the law and public attitudes. Many of its components have taken a great deal of time to manifest, but the plan set an agenda in motion that brought such issues as economic equality, the special concerns of women of color, sexual preference discrimination, and national health security to the forefront of both national and local attention.

The advent of the Reagan years spurred Steinem to greater activism. At the same time, *Ms.* had earned enough status as a serious and educational publication—and was often used as supplementary reading in college courses—to become a non-profit publication and subsidiary of the *Ms.* Foundation for Women. Steinem had to increase her fund-raising efforts to compensate for its lack of support by advertisers more interested in fashion magazines. Additionally, she published her first book, *Outrageous Acts and Everyday Rebellions,* in 1983. The book became an instant best seller. It profiled women as diverse as Steinem's mother Ruth, Marilyn Monroe, Alice Walker, and Linda Lovelace (whose real name was Linda Marciano). Her interviews with Marciano, who had been beaten and imprisoned into her role in the pornographic hit *Deep Throat* brought out her compassion and her ever-present role as rescuer. She placed a great deal of personal effort to help Marciano, who had been horribly abused, overcome the trauma of her past and begin a new life. Steinem even helped her get the medical treatment she needed as a result of severe beatings she received from her former manager.

Meanwhile, Steinem kept up her usual harrowing schedule, combining book tours with speaking engagements at shelters for abused women, local benefits for women's groups, and conferences. Steinem's years of self-sacrifice were not without cost. In 1986 she was diagnosed with breast cancer. In assessing her treatment options, Steinem personally experienced the benefit of her own efforts on behalf of women. She realized that had she been diagnosed earlier, before *Ms.* and various women's organizations began to crusade for better health care and to oppose unnecessary surgery, her diagnosis would have meant an immediate mastectomy. As it was, a minor lumpectomy and radiation cured her cancer. The experience nonetheless forced her to admit she could no longer take her excellent health for granted. As she stepped back to gain perspective on her life, she realized she had spent only one week during the last twenty years when she was not on a plane at least once.

Fortunately, two Australian feminists persuaded their company, Fairfax, to take over *Ms.* and provide more investment in the late 1980s. For the first time in almost twenty years, Gloria unpacked her boxes, decorated her walls, and established a real home in her New York apartment. She began to spend more time with friends and family, and while she kept up her commitments to causes and political campaigns, she vowed to achieve more balance. She went to work on her book, *Revolution from Within,* focusing on self-esteem as the source of revolution, and providing examples from diverse lives, including her own. The book got mixed reviews but an overall positive response, especially from some feminists who had turned away or been turned off by the women's movement when it became more political, with less of the personal and internal balance which had been its wellspring in consciousness-raising groups. Many told Steinem they were glad to discover that feminism could be about strengthening from the inside in order to change the outer world. Again, Steinem had become a new kind of role model, linking the internal and external halves of revolution and avoiding the polarization of patriarchal thinking.

Steinem's current pace has been described in the "lower range for workaholics." She continues to tour and speak and to work for a feminist world view that stresses the full humanity of each person. She assisted the *Ms.* Foundation in launching the "Take Our Daughters to Work Day," the first national event ever devoted to girls, and has helped organize women who are trying to break into male-dominated industries, such as mining. She continues to assist at battered women's shelters; in programs to help women become economically independent through cooperatively owned businesses; as well as at *Ms.*, which is now successful without advertisers.

As she enters her sixties, Steinem's role as peacemaker seems to be a top priority. She urges better communication between women, along with encouragement and support among all who share common goals of equality and fair opportunity for all people. She warns that we have just begun.

GERALDINE A. FERRARO

1935 –

GERALDINE FERRARO ONCE HAD AN OFFER FOR A JOB AT THE Manhattan district attorney's office withdrawn when she told the hiring attorney she was getting married. When she did rise to the position of bureau chief in the Queens district attorney's office, she received a lower salary than males in the same position. Upon her graduation from Fordham Law School, she was put through four difficult and detailed interviews with Dewey, Balentine, Bushby, Palmer and Wood, a Wall Street firm that eventually told her in her fifth interview that they "would not be hiring any women that year." After serving three years in Congress a creditor denied her an account in her own name, despite the fact that she had good credit. Yet Geraldine managed to achieve nomination, and win a strong showing among voters, for the second most politically powerful position in America.

One week before the 1984 Democratic National Convention, Geraldine Ferraro was a third-term congresswoman from Queens, wife of businessman John Zaccaro, and mother to three college-aged children. A mere week later, she changed American history when she was nominated as the first woman to run for the office of vice-president on a major party ticket. In her book, *Ferraro: My Story,* she speaks of the surreal experience of going from the freedom of her relative anonymity, in which she could do as she pleased, to becoming a hub in the wheel of a national campaign.

Ferraro's path to political success was not easy. Her father died suddenly of a heart attack when she was eight. Ferraro has tremendous respect for her mother, who remained proud, independent, and never complained through the trials of raising two children alone. The Ferraros moved to a tiny apartment in the South Bronx to be closer to other family members. It was a rundown area, and Geraldine was sent to boarding school a short time later. Ferraro kept her name in professional use after her marriage to honor her mother.

Ferraro later recalled that her father's death brought drastic change and important lessons. Since that time, for every plan she has made she has arranged for an alternative to fall back on. Her mother was a strong believer in self-sufficiency. To pay Geraldine's tuition at the Marymount Boarding School, Antoinetta Ferraro made a deal whereby rent from property left by her husband in Italy, inaccessible to the family because of World War II, could be paid to Marymount in Rome. The nun who arranged the deal, Sister Catherine, agreed to take in Geraldine, with whom she is still close. Meanwhile, Antoinetta supported the family by crocheting beads onto evening dresses for women able to afford such luxuries.

Geraldine learned to be resourceful while still quite young, and showed an early patriotism—family photographs reveal a nine-year-old Gerry in costume as Uncle Sam. She often held two or three jobs simultaneously while in college, and upon graduating taught grade school during the day while attending law school at night.

After marrying businessman John Zaccaro, Ferraro spent fourteen years at home raising their children, occasionally doing legal work for John in his real estate office. She has described the change from full-time mother to assistant district attorney in Queens as the toughest transition she ever had to make. Among other things, she had to learn a new criminal code that had been passed since her law school studies. Yet she learned quickly and did well. In 1977, Ferraro was named bureau chief of the division responsible for prosecuting all sex crimes, child abuse cases, and violent crimes against the elderly, as well as for implementing new battered-spouse legislation. The bureau's purpose was to assist the most vulnerable victims in navigating the court process as painlessly as possible.

Ferraro found the work heartbreaking, and she anguished over each victim. It wasn't enough to punish offenders if society did't also address the root of the problem. She saw the need to change neighborhoods and the circumstances that produced the criminals, to break the cycle of poverty in order to break the cycle of crime.

One evening as Ferraro discussed her frustrations with New York governor Mario Cuomo, he suggested she run for Congress. So in 1978 Ferraro made a bid for the Democratic seat in the Ninth District of Queens, New York, and won. She insisted on a visible, accessible storefront office to serve her constituents and hired caseworkers who roamed Queens in a mobile office to meet those who could not come to her.

Like many women in similar circumstances, Ferraro realized she had to pay close attention to the smallest details and actually surpass her male colleagues to avoid becoming a target for gender-bashing. She studied transcripts of past committee hearings so she could ask intelligent questions; and she concentrated on issues important to her constituents and joined the Public Works Committee that provided federal funds to build and repair the New York City infrastructure. Senior citizens and women's issues were always at the forefront of her efforts. Ferraro had a personal stake in such matters, since 12 percent of the households in her district were headed by women, and she carried her own memories of growing up in a home run by a woman with little education.

Throughout her tenure in Congress, Ferraro consistently pushed for issues important to her own conscience. At the D.A.'s office she had learned she was paid less than the male bureau chiefs, her supervisors freely admitting that this was because she was a woman with a husband. And so, with Colorado representative Pat Schroeder, Ferraro introduced the Women's Economic Equity Act in 1983, a compound bill with provisions for pension equity and child-support enforcement, plus tax credits for employers of homemakers, civil service pension reform, and tax relief for single heads of households. Many of these measures passed, but the wheels of reform moved slowly. Ferraro's pension equity bill did not become law until three and a half years after she introduced it.

One of Ferraro's goals in Congress was to gain a seat on the House Budget Committee, although her eventual appointment there added more to her already exhausting schedule. Ferraro found it especially difficult to be separated for long periods from her family, referring to John Zaccaro as her "rock of Gibraltar." Yet Ferraro juggled her commitments. While in Washington, she served on four committees in six years, including the Budget Committee, which she pursued with particular enthusiasm.

While Ferraro was still waiting to learn whether she had won the seat on the Budget Committee, John Riley, Walter Mondale's top political adviser, asked her to serve as the national chair for Mondale's upcoming presidential campaign. Ferraro was torn, but after much contemplation decided the time was not right and turned down the position. A short time later, however, Gary Hart, another contender for the Democratic presidential nomination, casually suggested to her that the time might be right for a female vice-presidential candidate. She later recalled how shocked she was that the idea had even occurred to a potential candidate.

Before long, Hart's thoughts were echoed by others. The National Organization for Women and the National Women's Political Coalition were actively calling for a female vice-presidential nominee. Ferraro was well aware that women were becoming a more powerful voting force, and that such issues as the persistent disparity in financial equity were bearing increased scrutiny.

The polls also showed female voters becoming increasingly disenchanted with the policies of the Reagan administration, particularly concerning the threat of nuclear war and environmental and family issues. At the same time, the Reagan administration attempted to attract the female vote by such actions as appointing Sandra Day O'Connor to the Supreme Court and naming Elizabeth Dole and Margaret Heckler to Cabinet posts.

Ferraro's name was mentioned as a potential candidate throughout the first half of 1983, but flattered as she was, Ferraro dismissed the idea as essentially unrealistic. Then, later that year, a small group of politically connected women, including Joanne Howes, the executive director of the Bipartisan Women's Vote Project; Ferraro's administrative assistant Eleanor Lewis; and Nanette Falkenberg, the executive director of the National Abortion Rights Action League, invited Ferraro to discuss her political future. Over a takeout Chinese meal, these women, known as the "A Team," explained that after careful research they'd concluded that of various potential female vice-presidential candidates, Ferraro was the top choice. When she cracked open her fortune cookie that evening, the message read "You will win big in '84." The fates seemed to be pulling her inevitably toward the candidacy.

Meanwhile, Ferraro set her sights on a position she considered more attainable. She wanted to chair the Platform Committee, responsible for putting together a national agenda for all Democratic candidates. This, she felt, would be a breakthrough achievement for her and for women in general. The A Team thought it would help her gain experience and visibility for the nomination. She won the appointment, thereby furthering both agendas.

Yet Ferraro still did not take the groundswell seriously. She was exhausted from her platform and congressional work and was wary of the media. A woman in a man's game would be constantly tested in the press. But support continued to build. Ferraro got a kick out of seeing Mondale-Ferraro and Hart-Ferraro buttons on the lapels of members of the Platform Committee. The "veepstakes," as the media had dubbed it, were heating up.

In summer 1984 Ferraro shared a *Time* magazine cover with another front-runner for the nomination, San Francisco mayor Diane Feinstein. A few weeks later, she was interviewed on television's *20/20.* Just weeks before the Democratic National Convention, Ferraro still didn't believe she would actually be nominated. A turning point came when she heard New York mayor Ed Koch refer to her candidacy while she watched television in her own home. It was then that she and her husband discussed the possibility seriously for the first time.

It was a time of change for the family, with their youngest child preparing to start college. John had consistently supported Geraldine's independence, career, and goals, often at personal sacrifice to himself. Again, he pledged his support. On July 11, Mondale asked Ferraro to be his running mate, and she accepted. Her mother, she recalls, was not the least bit surprised by the decision.

Women's organizations and female leaders were thrilled. New York congresswoman Bella Abzug passed out cigars inscribed "It's a girl!" Ferraro recalls feeling only enthusiasm and optimism as she stood by Mondale's side on the platform at the convention when the nomination was announced.

Once nominated, the pressure on Ferraro became immediate and intense. Her briefing began two days later at a marathon session at Lake Tahoe. Ferraro had an enormous amount of information to absorb quickly, but fortunately she also had experience, plus natural talent in many key areas, and she and Mondale agreed on most issues. She strongly believed that voters had a right to have questions answered and complex issues like arms control demystified. She won much admiration for her ability to explain budget matters, international policy, and other complicated agendas in language her audience could understand.

Ferraro's candidacy created a media frenzy. She described her office, constantly surrounded by a sea of press, as "bedlam." Gifts poured in, along with the occasional bomb threat, and sometimes the two were oddly confused. On one occasion the bomb squad was called in to dismantle a suspicious-looking salami. During the four months of her candidacy, Ferraro received 50,000 pieces of mail. Suddenly, she and John found themselves under siege.

Ferraro's detractors attacked quickly. Her decision to take the statutory exemption from disclosing information about her spouse's finances in the yearly disclosure statements filed in Congress—an action routinely taken by numerous members and never before questioned—was publicly challenged. John Zaccaro's business dealings were suddenly the topic of suspicion and innuendo.

Yet Ferraro managed to enjoy the warm reception of growing crowds and had a good deal of fun on the campaign trail. At every stop, shouts of "Ger-ee" formed a welcoming roar from her supporters. Many of Ferraro's former grade-school pupils from P.S. 85 in Queens turned out to help in her campaign. There were endless questions of protocol, but with her customary energy and enthusiasm, Ferraro coped well. Occasionally, though, her natural candor backfired. Under mounting pressure, John Zaccaro had agreed to release a financial statement but felt his business interests would be adversely affected if his tax returns were made public. Ferraro spontaneously replied to a reporter that John's tax returns would be released. This minor gaffe created a monster. Furor about the couple's finances grew. Bigoted suggestions of links to organized crime based solely upon their Italian surnames also began to surface.

Ferraro knew she and her family had nothing to hide. She had survived dirty campaign tactics before. Yet both the triviality and the depth of the barrage she now faced were unprecedented. A new firestorm broke over her campaign loans, dating back to 1978. Ferraro had arranged certain loans on the advice of a former Federal Election Commission lawyer, then learned just before the primary that the loans were not proper under FEC rules. Ferraro had promptly sold her own property to pay them back, and the transaction was a matter of public record. However, David Stein, the attorney who had advised her, was now claiming that he had told her the loans were improper. In fact, the opposite was true, and Stein had been fired from the FEC for substandard work.

Ferraro had known the campaign would be tough, but she didn't expect it to be so dirty. As she stated in her book, "It wasn't enough to be street smart in this campaign. I had to be gutter smart as well."

Ferraro and Zaccaro finally decided to release all their tax returns from 1978 forward, going far beyond the legal requirements and revealing more personal financial information than any candidate had in the history of a national campaign. When "disclosure Monday" arrived, Ferraro filed the mountain of documents with the FEC eleven minutes before the official deadline. Literally hundreds of media people pounced. At a press conference the following day, Ferraro faced down a brutal crowd with grace and competence. Mondale himself held a conference reinforcing his support for his running mate.

In the backbreaking pace of the campaign, Ferraro worked hard to set aside one day a week, usually Sunday, to spend with her family. But the relentlessness of her schedule did not ease up. Ferraro preferred meeting with small groups, and especially appearing before high school students. She was deeply moved by a twelve-year-old girl who wished she were old enough to vote, and an eighty-two-year-old woman who had registered to vote for the first time.

Ferraro was also impressed with the way her own children blossomed during the campaign. Her two younger children, formerly too shy to speak at school events, became excellent public speakers. The Zaccaro and Mondale offspring often campaigned together as "the Monderos." Eighteen-year-old Laura Zaccaro delayed her freshman year in college to speak on campuses throughout the country. Likewise, John Jr. delayed his junior year to stomp the campaign trail, while twenty-two-year-old Donna took time off from her work. Ferraro noted with pride that her children all managed to weather hecklers and abuse with dignity, and she and her husband were thrilled by the attention and praise they received.

At the same time, however, the Zaccaro children were shocked and hurt by attacks on their father. John Zaccaro was devastated when he was removed by a court from a previous appointment as conservator for an elderly woman's estate. His offer to resign when he learned that some of his investments for her, though beneficial to her estate, were improper, was refused as being unnecessary. Because of media pressure, even though the court found no evidence of malice or dishonesty in his handling of the matter, he was publicly disgraced. Ferraro found this event especially painful as well, because she could not be with her husband as the campaign barreled on.

Naturally, Ferraro was attacked by religious extremists who couldn't accept a pro-choice Catholic. She was constantly amazed by the extent of the bigotry, sexism, and viciousness she faced. When her voting record in Congress was distorted, she felt such blatant dishonesty was hitting below the belt. Worse, however, was having her religious faith questioned. Over and over, Ferraro had to explain that although she personally would not choose to have an abortion, the issues wouldn't be so clear if she were raped. She had seen too much suffering in her position as bureau chief of the victims division in Queens—children who had been brutally raped, victims of incest, horrifying child abuse. Neither she nor the Church, she felt, had the right to force a pregnant thirteen-year-old who had been sexually assaulted to compound her trauma by bearing a child. Yet she handled hecklers with dignity, often agreeing to hear them out later, which she did to the chagrin of the Secret Service.

One of the key hurdles Ferraro faced in the campaign was her debate with George Bush. She prepared extensively with endless research, even studying Jimmy Stewart's demeanor in *Mr. Smith Goes to Washington*. Predictably, there was massive discussion of what she should wear for the debate, but Ferraro insisted throughout the campaign that she make her own decisions on matters of style.

Ferraro compared her feelings prior to the debate to the experience of driving to the hospital to give birth to her first child. She wondered how she had gotten herself into such a predicament but knew she had no choice but to go in and deliver. The debate went smoothly, although Ferraro was annoyed at Bush's persistence in calling her Mrs. Ferraro instead of the correct Congresswoman Ferraro. (She was Mrs. Zaccaro, her mother Mrs. Ferraro.) Her temper flared only once, when Bush became patronizing over foreign policy. She ad-libbed a stunning rejoinder that many assumed she had rehearsed.

The polls either gave Bush a slight edge or called the debate a draw, but Ferraro was pleased with her performance. She felt revitalized. With a little over three weeks to go, she was covering as many as five states in a single day. Her campaign team, however, was showing signs of wear.

Members of the traveling media crew, in a new sport they called "sky-surfing," would zip down the aisle of the campaign plane as it tilted on takeoff, riding the plastic emergency cards like surfboards. At one point Ferraro looked up to see her daughter Laura leading the entire press corps in a conga line down the aisle.

Meanwhile, Ferraro was beginning to gain historical perspective on her role. Four days before the end of the campaign, she began recording her thoughts. She never thought about losing until the very end, and in the final days continued with subway whistle stops, appearances at neighborhood Italian markets, and handing out candy to children on Halloween. Even though the Democratic ticket was slipping in the polls, Ferraro had become a heroine to many. She and astronaut Sally Ride were named as the top two role models for women in a public-opinion poll.

Ferraro spent election day attending church, stopping by her office, and voting. She ended the day at a senior citizens' center, introducing those constituents to the new representative who would replace her. Given an honorary membership in the center, she later recalled how she'd felt old enough to qualify. Then she went to the New York Hilton to await results with her team.

Ferraro was determined to keep spirits up, reflecting on the need for unity, what her campaign had achieved, and the work yet to be done. Although the election was lost, a victory had been won for the future of women in America. Looking back a short time later, Ferraro had no regrets.

After the election, Ferraro and her family took a much-needed vacation to St. Croix to unwind. Despite the dirty campaign and ultimate defeat, Ferraro had many reasons to be proud and gratified. Polls following the election showed that the gender of a candidate was no longer a significant factor to most voters. Letters poured in, telling her what the campaign had meant to women, men, and especially their children. Throughout the campaign Ferraro never lost her sense of humor, and when she was hit the hardest by her detractors, the supportive mail peaked.

Ferraro's challenges—or the media frenzy that followed them— did not end when her campaign was over. In 1988, John Zaccaro Jr. sold a small amount of cocaine to an undercover policeman while at college in Vermont. Ferraro told *The New York Times* in a subsequent interview that she did not excuse her son's actions for one minute, but felt her prominence had impacted negatively on how he was treated by the system. She emphasized her pride in his work for Covenant House and his successful law studies at Catholic University.

By 1992, Ferraro declared these problems finished. John Jr. had entered law school and was running a pasta business as well. Ferraro felt it was time to return to the political arena. In 1992, she entered the race for the Senate. She hoped to win the Democratic nomination, then defeat Republican incumbent Alfonse D'Amato. Ferraro told *Working Woman* magazine in July 1992 that she had decided to run for the Senate because she was anxious to "put my energies where my mouth is."

After the intense scrutiny of her personal and financial life in 1984, Ferraro believed there could be no surprises during this campaign. When the *Village Voice* tied twenty-four people allegedly affiliated with the mob to Ferraro or Zaccaro, she staunchly denied any wrongdoing and blasted journalists who practiced what she referred to as "smear by innuendo and guilt by ethnicity."

Ferraro had emerged from the 1984 campaign with a strong image combining political fame and a down-to-earth, middle class sensibility. She had also honed her ability to laugh at herself, often a rare commodity in politicians. Ferraro frequently recalls such gaffes as her first major speech in Congress, in which she stated her views against proposed aid to Turkey. Running out of time, she closed the speech by stating, "And I must tell you, we should not give aid to the Turkeys." Mortified, then stifling giggles, she returned to her office to find a sign on her door that read, "Congratulations, Gobbledine."

Thus Ferraro entered the 1992 campaign for Senate a seasoned veteran with high hopes. At one point in the race she was considered a shoe-in, but her eighteen-point lead was destroyed in the last two weeks of the campaign when one of her opponents went on television with a half-million dollar's worth of negative advertising, reviving the anti-Italian slurs of 1984. She lost the vote to State Attorney General Bob Abrams, who was in some measure defeated because of his attacks on Ferraro by D'Amato in the general election.

As always, Ferraro moved on to the next challenge. Ten months later, she joined the New York law office of Chicago-based Keck, Mahin and Cate, her first foray into private practice. As a managing partner of the New York office, Ferraro concentrated on international trade and government lobbying.

Ferraro has hardly turned her back on public service. Appointed to the United Nations Human Rights Commission by President Clinton, she has also continued to actively support Democratic political candidates. As she told *Working Woman*, she enjoys feeling appreciated: "I told my husband that nobody has wanted me this much since he wanted me to marry him." Today, Ferraro appears as a co-host of CNN's *Crossfire* and lectures around the country.

Ferraro's contribution to history is undeniable. She has been called a "bridge" candidate and credited with opening doors for other women to follow into high political office. Noting the effect of high-office victories by women, she relates a British joke that followed Margaret Thatcher's tenure as prime minister. Two children are overheard playing grown-up. The boy turns to the girl and states, "I want to be the prime minister." "You can't," the girl replies. "You're a boy."

BARBARA
JORDAN

1936 – 1996

B ARBARA JORDAN WAS BORN IN A BLACK NEIGHBORHOOD IN Houston, Texas, in 1936. As a child, she was very close to her grandfather John Ed Patten. A perennial entrepreneur, he operated a café, a confectionery shop, and later in life a junk business that Barbara remembered fondly. Patten drove a wagon pulled by two mules, and Barbara loved to help him sort the things he collected and then take them to resell. In turn, he gave her a zippered money belt and shared his earnings with her. He urged her to follow her own way, saying, "You just trot your own horse and don't get into the same rut as everyone else." His words were to prove prophetic.

One of Barbara's favorite rituals with her grandfather was to share a bag of "reg'lars," the end pieces of barbecued beef roast, ribs, and sausage given away by a local barbecue restaurant. As they shared this treat, Barbara's grandfather would talk to her about the Bible, the importance of holding high standards, and of self-sufficiency.

Barbara felt her most important lessons came from these Sunday night sessions with her grandfather. She later credited him with giving her money, food, God, autonomy, and a guarantee he would always be there.

The Jordan family provided other role models as well. A cousin was the first black doctor in Houston, who delivered Barbara when she was born. Barbara's mother was an eloquent church orator, who often gave the welcoming address for state, district, and national Baptist conventions. Bright and gifted, she wrote all her own speeches. Her father attended Tuskegee College and eventually became a preacher.

Jordan attended a segregated school where integration was discussed but the status quo accepted, although it never felt right to her. Barbara was elated by the Supreme Court's 1954 *Brown v. Board of Education* decision, mandating integration of public schools. Yet her joy soon turned to frustration as she witnessed the snail's pace at which efforts toward integration progressed. Meanwhile, Barbara was plotting her own path to success applying her natural talents and perseverance. Her leadership abilities emerged among the groups of neighborhood children, and she became known as a good singer and a skilled debater. While in high school, Barbara got into the habit of announcing she was going to be a lawyer, though she had no real idea of what the profession entailed. She began to pile up accolades, garnering such honors as Girl of the Year. She also won a national oratorical contest and a scholarship. Her father told her he would support her as far as she wanted to go and in anything she wanted to do. She simply had to decide the kind of career she wanted, Jordan reflected later in a 1990 interview, and then she "got after it."

Barbara entered Texas Southern University, the alternative school for blacks created by the Texas legislature to sidestep efforts to integrate the University of Texas. There she joined the debating team and traveled extensively. The team was outstanding, once tying a match with Harvard. But members frequently still had to stay in "colored only" accommodations and eat at the back doors of restaurants. Often, they stopped at gas stations that provided clean rest rooms for "men" and "women"—plus an outhouse in a field for "colored." These experiences left Jordan deeply affected.

After college, Jordan's family pooled their resources to pay her tuition to Boston University Law School. Barbara struggled with the program at first, coming to realize that her "separate but equal" undergraduate education had been far from equal.

Yet she was determined, despite the prevalence of "ladies' days" (in which professors who disapproved of female students singled them out for ridicule), financial hardship, and the difficulty of the material. The black students formed their own study group and helped one another succeed.

When Barbara graduated, her father was so excited he bought a brand-new Oldsmobile 98 and drove the family north for the ceremony. Barbara considered staying in Boston to practice but returned to her family home, where she operated her law office out of the pink-and-green family dining room. Meanwhile, she worked on the Kennedy-Johnson campaign and taught at Tuskegee University long enough to save money to open a real law office, which she shared with two other lawyers.

Jordan began her practice in the early sixties, when civil rights issues were escalating throughout the South. Numerous lawsuits had been filed to force the integration as required—but ignored—under the *Brown* decision. It was then that Jordan began to think about politics. Working on the Kennedy campaign had sparked her interest, and she often spoke before various civic groups on political issues.

In 1962, Jordan ran her first campaign for election to the Texas House of Representatives. Although she made an impressive showing at the polls, she ultimately lost the election. Again she ran in 1964, gaining more votes but ending with the same unhappy result. At this point she thought seriously about giving up politics. Her family was pushing her to marry, to which she always replied, "Down the road a piece."

Jordan was devastated by the Kennedy assassination but impressed with President Johnson's vows to end segregation and implement civil rights. His advocacy of these issues served as a milestone in Jordan's own career plans. She was working as an administrative assistant to a judge from nine to five each day, then tending to her own growing law practice in the evening. Harris County, which encompassed Houston, had been redistricted so as to be more fair to minority voters. This had resulted in several new congressional seats, and Jordan decided to run once again, this time seeking the new state senate opening. She won by a two-to-one margin, making national headlines as the first black woman elected to the Texas legislature.

Jordan knew that it would be difficult to fit into this well-established old-boys' club, but she studied the structure of the senate and slowly learned the ropes. She built respectful relationships with key people and put other senators at ease by assuring them she wasn't there to stir things up and would not be offended by their salty language; she simply wanted to do her job along with the rest of them. She made such a good impression on her colleagues that she was invited to an annual quail hunt that had previously been an all-male event.

At the same time, Jordan maintained balance in her life by preserving her close ties to old friends, with whom she could escape on camping and fishing trips and completely be herself. She always loved a party, and her guitar playing and singing made her popular in both worlds.

In 1967, Jordan was summoned to Washington to confer with President Johnson on fair-housing legislation. The president was impressed with her intelligent ideas, and she gained the respect of those in national government. After serving six years in the Texas senate, she decided to run for the U.S. House of Representatives in 1971. Lyndon B. Johnson attended a gala fund-raiser and offered his support. As part of the event, she was named "Governor for a Day" of Texas and was sworn in as her parents stood alongside her on the platform. Her joy was marred when her father suffered a stroke and died the following day, although she later recalled he was still beaming with delight in the hospital.

Jordan won the election and faced quite a change when she joined the 435-member House of Representatives in 1973. She and Andrew Young became the first blacks elected to Congress since

Reconstruction. At the suggestion of her friend Lyndon Johnson, she joined the Judiciary Committee. Soon afterward, when Johnson died, she gave a moving eulogy on the floor of the House as her first formal address. One of Jordan's primary concerns in Congress was minority legislation. Early in her tenure, she saw her name attached to civil-rights legislation and participated in a new and more effective Voting Rights Act.

When the first Watergate rumblings began, Jordan discounted them, thinking nothing so drastic could happen to the presidency. The revelation of the tapes shattered that illusion, and with the rest of the Judiciary Committee she became embroiled in the Watergate scandal. When the closed-door sessions ended and a press conference was called, stunned audiences across America saw Jordan in her first televised appearance. She emphasized her faith in the Constitution and quickly won the respect of the nation. She spoke eloquently of what the Constitutional impeachment provisions meant, explained what had to be decided, and urged reason, not passion, to be the guide. A flood of letters praised her honesty, her forthrightness, and her ability to succinctly explain a shocking and confusing state of affairs. Jordan did not like the idea of impeachment, but her loyalty, she felt, was to the Constitution rather than to any one individual.

In 1976, Jordan was appointed one of the keynote speakers at the Democratic National Convention, again the first black woman to earn this honor. Her moving speech created a sensation, as well as a drive to have her added to Jimmy Carter's ticket as the vice-presidential candidate. A cabinet post in the Carter administration was also discussed, yet Jordan felt she needed a change of a different kind.

After serving three terms in the House, Jordan decided she did not want to spend the rest of her life in Congress. She was drawn to a more instructive role in national issues, fueled by a desire to get people more involved in government. The lack of privacy and constant demands on her time were also beginning to take their toll. And so, in 1979, Jordan joined the faculty of the LBJ School of Public Affairs at the University of Texas.

Jordan long emphasized that a woman's own liberation begins with a healthy self-concept. "The first place to look if you've got a difficult situation," she once stated, "is the mirror. If you see looking back at you someone without a depth of concern about her environment, someone who is an idle onlooker and not an involved participant in making life better, then try to improve that image which looks back at you from that mirror. The first thing we have to do, before we can make others see us as leaders or people with a plan, is to believe in ourself."

In 1991, Jordan was named to the unique post of special counsel on ethics for Texas governor Ann Richards. In a *Time* magazine interview, Jordan described her role in the job as "the ethics guru." She was responsible for questioning and instructing the governor's proposed appointees, counseling the governor on any concerns about proposed appointments, and speaking at training sessions for appointees. Jordan, emphasizing the necessity to constantly remind public servants of the importance of ethical behavior, once said, "It's the things that are not blatant that get you into trouble."

At the same time, Jordan acknowledged that ethics are difficult to teach. When Jordan taught a course at the University of Texas called Political Values and Ethics, she tried to sensitize students to identifying an ethical morass before they stepped into it. Jordan also told her students that if they ever decided to try to get rich in a public-service position, then they had better get out of government, because if they didn't, she would visit them in jail.

Jordan continued to accept speaking engagements even after she became confined to a wheelchair with multiple sclerosis. In 1995, the year before her death, she served as chairwoman of the Commission on Immigration Reform. In this capacity she addressed Congress in opposition to a proposal that would deny automatic citizenship to children of illegal immigrants who were born in America. With familiar passion and eloquence, she stated, "To deny birthright citizenship would derail this engine of American liberty."

Jordan always carried a copy of the Constitution in her purse and once described her faith in that document as "whole, complete, and total." She made her voice heard through dignity and wisdom, rather than confrontation. As she explained to an interviewer during her first campaign, "All blacks are militant in their guts. But militancy is expressed in different ways."

Barbara Jordan did not believe in limits. She believed that setbacks should be viewed as a spark to energize people and spur them to action. During the toughest times of her life, Jordan never lost her fundamental optimism. She strongly believed that public servants should set an example to their constituents by upholding the common good. As she stated in her keynote address at the 1976 Democratic National Convention, "More is required of public officials than slogans and handshakes and press releases. More is required. We must hold ourselves strictly accountable. We must provide the people with a vision of the future."

When Jordan died at the age of fifty-nine in January 1996, she was remembered as an American original and a national treasure who, in the words of her pastor, intuitively understood where to invest her hope. *The New York Times* characterized the memorial service as a celebration, with honorary words offered by President Clinton, former Texas governor Ann Richards, and actress Cicely Tyson, who stated, "If I were sitting on a porch across from God, I would thank him for sending you to us." The Baptist church was filled to capacity, and hundreds of citizens gathered outside, where the service was broadcast by loudspeakers. As stated in a *New York Times* editorial of January 19, 1996, ". . . few lawmakers in this century have left a more profound and positive impression on the nation than Barbara Jordan . . . ."

ROSE ELIZABETH
BIRD

1936 –

IN 1977, ROSE BIRD WAS NAMED CHIEF JUSTICE OF THE CALIFORNIA Supreme Court amid a flurry of controversy, both because of her young age—she was only forty at the time—and her unrepentant liberalism. Like many women of her era, Bird endured a considerable struggle before rising to the heights she eventually achieved. Bird was raised near Tucson, Arizona, on a chicken ranch, where her mother worked in plastics factories to help support her three children. Bird's parents separated when she was five, and her father, who sold hat materials, died a short time later. The family then moved East, where Bird attended Long Island University on scholarship. She returned to the West for graduate studies in political science at the University of California at Berkeley, where she met future governor Jerry Brown, also a student there. Bird earned her law degree at Boalt Hall in Berkeley in 1965, then became the first woman hired as a law clerk for the chief justice of the Nevada Supreme Court. While in law school, she was discouraged from going into trial work, but after her clerkship she landed a job at the Santa Clara County public defender's office to begin her career as a litigator. In 1966, Bird was the first woman hired by that office as a deputy public defender. She managed a busy criminal trial practice for eight years and became chief of the appellate division of the office. In one of her first cases as a public defender, a judge of the San Jose Municipal Court ordered her out of his courtroom; unable to conceive of a female attorney, he thought she was a bail bondsman. As a judge on the state's supreme court, Bird later had the opportunity to review the same judge's decisions—"Objectively, by the way," she stressed to *Barrister* magazine in a 1983 interview.

As a young lawyer, Bird was anxious to make a successful showing as a trial attorney, to demonstrate to those who did not think women were suited for courtroom work that she could be as effective a litigator as a man. But she told *Barrister*, she rarely actually experienced sex discrimination in practice because she was so often the first woman to appear in various positions—the first female clerk, the first woman in the public defender's office, one of the first female professors at Stanford Law School, the first female cabinet member in California's history, and ultimately the first woman appointed to the California Supreme Court.

Bird moved on from the public defender's office to teach at Stanford Law School, where colleagues considered her a rebel and a pioneer. Bird helped Jerry Brown in his campaign for governor, and after he was elected he named her head of the Department of Agriculture, the first female cabinet member in the state's history. As secretary of Agriculture and Services, Bird administered twelve state agencies. The job carried tremendous responsibility, with 16,000 employees and a $227 million annual budget. Bird later rose to direct the Division of Occupational Safety and Health. She found great personal satisfaction in her efforts to end serious problems faced by workers, especially exposure to toxic chemicals, which had affected her own mother's health. During her stint with the division, she also began a practice of appointing laypeople to boards to license contractors, doctors, and dentists.

Bird was appointed chief justice of the California Supreme Court in 1977 by Governor Jerry Brown. The appointment drew fire from the beginning, but Bird plunged into the job with reformist enthusiasm. She quickly began to change the administration of California's court system, which she considered an old-boy network. As head of California's Judicial Council, responsible for policy making, she appointed numerous women and minority members. She held meetings of the council in state buildings rather than plush resorts, put an end to California's practice of adopting tentative court rules without public comment, and appointed panels to gather suggestions on problems such as court congestion. She also invoked a strict rule prohibiting employees of the council from accepting gratuities offered by lobbyists.

Bird made swift changes as well to the supreme court itself. She lengthened the workday and acquired word processors for the clerical staff. She brought in Lexis computerized legal research and instituted a personnel system that hired on merit, rather than on whom the applicants knew. Ever mindful of waste, she also sold the limousine provided for the chief justice and insisted her staff stay in inexpensive hotels when the court, based in San Francisco, traveled to Los Angeles.

Bird compares her entry into the California Supreme Court to taking a journey back to the horse-and-buggy days. She also compared joining the judiciary to entering the priesthood. She did not set out to deliberately ruffle feathers but was determined to streamline outmoded practices.

Bird was greatly disturbed to learn that approximately 95 percent of the opinions issued by the California Court of Appeals were never published or otherwise open to the public. She thought the court was under the thumb of special-interest groups, and her suspicions were borne out on many occasions.

Bird was criticized not only for disrupting the close-knit court system but also for allegedly being confrontational, overly suspicious, and placing loyalty above experience in choosing her associates. The harshest criticism, however, sprang from the decisions she made on the bench.

Bird, a devoted civil libertarian, handed down many decisions protecting the rights of the accused. Some felt this reflected a far too gentle approach to crime. She supported extension of the exclusionary rule for illegally seized evidence, voted for strict standards as to when confessions could be admitted, and steadfastly opposed the death penalty. Although Bird never succeeded in seeing California's death penalty overturned, she wrote a strongly worded dissent in a 1977 case, in which the court upheld that law, voting 4–3. In her dissent, Bird explained her staunch opposition to the penalty, noting that in many cases an indigent defendant did not receive adequate legal representation, thereby thwarting due process.

During her nine-year tenure, Bird resisted eight recall campaigns, which she dismissed as nothing more than harassment. Critics who presented potentially legitimate points she met head on. For example, when she was accused of being soft on crime, she pointed out that California incarcerated more individuals on a per capita basis than any country except the Soviet Union and South Africa, and emphasized that 90 percent of those cases that were overturned were sent back for retrial. Bird once explained, "When you are upholding the Constitution, you are not being pro defendant or pro prosecutor. You are doing your job in following your oath of office."

Bird's hard work and dedication won her the admiration of many of her colleagues. In a 1986 article in *The Nation*, William Warren, a California legal scholar, stated that Bird "has all those qualities we in society admire. She is a hard worker, a humanitarian, a champion of the underdog."

But these same qualities were largely responsible for the uproar that dogged Bird throughout her years on the California Supreme Court. Conservatives constantly harped on her concern for the rights of defendants. Prior to the 1986 confirmation vote, a Republican activist formed a group called "Bye Bye Birdie." Bird, undaunted, summed up her feelings to *The Nation*: "Our role is an unpopular one because it is to ensure that the Constitution is preserved. When you have majority rule, often you are protecting the rights of people who are unpopular. It is always the minorities who aren't a part of the mainstream, who define what the limits of the state, or the limits of the majority, are going to be. And as a result, the courts are the ones to step in. My role isn't to be politically smart. My role is to do what is right under the Constitution. And if that's politically unpopular, so be it."

The 1986 election unseated Bird, as well as two of her colleagues. Many felt that this marked the end of a long era, in which the California Supreme Court held a position of leadership in the evolution and development of new law. Long before Bird's appointment, the court had become known as an innovative, bold tribunal that frequently forged new ground, particularly in constitutional, criminal, and tort law. Its decisions often marked the initial acceptance of new legal principles that other states soon adopted. Visionary justices such as Phil S. Gibson and Roger J. Trainor wrote precedent-setting opinions in cases that struck down laws against interracial marriage, held manufacturers strictly liable for injuries caused by defective products, and adopted the principle of comparative negligence to apportion damages in tort cases. When Bird was appointed, she continued the court's pioneering trends with increased reliance on the state constitution to establish rights not yet recognized by the United States Supreme Court.

Since Bird's ouster, some feel that the court's tradition of judicial activism has come to an end. Writer and attorney Bill Blum commented in the *ABA Journal* in 1991, "Where once the court was unafraid to lead the law into new and untracked areas, now it seems content to leave the leading to others." Not surprisingly, the new, more conservative California Supreme Court, led by Chief Justice Malcolm M. Lucas, has acted quickly to affirm the majority of death penalty cases that come before it for review.

Since leaving the bench, Bird has taught at the Golden Gate University School of Law and served as president of the board of directors at Hastings College of Law. She was also a visiting professor at the University of Sydney, Australia. She took a new direction in 1988, when she became a television commentator. Bird has also worked with the San Fernando Youth Foundation and established a private law practice in Palo Alto, California.

Bird hopes she will be remembered as a judge with intelligence and courage. She told *Barrister* that she was proud to see the opening up of the judicial process to minorities and women. A great supporter of diversity, Bird believes that the judiciary will be enriched and strengthened by greater involvement of people from different backgrounds—something she believes will strengthen the entire society.

JANET
RENO

1938 –

WHEN JANET RENO BECAME THE FIRST ATTORNEY GENERAL of the United States on March 12, 1993, she resolved to always ask, "What is the right thing to do?" And she vowed that she would do it, even when it was politically unpopular. Reno has stayed true to her word and refused to compromise her integrity, even when she has faced painful decisions potentially threatening to her career.

Reno is known for her big, deep laughs, her long stride, and her formidable height. At six feet, two inches, in her usual low-heeled shoes, she can be intimidating. But she is also known as a warm and caring person with a love of the outdoors who would rather hike the Everglades or sail Biscayne Bay than attend a White House ball. Her down-home style has been an asset in her political career, and she likes nothing better than to get out and meet the people she actually serves.

Reno comes from a close, loving, and eccentric family. When she is not in Washington, she still lives in the same rustic, rural Miami home her mother built with her own hands in 1949. Reno's parents met when they were both working as reporters for the *Miami Herald*. Janet's family introduced her to the law early in life. Her mother's father was a lawyer, and her father worked for many years as a police reporter. He was also renowned for the flowers he raised, often sending roses and gardenias to his daughters while they were at college, wrapped in damp tissues in a cigar box. He even brought one of those familiar cigar boxes to Washington for Janet's confirmation as United States attorney general.

But it was Reno's grandmother, mother, and the other strong women in her family who established her conviction that she could be anything she wanted to be. These women included a battlefield nurse, a World War II WASP pilot, and a journalist. Reno viewed her aunts as heroines when they came to visit in their uniforms.

Reno's greatest influence was likely her mother, who consistently wrote the script for her own unconventional life without apology. Jane Wood Reno was quite a character around Miami. Strong and extremely independent, she frequently took off alone on a hundred-mile hike after she was a grandmother. Known as a hard drinker and eccentric dresser, she taught her children such diverse skills as baseball and baking. Reno recalls that her parents loved their four children absolutely, and treated them as equals. Henry and Jane Reno took their children camping and hiking, where they instilled a deep love of nature in all of them, often in unique ways. One spring the Renos tucked peacock eggs beneath the hens that always roamed the property. Descendants of the original brood can still be seen in the area, bordering the Everglades, and Reno keeps a spray of their feathers in her Washington, D.C., office.

The Reno children had few rules to follow. They could be wild, adventurous, and enthusiastic, but they were also expected to be scrupulously honest and not to do things they knew to be wrong or unkind. Education was highly valued. Janet took on the role of leader during her childhood and was respected for her intelligence. Her sense of public duty was also imparted early in life. In 1951, her father and his partner won a Pulitzer Prize for public-service journalism, reporting on the underworld grip of gambling on Miami. Jane Reno also did undercover reporting for the *Miami News* and participated in an exposé for the newspaper about baby selling. She sometimes wrote under a male pseudonym at the request of her editors.

In high school, Reno was considered scholarly and athletic, as well as an excellent debater, and was voted "Most Intelligent." One year she won the state debate contest and went on to compete at the national meet.

Janet attended Cornell University and clerked during the summers with the Dade County Sheriff's Department. She loved to be around the county courthouse, often accompanying her father to watch trials. Encouraged by her mother in her early desire to become a doctor, she started at Cornell as a chemistry major.

When a summer job in medical research convinced her that science was not her field, Reno switched to law. She was accepted by Harvard Law School, becoming one of 16 women in her class of 522 students. It was not easy for female students at the Harvard of 1960, whose law school had been admitting women for only ten years. However, Reno was impressed with the history and reputation of the college, and she graduated in 1963 with a promise to herself never to do anything she did not enjoy.

After her second year of law school, Reno sought a traditional summer clerkship. She applied to a large, well-respected Miami firm but was turned down solely because she was a woman. Disappointed but far from shattered, Reno went on to win a spot with another highly regarded Miami firm. When she graduated the next year, she returned to that firm and began her legal career with a focus on real estate work. She was especially interested in the field of eminent domain, and frequently defended property owners against government condemnation actions. This gave her a good deal of court experience.

Like many of her predecessors, Reno was troubled with the concept of charging a fee to protect a person's rights. When she spoke at a thirty-year Harvard class reunion, she told classmates that lawyers are too concerned about their own incomes and do not do enough to bring the legal system to the poor, the working poor, and children.

The day before her speech, a proposed public-service requirement as a condition of admission to Harvard Law School had been overwhelmingly voted down.

Reno was a great admirer of the Kennedys, especially Robert, respecting their commitment to civil rights and public service. She joined the Young Democrats Miami Chapter early in her career, where she actively campaigned for Jerrold Lewis, an attorney running for the state House in 1966. After Lewis was elected, she left her firm to become his law partner. She opened her practice with her grandfather's law books on her shelves. Reno soon became known for her integrity, her organizational skills, and her reputation as a formidable cross-examiner.

Reno began her career in public service in 1971 when state representative Sandy D'Alenberte hired her as general counsel to the House Judiciary Committee. Reno went to work with her usual enthusiasm. During her first months on the job, she wrote Florida's no-fault divorce law and worked on a constitutional amendment to reform the state courts. During this time she received some valuable advice on political survival from friend and former legislator Jack Orr, who counseled her not to pussyfoot and to say what she believed at all times, rather than try to please everyone.

Reno campaigned to become the state representative from Dade County in 1972. She ran a determined and straightforward campaign that led to victory in the primary, but she lost the general election to her Republican opponent. Everyone was surprised at the outcome of the election, including her opponent himself, who had been heard to remark that he hoped he would not get beaten too badly.

The day after the election Reno was offered a job by Dade state's attorney Richard Gerstein, who later won the first conviction in the Watergate trials. Reno hesitated, having sworn she would never be a prosecutor, based on her belief that prosecutors were more interested in securing convictions than in seeking justice. Gerstein convinced her to accept the job by remarking that she could do a lot to change that perception of prosecutors. Reno accepted, committed to her personal credo that a prosecutor's first objective should be to make sure innocent people are not charged, and second, to convict the guilty according to due process and fair play. One of Reno's first tasks as a prosecutor was to set up a juvenile court division, which had been created under the new amendment she had written redefining the roles of state's attorneys.

Three and a half years after joining the state's attorney, Reno left; she missed private practice. Steele, Hector & Davis, the firm that had refused to hire her as a summer clerk fourteen years before, now welcomed her. Despite the demands of working for a large law firm, Reno remained devoted to public service. She assisted in programs to help the poor receive legal aid and served on the board of directors of the Greater Miami Legal Services Corporation.

But Reno was not destined to remain in the private sector for long. When Richard Gerstein announced that he would resign as D.A. in late 1977, Reno was recommended as a potential successor. The governor appointed her as the first female state's attorney in Florida. At the age of thirty-nine, Reno found herself in a job of tremendous power and responsibility, overseeing 286 employees, including 91 attorneys, and administering a $4.5 million budget. The Dade County office was prosecuting 40,000 misdemeanors and 15,000 felonies a year.

Reno remained active within the community as she settled into her new post, often speaking at community gatherings. She took classes in Spanish to better communicate with Miami's large Spanish-speaking population and kept a sleeping bag at the office for evenings when she was too busy to go home. Reno drew accolades for her strong sense of ethics. She refused to take price cuts from local merchants or to tolerate her staff's accumulation of parking tickets. When she was called for jury duty, she insisted on participating in the process like any citizen, and was chosen to serve on the jury of a two-day civil trial. Reno felt strongly that she should be accessible to the public, and her phone number remained listed. She even took 1:00 A.M. calls from irate citizens complaining about such things as noisy roosters in the neighborhood—and followed through, once sending a zoning inspector out the next day to deal with that very complaint.

Reno won the election the November following her appointment. She thought her major hurdles were behind her for a time. But a nightmare erupted just three months later when five Metro Dade policemen raided the wrong house for drugs and beat the occupants, a locally popular teacher and his son who resisted the plainclothes intruders because they believed them to be robbers. Reno's office investigated, finally announcing that there was insufficient basis for a criminal prosecution of the officers. Then, a short time later, her office charged several prominent black citizens with crimes of corruption. She began to receive harsh criticism from some black community leaders.

But all of these challenges were only opening acts for the worst, which was yet to come. When Arthur McDuffy, a black man, led the police on a high-speed chase, he was handcuffed and beaten to death by several Metro Dade officers. The policemen tried to cover up the crime and make it look like an accident. The state's attorney's office launched an intense investigation, and the five officers involved were charged with manslaughter and the cover-up.

Due to local publicity, the trial was moved to Tampa, where the defense managed to strike all women and blacks from the jury. When the five policemen were all acquitted, the Liberty City section of Miami exploded in a riot that quickly spread to other neighborhoods. The city raged out of control for four days. The National Guard was called in, and when it was over, sixteen people were left dead, hundreds were injured, and over a thousand had been arrested.

Reno quickly filed charges against those arrested in conjunction with the riot. This unpopular decision earned her such labels as antipolice, antiblack, and even led to some calls for her resignation. Reno remained calm, despite a number of death threats. The charges of racism hurt her deeply, because she had always been strongly committed to civil rights and had hired many black attorneys. She quickly went into the black neighborhoods to talk to community groups, and explained her position to journalists and talk-show hosts. She opened all files on the case to public scrutiny and spoke of her regret at the acquittal after putting five months of energy into the prosecution of the policemen who had killed Arthur McDuffy.

These actions regained Reno the respect of many people. Throughout the fiasco, she would not apologize; she'd done the best she could with what she had to work with. She walked in the annual Martin Luther King Jr. Parade through Liberty City, shaking hands, while other politicians rode in cars.

Yet the crises seemed endless. In less than five months during 1980, 120,000 Cuban immigrants arrived in Miami, the majority sponsored by friends and family already in Florida but a large number were former Cuban prisoners involved with the drug industry. Between 1980 and 1981, felony cases filed in Miami soared from 15,000 to 25,000. There were so many homicides that the Dade medical examiner had to rent a refrigerated trailer from Burger King to house the overflow of bodies. Not surprisingly, when it came time for election that year there were no challengers for her job. Reno was also confronted with widespread corruption, as the lure of easy drug money reached even her department. Three attorneys and three secretaries in the state's attorney's office were arrested after dealing drugs out of a rest room in the Metro Justice Building.

Yet Reno maintained her stamina and panache. She still found time to enjoy entertaining family and friends at the Reno home. Dinner might be followed by reading George Bernard Shaw's *Saint Joan,* or reroofing the hand-built house. One form of entertainment she declined was watching the hit television show *Miami Vice,* after its debut in 1984. When asked if she watched the show, she once remarked she had enough Miami vice in real life.

Racial tensions again flared in 1984 when another white policeman accused of killing a black suspect was acquitted after trial. This time her reelection was opposed, and she had to run a vigorous campaign, fueled by the *Miami Herald*'s criticism of her and endorsement of her opponent. Again she stumped the neighborhoods, shaking hands. She even marched through Little Havannah and Liberty City, sometimes accompanied by a band. Her grassroots campaign and personal contacts, combined with her determination, won her victory by a nearly two-to-one margin.

Meanwhile, the media came to relish reporting on the escapades of Janet's mother, dubbing her "Calamity Jane." Sometimes the name seemed uniquely appropriate. When Jane was arrested for driving while intoxicated, Janet and her sister Maggie insisted she serve her sentence like any other citizen.

Jane Reno's eccentric ways continued all her life, usually to her children's amusement. She even became an alligator wrestler, prompting Janet and her brother Bob one time to corral an errant specimen in the fireplace with brooms and chairs, after the tape around its jaw had loosened and it had nipped Jane, who left to get reinforcements. When Jane retired from full-time work at the age of sixty, her children presented her with a chain saw. Her father, too, stood out from the crowd, so highly respected by local law-enforcement officials that he was made an honorary Miami policeman. He is still remembered as fair, honest, and accurate in his reporting.

Reno faced yet another challenge when her race for reelection in 1988 turned ugly. Her opponent, Jack Thompson, an icon of the religious far right, spread false accusations about Reno's character and sexuality. Predictably, Reno never lost her cool. Much later when she was asked to comment on Thompson's allegations, she remarked to a reporter from the *Miami Herald,* "He has nothing to worry about. I am attracted to strong, brave, rational, and intelligent men." She won reelection in 1988 and again in 1992, for her fifth term.

Reno has steadfastly insisted that her gender has no effect on her role as a prosecutor—or, apparently, in managing her personal life. When Reno's purse was snatched in Brooklyn, Reno and her sister, both over six feet tall, raced after him in their heels yelling, "Stop, you son of a bitch!" The thief dropped the bag and kept running.

Reno may be proudest of her more creative, lower-key achievements. She not only successfully forced renovation of privately owned tenements in Miami but enforced the housing codes against substandard public housing as well. She was instrumental in stopping a plan that would have led to demolition of the old Miami Beach art deco hotels, which were home to many elderly Jewish people who had formed a community in the area. Her efforts paved the way for historic preservation and renovation of South Beach, which remains home to many of the elderly but has also become a mecca for artists and entertainers.

Reno has also brought many children under her wing, in one way or another. She served as a mentor for a public school student and became the legal guardian of a friend's fifteen-year-old twins after the friend's death. She gained public accolades for her vigorous prosecution in child abuse cases, including some of the first to involve children abused by institutional caretakers. In these cases she helped pioneer new techniques such as videotaped testimony to make the experience less frightening for the children. Her prosecution of a couple who were charged with sexually abusing children at a baby-sitting service they ran in Miami's upscale Country Walk suburb drew national press coverage. The case brought Reno to the attention of Marian Wright Edelman, founder of the Children's Defense Fund, and Hillary Rodham Clinton. Both later advocated for her nomination as United States attorney general.

Reno revived the concept of "community policing," based on the old idea of cops walking the beat in a neighborhood. She helped found a program of neighborhood resource teams in 1992, in which a police officer, a social worker, a public health nurse, and a housing adviser went door to door in neighborhoods to assist people in addressing their needs and problems.

When President Clinton was elected in 1992 and began to assemble his cabinet, Reno did not expect to be seriously considered for the post of U.S. attorney general. After the nannygate fiasco removed Zoe Baird and Kimba Wood from consideration, however, Reno's name moved high on the list of contenders. Senator Joseph Biden, chairman of the Senate Judiciary Committee, along with Marian Wright Edelman and Hugh Rodham, the first lady's brother who works as a Dade County public defender, began to endorse her.

Reno breezed through the initial screening process, enjoyed a warm meeting with President Clinton, and passed scrutiny of her private life—detailed, personal, and exhaustive—with flying colors. Endorsements piled up quickly, including one from the National Organization for Women and another from the National District

Attorney's Association. Her supporters spoke of her competence, her brilliance, and her experience in prosecution, as well as her ability to function in the midst of political turmoil. Conservatives liked her toughness on crime, while liberals praised her commitment to fairness and the innovative programs she had established. At a press conference in February 1993, Clinton said he was "literally amazed at the quality of recommendations that I have received for Janet Reno." As her confirmation drew closer, friends and family flooded to Washington to help her celebrate. Reno coolly responded to repeated and annoying questions about her sexual orientation by describing herself as "an old maid who prefers men." She had a homespun appeal that people could appreciate.

Naturally, Reno was not free of detractors. Right-wing opponents attacked her stance on gun control, pointing out that she had brought a referendum to the Florida ballot to require a five day cooling-off period for handgun purchases. Her former opponent, Jack Thompson, continued to claim that she was a lesbian. Ironically, a radical gay rights organization also criticized her for "not coming out of the closet," despite common knowledge that she was heterosexual.

Reno later remarked that preparing for the Senate confirmation hearings reminded her of studying for the bar exam. She worked with her primary advisers, Ron Klain and Ricki Siednan, to learn more about issues of federal law on which she would be quizzed as part of the hearing. Meanwhile, the nation warmed to the statuesque woman from Florida who steadfastly refused to hedge on issues that were important to her. She would not, she told her advisers, hide her support for a woman's right to choose abortion or her personal opposition to the death penalty.

In the end, the committee voted 18–0 to recommend her approval to the full Senate, with a waiver of the usual ten-day waiting period. The media dubbed the proceedings a "love fest." Even ultraconservative Jesse Helms praised her as honorable. After mentioning issues upon which they disagreed, Helms acknowledged that he could get along with people who disagree with him as long as they have character—and he believed that she did. Reno went on to be unanimously confirmed by the full Senate. Thus, on March 12, 1993, she became the seventy-eighth attorney general, and the first woman to hold the office.

Reno had vowed to streamline operations in the Justice Department and to eliminate waste. One of her first acts was to shut down the private dining room that served the attorney general with a personal staff. Reno could not understand why such a service was necessary when there was a perfectly good cafeteria in the basement of the building. She decorated the office to reflect the essence of her personality. A cross-stitched picture, brought from the Miami office, hangs behind her desk with the legend "The burdens of the office stagger the imagination and convert vanity to prayer." A portrait of early hero Robert F. Kennedy also graces the room. But Reno's mischievous side sometimes prevails. She seemed to delight in the confusion she caused by appearing in the cafeteria carrying a friend's baby one day and lunching with actor Don Johnson the next.

Reno faced a daunting task from the start. The Department of Justice, a hundred times larger than the office she administered in Dade County, has 93,300 employees. And she had virtually no time to relax and settle into her new role. Almost immediately after her confirmation, the crisis at Waco, Texas, came to a head.

Reno was deeply concerned about the standoff that continued at the Branch Davidian compound, particularly when she learned that two dozen children were among the ninety-five people blockaded inside. A media slip had triggered the showdown of February 28, 1993, with the Alcohol, Tobacco, and Firearms agents who were trying to serve a warrant upon David Koresh. After a shootout that left four federal agents dead, sixteen wounded, and an estimated six cult members dead, President Clinton ordered the FBI to end the siege.

On Janet Reno's thirty-eighth day as U.S. attorney general, she faced one of the toughest decisions of her life. She authorized the FBI raid on the compound, spurred in large part by reports that Koresh continued to savagely beat children and have sex with girls as young as twelve during the siege. When the plan to storm the compound was presented to her, Reno grilled the agents and consulted with army experts, including a toxicologist she questioned about the effect of the tear gas on the children. After questioning, pondering, and agonizing, she was advised that the likelihood of mass suicide was remote. She concluded that she must take steps to protect the children inside the compound. Finally, she authorized the raid, on a day she later called the worst of her life.

When the Branch Davidians began their suicidal burning of the building, Reno was horrified. When it was over, she was grief stricken, especially over the death of the twenty-five children. But she stood by the FBI, characterizing such decisions as the hardest in the world to make. She quickly accepted responsibility for the plan to gas the compound, with a show of fortitude rare in Washington. She was widely quoted in the press for her statement "The buck stops with me."

Like her experience in Dade County, Reno's tenure as U.S. attorney general seemed plagued by crises. Later in her first year, she faced the FBI upheaval involving removal of William Sessions as its director. Despite the efforts of President Clinton and Reno to convince him to resign, the troublesome director refused, in the face of ethical breeches and various wrongdoings. But his ousting came at the worst possible time for the FBI. In addition to the Waco crisis, the FBI was occupied with investigating the World Trade Center bombing, the terrorist plot to bomb the United Nations and other Manhattan sites and to assassinate a number of leaders, and a growing threat from neo-Nazis plotting schemes to spark race wars. But Sessions was quickly replaced by Louis J. Freeh, who immediately began to work with Reno in restructuring and streamlining the FBI to deal more efficiently with domestic terrorism and other problems facing the nation.

One of Reno's early priorities was to institute a better working relationship among the FBI, the DEA, and other law enforcement agencies within the federal government. No stranger to turf battles among such agencies, having clashed with the DEA during her years in South Florida, Reno had been upset to discover that the various federal agencies with overlapping duties did not routinely share information, training facilities, equipment, or even radio communication networks. Vice President Al Gore recommended the merger of the DEA, FBI, ATF, and other agencies to increase efficiency and cut costs, and Reno, who had issued a stern order to the agencies to "share your toys," wholeheartedly supported the idea. When wholesale merger met with widespread opposition, Reno worked with Gore and others to forge a less drastic proposal to make the agencies cooperate, coordinate, and compromise. While not all were pleased, the new FBI director and many others praised the plan as innovative.

Reno is also committed to implementing on a national level the community-based law enforcement programs she supported in Miami. In addition to cops on the beat, she promotes community support for Head Start, after-school programs, health care options, and other programs she believes will save the taxpayers money in the long run through lowered medical care, law enforcement, and welfare costs.

A strong believer in prevention, Reno has long urged a national agenda for children, in order to prevent society from raising a new crop of criminals. She believes it essential to prevent teen pregnancy and family violence, and that alternative conflict-resolution programs be taught in the public schools. She urges more citizen involvement in these efforts. She teamed with drug czar Lee Brown, who as police commissioner in Houston and New York City successfully re-established neighborhood beats in those cities.

Reno worked hard to achieve passage of the crime bill of 1994, especially the section that dealt with community policing. As always, the proposal was controversial, drawing criticism from conservatives for its gun-control provisions and from liberals for its tough anticrime and punishment components. After various changes, the final bill included funding for new police, tough antigang laws, programs to prevent violence against women, and alternate punishment for juvenile offenders. She was extremely pleased to see the passage of the Brady Bill, requiring a five-day waiting period on handgun purchases, in response to pressure from a public fed up with gun violence.

Throughout her first years in office, Reno has weathered extremely tough issues and continues to be embroiled in difficult matters on a daily basis. The controversy over gun control rages on. One of her most recent challenges has involved crime in cyberspace, a situation requiring a balance between protecting free speech and controlling criminal use of the Internet. Yet the public always knows where she stands, and she has remained true to herself and her agenda.

There is constant speculation on where Reno will go next when her term as attorney general ends. Some predict she may be appointed to the Supreme Court, but others wonder if she would accept such a position, as she has turned down opportunities to become a part of the judiciary in the past. Some believe she will return to Florida politics, or perhaps to private practice in her home state. Whatever happens, Reno says she will one day return to the home her mother built. As she told the *ABA Journal*: "As I come down the driveway through the woods at night with a problem, an obstacle to overcome, that house is a symbol to me that you can do anything you really want to if it's the right thing to do and you put your mind to it."

MARIAN WRIGHT
EDELMAN

1939 –

A S A CHILD, MARIAN WRIGHT EDELMAN WAS TAUGHT BY HER parents to "make things better for somebody." Not only did Marian take these words to heart, she made a lifetime of putting them into practice—as a civil rights lawyer, an advocate for children, and a devoted public servant.

Marian Wright was born in Bennettsville, South Carolina, in 1939. All five of the Wright children were taught by their parents that serving their community was one of life's most important duties. She was raised to believe that any child, even a black girl growing up in the segregated South, could do or be anything to which she set her mind. Shortly before her father died of a heart attack when Marian was fourteen, his last words to her were, "Don't let anything get in the way of your education." Ten days later the United States Supreme Court outlawed school segregation in the landmark case *Brown v. Board of Education.*

Marian devoted herself not only to her own education but to preserving the right of a good education for others as well. Wright followed both the words and deeds of her parents, who used to take her along when they went to visit the sick. She learned early that character, not possessions, determined a person's worth, even in the stifling atmosphere of segregation. Since blacks were barred from using local recreational facilities, her father, a minister, built a playground behind his church. He also established a nursing home for elderly blacks, where the Wright children helped care for the residents.

Marian felt the humiliation of having to sit in the balcony of movie theaters and drink only from water fountains designated for blacks. She was especially horrified on one occasion during her youth when she witnessed an accident near her family home in which a white driver rammed his truck into a car filled with black migrant workers, including children. An ambulance arrived to take the slightly injured white man to the hospital, but left the severely injured black people lying in the road without offering assistance. Wright never forgot the image of black children like herself bleeding as the ambulance drove away.

After her graduation from Marlboro Training High School, Wright attended Spellman College, a black liberal arts school for women in Atlanta, Georgia. She spent a year traveling overseas, an experience that broadened her perspective and made it all the harder to return to a world stifled by segregation. She soon became active with the NAACP, gathering evidence of pervasive discrimination.

After graduating as valedictorian from Spellman, she began law school at Yale and continued her civil rights activities. In 1963, she went to Mississippi to assist with voter registration. Wright's work was often dangerous, especially when she traveled through the South, where the Ku Klux Klan had attempted to bomb the voting-rights workers. In some places they were met by club-swinging policemen who turned loose vicious dogs and arrested the voting-rights marchers. In Greenwood, Mississippi, Wright was outraged as she saw the FBI stand aside and watch the workers being attacked.

Wright's anger fueled her determination. After earning her law degree, she returned to Mississippi as one of the first two NAACP legal defense and education interns. She was the first black woman to pass the Mississippi bar, and soon she had a busy practice representing demonstrators who had been jailed, handling school desegregation cases, and serving on the board of the Child Development Group of Mississippi, involved with one of the largest Head Start programs in America at the time. Eventually, she opened a branch of the NAACP Legal Defense Office in Jackson, Mississippi. Most of her clients were jailed and beaten, and one young man she represented was killed while incarcerated. The image of the murdered man and his parents' grief troubled her deeply and gave her nightmares.

In 1968, Wright received a Field Foundation grant and went to Washington, D.C., where she founded the Washington Research Project, with the goal of learning how new and existing laws could be made to better serve the poor. During the sixties, she worked on the front lines of the civil rights movement. She served as NAACP attorney and testified before the Senate for civil rights legislation.

In 1967, after testifying before Senate hearings on southern poverty, Wright offered to take the senators through the Mississippi Delta so they would see firsthand the level of desolation and despair. As she guided them through the shacks, she recalls that Senator Robert Kennedy was especially moved by the sight of children starving in America.

It was on this trip that Wright met the man who was to become her husband, a young Kennedy aide named Peter Edelman. When the couple married and Marian moved to Washington, D.C., to be with her husband, she became the voice for poor children in the nation's capital. The Edelmans moved to Boston in 1971, where she became director of the Harvard University Center for Law and Education. Yet she regularly returned to Washington to attend to her work on the Washington Research Project, which became the Children's Defense Fund (CDF) in 1973. As director of the group, which was considered the most effective advocate for children in the country, Edelman became known as "the children's crusader."

Since the 1970s the Children's Defense Fund has fought to

preserve support for Head Start and other programs working to educate children and keep them healthy. For a period during the 1970s, Hillary Clinton chaired the fund. Edelman was one of the first pioneers to expand the rights of children beyond early laws that accomplished little more than limiting the number of hours that children could work in fields or factories. Edelman worked for passage of the Child Welfare Act in 1980 and successfully fought off efforts by the Reagan administration to repeal it.

Edelman emphasizes that every child is important and essential to our future. "We don't," she has often stated, "have a child to waste." Any nation, Edelman believes, that will allow children to be the poorest of its citizens is spiritually impoverished—and she notes that children are, indeed, the poorest Americans. In her book *Families in Peril: An Agenda for Social Change,* Edelman urges Americans to recognize the importance of investing in all of our nation's young people. She emphasizes such essential goals as a national campaign to prevent teen pregnancy, infant mortality, and early childhood deprivation. Because children are America's most precious resource, they must be given priority.

Edelman is realistic enough to know that all Americans must work together, with joint efforts among black and white, rich and poor, public and private sectors, if these problems are to be effectively addressed. "We invest in children," she writes, "because the cost of public sickness, ignorance, neglect, dependence, and unemployment over the long term exceeds the cost of preventative investment in health, education, employed youth and stable families." Edelman offers a battery of statistics to prove her point.

She stresses that parents bear the primary responsibility for meeting the needs of their own children, but she also points out that since our country's frontier days, families have requested and received government assistance in the form of public schools, tax incentives, housing subsidies, libraries, parks, and playgrounds. Edelman blasts the skewed perspective of those who tout traditional family values yet cut billions from basic survival programs. She offers proof that the War on Poverty programs of the 1960s had a positive effect in reducing poverty, while the cuts and repeals of the 1980s have added one million children per year to the poverty rolls. She is never hesitant to be blunt, even to friends such as President Clinton whom she has admonished that keeping a safety net for poor children is the moral litmus test of his presidency.

Edelman also characterizes teenage pregnancy as an epidemic. Each year one in ten American girls become pregnant, approximately three thousand per day, and the cost to families and society is tremendous. As always, Edelman not only delineates problems but offers solutions: Teenagers must be shown opportunities for building self-esteem, nonacademic avenues for success, and sound academic skill building. She also urges work exposure and skill training at an early age, as well as consistent education on family life and family planning. She favors comprehensive health services in the schools to offer general health care and contraceptives, pointing out that existing school-based clinics have been highly effective. She stresses the importance of giving teens ways to feel good about themselves beyond their sexuality. The CDF has established a sequential program that offers new incentives each year, with the goal of reducing the incidence of first and repeated teen pregnancies, the dropout rates due to teen pregnancy and parenting, and the number of babies born to impoverished mothers who did not have adequate prenatal care.

Perhaps Edelman's greatest challenge is the persistent apathy of so many citizens. "Albert Einstein," she writes, "believed the world to be in greater peril from those who tolerate evil than from those who commit it. Democracy is not a spectator sport." She firmly believes that if tackled step by step, with confidence and persistence, the problems of our nation can ultimately be solved. "Each individual has a responsibility to try and make a difference," she states "to give imaginative flesh to the ideal of justice. We should aim high."

Edelman's work for children has been continuous, broad based, and tireless. She has served on the boards of the March of Dimes, Unicef, and the Carnegie Council on Children, as well as various other political organizations. She also became the first black woman elected to the Yale University Corporation.

An eloquent and impassioned communicator, Edelman has published several books, including *Children out of School in America, Portrait of Inequality: Black and White Children in America,* and *The Measure of Our Success: A Letter to My Children and Yours.* In 1990, she became the first black and the second woman to chair the Spellman College Board of Trustees. She has been awarded honorary degrees from over thirty universities, was named a MacArthur Foundation fellow in 1985, and was inducted into the National Women's Hall of Fame in Seneca Falls, New York, in 1993.

With one in five children living below the poverty level, Edelman faces an overwhelming task. Yet she perseveres, sustained by a strong sense of hope and the steady progress she has witnessed. She has raised three sons of her own and watched with pleasure as the children of sharecroppers she worked with in 1960s Mississippi have gone on to college. She continues to pursue her calling in innovative ways. In 1996, she was one of the organizers of a rally at the Lincoln Memorial in Washington, D.C., called "Stand for Children." The nonpartisan event, which drew the support of some thirty-five hundred organizations and innumerable individuals, marked Edelman's latest effort to unify, renew the spirit, and refresh the commitment of those urgently concerned with the welfare and future of America's children. Edelman sustains herself by these victories, the love of her family, and the blessings she sees around her. "I try to find the grace around us," she told an interviewer in 1993. "It is easy to be joyful."

ARLENE
VIOLET

1943 –

IT IS HARD TO IMAGINE A MORE PECULIAR COMBINATION OF careers than nun and prosecutor. Yet in 1984, Sister Arlene Violet, a member of the Sisters of Mercy for more than two decades, was elected as the first female state attorney general in the history of America.

From childhood, Violet, described as feisty and fiercely independent, assumed she would follow the traditional path of marriage and children, like all of the other women she knew. Yet she was torn between childhood dreams of becoming either a nun or a police officer. Through an odd twist of fate, she was eventually to become both.

Arlene Violet grew up in blue-collar Providence, Rhode Island, in a three-decker tenement on Plain Street, a traditional Catholic neighborhood. Her father, a warm and loving man, was unfailingly generous to those in need and highly respected in the neighborhood. He eventually served as an alderman and later as campaign manager for the governor. He also set an example of community service in his charitable activities, working for a sports program that successfully kept young people out of trouble, and throwing an annual ice cream party where he scooped cones for thousands of children over the years that the popular summer ritual endured. His honesty, strength, and love of people were a tremendous influence on Arlene as a child.

In her book, *Convictions: My Journey from the Convent to the Courtroom*, Violet describes her mother as the quintessential home-maker, attentive and loving, as well as a knockout with a strong resemblance to Bette Davis—whom Violet says paled by comparison. Violet admired her mother's ability to stretch beyond the limits of her innate shyness. The book is dedicated "To my mom, who taught me the lesson of the high wire. Why walk across it when you can dance?"

As a young girl, Arlene was a tomboy who loved to roughhouse with her brother, play baseball and football, and do anything that involved getting dirty. She recalls that she was a happy kid "in constant motion and constant trouble." No scholar, Arlene did poorly in school during her elementary years, both because she disliked being cooped up inside and because she concealed her poor eyesight, not wanting to be bothered with glasses. Once the problem was discovered, her grades improved.

Violet's life was suddenly transformed when her father died unexpectedly when she was fourteen. Yet she gained new strength and insights in coping with her grief. As a teenager, she became serious about three things; school, theater, and boys. She passionately wanted to be an actress and frequently went to New York to see plays. Life was fast and festive, and Arlene was determined she wouldn't miss out on anything. But she experienced a turning point when, after encountering a troubled, drunk girl at the elevator on one of her big-city jaunts, she stopped in the midst of the whirlwind trip to take stock and reflect on her life.

At this time Violet was rapidly falling in love with Bob Turner, a handsome young college man. Yet at the same time her admiration for the nuns she knew had deepened. She saw them as focused activists, women with guts and conviction who were really making a difference in the world, guided by love. Her senior year in high school, she made a wrenching decision. She broke up with Bob and applied to join the Sisters of Mercy Convent.

Though some of the nuns in the order expressed trepidation over Violet's scattered enthusiasm and headstrong ways, she was accepted. Within six months of entering the convent in 1961, Violet settled in and became devoted to her new life, though she still enjoyed gossiping about boys with her sister postulants. She found her time as a novice to be a period of great testing in which she had to face the challenge of measuring up to her own ideals. But she persevered and flourished in the religious life. She soon volunteered to counsel incorrigible girls at a training school on state prison grounds. There she met twelve-year-old mothers, was threatened with switchblades, and became increasingly troubled by a system that offered little in the way of comfort to the teenagers.

In 1969 Violet took her final vows and began teaching at an inner-city high school. Deploring prejudice, she worked hard to break down the barriers between races. She often spoke out publicly at a time when nuns where not supposed to draw attention to themselves. Given her outspoken nature, run-ins were inevitable, and she eventually left the school after pointing out to the arrogant and powerful monsignor the absurdity of his installing a marble floor in the gymnasium.

Violet moved on to work in the ghetto, living with five other nuns in a dismal housing project. The nuns were devoted to bringing a better quality of life to the local people, and joked that their vow of poverty fit in well. The group became the first Sisters of Mercy to live outside the convent setting.

Violet found the people of the ghetto suspicious at first. She compared her efforts to build community values and pride to trying to raise the *Titanic* with a piece of string. Yet this was to be one of the key experiences of her life, and it greatly shaped her future. For the first time she saw injustice in action, and it touched her in a personal way. She saw the people she befriended suffer as crime victims, while the perpetrators got off with a slap on the wrist. She watched as poor people were exploited by dishonest businessmen, with little legal recourse. She saw, in short, a "different system of justice for the poor," she later wrote.

This led Violet to turn to the law. With the blessings of her order, she entered law school at Boston College. She loved law school, especially commercial law, which she envisioned as a tool she could use to help her impoverished friends gain power as consumers. Yet she also witnessed competition, viciousness, and humiliation there, and began to suspect that law school was one of the factors that put the distance between so many lawyers and their ethics.

During law school Violet worked summers for Rhode Island Legal Services, then went on to clerk for Justice Thomas Paolino of the Rhode Island Supreme Court for a year after her graduation. These experiences taught her to make sound legal judgments and gave her an overview of the workings of the justice system. At the end of her clerkship, Violet joined the attorney general's office as the special assistant attorney general in charge of the Consumer Division. Again, she was the first nun and the first woman to hold such a post.

Violet found her work in this office deeply rewarding. She attacked deceptive advertising, often finding her position as a nun an asset. Arrogant businessmen frequently treated her with condescension, allowing her to set an effective trap to nail them. She honed her litigation skills during her many court appearances. She even picketed and sued a bishop who illegally closed a day care center. For her efforts, she was threatened with excommunication.

In 1977, Violet opened her own office in Providence, specializing in public-interest law. A trip to Central America during this period strengthened her commitment to effecting change on behalf of the poor. She gained a new perspective on her travels, encountering extremely poor yet generous and loving people.

At the same time Violet became involved in environmental law. She represented the Conservation Law Foundation in many actions to force an end to illegal pollution. In one such case, against a man known as "Wild Bill" who was illegally dumping hazardous waste, she was threatened with a shotgun. The policeman who accompanied her to the defendant's property to provide protection shrank in fear, but Violet stood up to the offender, who was later sent to prison during her tenure as state attorney general. Her initial victory against the bully helped her gain visibility, and her business rapidly grew.

She earned the nickname "Attila the Nun" when she represented retarded citizens in an effort to improve conditions and end brutal abuses at state homes. Having built a reputation for winning cases on behalf of the handicapped, she had no fear when she went up against a battery of specially hired high-powered lawyers. She refused to be intimidated by their tactics, and her steely determination, combined with a newfound political savvy, prevailed. A settlement was eventually reached.

Violet found disability law to be emotionally exhausting, yet this period became a turning point. She later reflected that she was grateful for the way it brought her "face to face" with herself. The victories led to great joy; the defeats, to unbearable heartache.

Violet's concern and empathy for the rights of crime victims led her to consider a run for the attorney general's office in the early 1980s. When she first approached Bishop Gelineau to discuss her idea, he waffled, then asked her to withdraw after she had announced her candidacy. She refused, and the diocese denounced her decision in the press. Yet Violet persevered. She entered the race late and did not raise nearly as much money as her opponent, but managed to win 42 percent of the vote.

In 1983, the Vatican declared that members of the clergy were discouraged from holding public office, but left it to individual bishops to make the final decisions for their individual dioceses. Bishops could grant an exception where it was deemed to be for the common good. Meanwhile, Violet considered a second run in the 1984 election, but Bishop Gelineau said that if she ran, she would have to leave the Sisters of Mercy permanently. Violet faced an agonizing decision, but her mother superior and sister nuns vowed to support whatever choice she made. After grappling with her options for several months, she finally decided she would rather be a "sister of mercy in reality than in name only."

The Sisters of Mercy have always been known for their rebellious spirit when rebellion has been necessary to pursue their convictions. The Mercy nuns had led the way for women to set out in the world and live among the poor. They pursued such helping careers as that of physicians and nurses, they supported birth control, and they urged the ordination of women as priests.

Violet began her campaign in earnest, gathering volunteers from among the nuns, parents of the handicapped children she had represented, old friends from the ghetto, and many others. Her name made the choice of a color theme easy, and everything surrounding her campaign was festooned with purple. Her opponent stooped to slams against her gender and charged her with lack of experience, not mentioning that she had won every case against his office when she had worked as a public-interest lawyer. His tactics backfired, and Violet won by a margin of five thousand votes. When she took the oath of office, she was the first woman ever to hold the post of attorney general for a state. Her mother held the Bible as she was sworn in.

Violet faced an enormous task, not only in confronting extensive corruption but also by virtue of the structure of the post of attorney general in Rhode Island. The office was responsible for criminal prosecutions, investigation of white-collar crimes, consumer fraud, and litigation of civil cases, as well as representing several state agencies, prosecuting certain traffic offenses, running the juvenile division, and conducting programs for first-time offenders.

Violet plunged in, undaunted by the magnitude of her job. Rhode Island was being called the most publicly corrupt state in the country. The chief justice of the Supreme Court was allegedly friends with organized-crime figures, and a 1984 *Newsweek* article characterized Rhode Island as the cocaine capital of the eastern seaboard, as well as the center of organized crime in New England. Violet launched a reform agenda, determined to root out corruption at all levels.

One of her first steps was to announce that everyone would be treated the same, politician or not. She filed complaints against judges who were allegedly incompetent or corrupt. She also installed a computerized case-management system, set up a victim/witness assistance program (which became a model unit followed by other states), and brought the appellate division to the level of being ranked number one in the country.

Violet did not shy away from prosecuting organized-crime figures and won conviction of Rudolph Sciarra, a top mob lieutenant. Her office did not hesitate to prosecute corrupt policemen and priests. Her crusade against white-collar crime stretched to the state's highest business and banking circles. It is easy to see why Violet once remarked, "Nuns are cantankerous people."

Anxious to get to work implementing the many changes and reforms she envisioned, Violet was appalled by some of the judicial misconduct that had become routine. She faced a big task in cleaning up the corrupt government and in reshaping public attitudes. Legislation was a priority, especially changes that would help crime victims. During her two-year tenure, Violet helped achieve passage of laws allowing videotaping of child sex-abuse-victim testimony, as well as speedier trials for victims of sex crimes that involved younger or older victims. The federal government selected Rhode Island's juvenile prosecution unit as one of four role models set before the rest of the nation.

Violet also took a zealous stand against polluters. She went after criminal violators and won every one of her hazardous-waste cases. She even filed suit against the Environmental Protection Agency at one point to enforce hazardous waste cleanup. Additionally, she designed a computerized case-tracking system, and her consumer protection unit returned a record amount of goods and cash to consumers who had been exploited. She pushed for neighborhood crime programs and helped communities set up the projects.

Violet was well aware of the need for both toughness and tenderness in dealing with the ravages of crime. She trained her prosecutors to be more sensitive to crime victims, but found it difficult when she had to prosecute priests and policemen, people who had always commanded respect. She was especially saddened by the prevalence of sexual abuse of children by priests. She called this crime the ultimate con job, as it betrayed the trust and innocence of the most vulnerable victims.

Predictably, Violet's even application of justice sparked controversy, but she was determined to clean up the state, especially after Morley Safer pointed out the deplorable public image of Rhode Island in a *60 Minutes* interview. Within the following year, her office prosecuted dozens of murder cases and took steps to retry Claus von Bülow after his first conviction was overturned by the Rhode Island Supreme Court on technical grounds. Although the resulting trial and media circus resulted in von Bülow's acquittal, there were also significant victories, as when David Roger Collins, suspected of abducting and sexually abusing over two dozen young people, was convicted and sentenced to a double life term plus twenty years.

Though Violet's record as attorney general was impressive, she was devastated by her losses and grew weary of the constant pressure. She enjoyed the breaks provided by her growing notoriety, including speaking engagements and various special functions. At a White House event she danced with Joe Namath and admittedly stepped on his feet, characterizing such occurrences as "welcome respites from constantly tending the battle zone." Violet received many awards for being a leader in her field, but she was often humbled by such things, and once joked with Elizabeth Taylor at an event where they shared a table, "At least you can act."

During Violet's tenure, a great deal of long-ignored public corruption was finally exposed, but this, too, came with a price. Efforts to change public attitudes toward white-collar crime were frustrated as important cases were thrown out. At one point, an attorney in her office was charged with prosecutorial misconduct, and even though subsequent investigations found no wrongdoing, Violet's bid for re-election to attorney general was lost.

Violet served only one term as attorney general, but the changes she made were vast and far reaching. She set an example by her courage and conviction, as well as her down-to-earth humor and devotion to the people she served. In a 1984 interview with the *National Law Journal* before taking office, she stated her desire to "go in, get the job done, put the system back on track and move on." Her record shows that this is precisely what she did.

Violet was to continue her outspoken ways as a "straight shooter," voicing her opinions on a popular talk radio show, where she continued to target corruption and scandal, especially among those who aroused her strongest outrage: abusers of the public trust.

PATRICIA
SCHROEDER

1940 –

P ATRICIA SCOTT WAS BORN IN 1940 IN DES MOINES, IOWA,
where her mother taught grade school and her father was a pilot
and aviation insurance adjuster. Patricia became a pilot herself in her
teens, and worked her way through the University of Minnesota in
the same business as her father, flying to crash sites to assess damages.

She met her husband, Jim Schroeder, at Harvard Law School,
where she was one of 15 women in a class of 550. The couple both
graduated in 1964 and moved to Denver, where Schroeder began
practice as a field attorney for the National Labor Relations Board, a
post she held for two years.

Schroeder then maintained a private practice in Denver from 1966
through 1972, including a stint as a hearing officer for the Colorado
Department of Personnel and another one teaching at the University
of Colorado Law School. Her husband was the first to enter the political arena, making an unsuccessful bid for the state legislature in 1970.

When Pat decided to run for Congress from Colorado's First District in 1972, nearly everyone thought it too soon for a woman to be elected, including the Denver Democratic Women's Caucus, which endorsed a male opponent. Schroeder went on to not only beat her opponent in the primary but win the general election, thus beginning a political career that would span nearly a quarter of a century.

When Schroeder arrived in Congress in 1973, she found the fraternity of what she called "old bulls" far from delighted with either her presence or her brazen attitude. Schroeder soon gained the reputation as a social liberal and a fiscal conservative. She authored innovative legislation establishing parental leaves, consistently supported reproductive freedom, and lobbied hard for the ERA. She rapidly earned much gratitude among her constituents for taking up the causes of senior citizens, pushing for pension and tax reforms. Before long, Schroeder was considered virtually unbeatable in her home district.

Schroeder began to build her reputation as an outspoken, consistent liberal during her first term in Congress. She has never used speech writers, preferring to improvise from her own notes. When she joined the House Arms Services Committee, she unabashedly called the chairman of the committee a sexist, suggesting he did not believe that anyone with a uterus can make a decision on military affairs. Her target, Democratic Representative F. Edward Hebert of Louisiana, refused to so much as provide her with a chair at committee meetings—she and a young black male representative whom Hebert disliked were expected to share a single seat. Schroeder in turn helped spark a revolt that led to his ouster in the next session of Congress, an early and significant triumph.

Though she resists being pigeonholed, Schroeder has always been keenly interested in women's issues, and served as co-chair of the Congressional Caucus for Women's Issues for nearly twenty years. Yet other causes have also been close to her heart. For example, Schroeder introduced a bill to help former military spouses receive retirement and survivor benefits. When the bill became law, it effected one of the most significant changes in domestic relations law in recent years.

Schroeder's causes frequently dovetail. While she has steadfastly opposed wasteful military spending, she has consistently worked to improve the rights of women in the armed forces. Following the invasion of Panama, she introduced legislation that would allow women in the army to take part in a full range of military activities, including combat.

In 1990, Schroeder introduced the Women's Health Equity Act, to insure that more women were included in medical research. She also authored the Family and Medical Leave Act guaranteeing workers that they could take time off from their job without jeopardizing the position in the event of birth, adoption, or serious illness in the family. She also introduced the school-aged childcare bill to fund community child-care programs for children of working mothers.

Schroeder has long been dedicated to environmental protection, reduction in military spending, and increased assistance to American families. In a 1988 speech, she pinpointed such upside-down priorities as spending by the Reagan administration the previous year that totaled $30,000 per soldier and $400 per child.

For a time, Schroeder was one of the top contenders in the 1988 Democratic presidential race, calling for a "rendezvous with reality." A Gallup poll taken the same year ranked her as one of the six most respected women in America. Although Schroeder decided on her own to drop out of that race, mainly due to lack of funds, she later stated that she was repelled by the dehumanizing nature of presidential campaigning, and this had played a part in her decision. When she shed tears at the announcement that she was leaving the race, she was chided by those who considered her show of emotion inappropriate for a presidential candidate.

Others, however, saw the irony in such stereotyping, including writer Philip Dunne. In a 1991 essay for *Time,* Dunne cited several occasions on which President Bush "indulged in a manly effusion of moisture." But when Schroeder was moved to tears by the outpouring of affection and support she received upon announcing her withdrawal from candidacy, "she was castigated, not only by supercilious males but also by a gaggle of super-heated feminists, as just another weak woman, temperamentally unfit for the presidency. If there is a moral to all this, it could be that in today's political climate, men may weep, but women must prove themselves made of sterner stuff."

With her characteristic sense of humor, Schroeder got a lot of mileage out of the uproar over her tears. She has claimed that if she runs for president again, she will definitely get Kleenex to be a corporate sponsor. She plans to raise campaign funds by selling teardrop jewelry, and maintains a "crying file" filled with clippings from newspapers, provided by supporters, that depict male politicians, sports heros, and evangelists bawling at emotional moments.

Since she first joined her colleagues on Capitol Hill, Schroeder has provided a breath of fresh air through the stuffy corridors of Congress. She once skateboarded to an appointment on Capitol Hill, and donned a bunny suit to amuse children at an Easter party held at the U.S. Embassy in China.

Schroeder is famous for her sharp wit. Columnist George Will once described her as "a rhetorical roughneck," going on to comment that "the honey of her voice is seasoned with lemon." She coined the term *Teflon president* to describe Ronald Reagan when it seemed that no scandal could stick to him. On one occasion, when asked how she could be both a politician and a mother, she retorted, "I have a brain and a uterus, and they both work." Yet Schroeder's quips represent more than a biting sense of humor. She is astutely aware of the need to break through the endless drone of Washington rhetoric to make her point in a way that will be noticed—and remembered.

Recently, bemoaning the lack of women in Congress, she remarked that if 1992 was the "Year of the Woman," 1994 was the "Year of the Angry White Male." Named to lead the female recruiting efforts of the Democratic Congressional Campaign Committee, she has been disappointed so far with the number of female candidates seeking office in 1996. Though only fifty-five, Schroeder is the senior woman in Congress. Schroeder also laments the present divisiveness in Congress after she worked so hard to establish and strengthen bipartisan caucuses. Her greatest concern, however, is the out-of-control spending that has become standard in high-level campaigns and the waste and influence-peddling that goes with it.

Like virtually all women in serious public positions, Schroeder has been subjected to wardrobe scrutiny. She has acknowledged that female politicians have less flexibility in their choice of dress than do men, with little middle ground between the unmade-bed look and the "Junior League" look. Schroeder also notes that female political behavior is judged differently, with what is regarded in men as crisp and decisive often considered aggressive and off-putting in women.

Schroeder, the mother of a son, Scott, and a daughter, Jamie, has never advocated the superwoman role. According to *McCall's*, when constituents wrote to her requesting a favorite recipe, she replied, "Find a bowl. If it's on the floor, wash it, because the dog was probably using it last. Find a box of cereal, preferably sugar coated, so you won't have to find the sugar. Find the milk but check the spoiled date before pouring. Then assemble."

In late 1995, Schroeder announced she would retire at the end of the congressional term. She had served twelve terms in the House, rising to the level of second ranking Democrat on the Judiciary Committee and top member of the Courts and Intellectual Property Subcommittee. She had also become third in rank as a member of the National Security Committee. During her tenure in Congress she also found time to author a book, which she characterizes as both personal and political, called *Champion of the Great American Family*. Schroeder explained her decision to retire by stating that she wishes to have a second career before ageism shuts the door for her.

Schroeder's decision to retire may have been motivated in part by a desire to quit while she was still at the top of her game. While her independent nature and propensity for flip comments undermined her authority in the eyes of some of her colleagues, Schroeder won the respect of many others who found that offbeat style refreshing. Schroeder has always appeared to enjoy tweaking the noses of those in power, both Republicans and members of her own party. At a news conference in 1995 to announce her retirement, she remarked to reporters, "I've always been hard to paper-train."

In an interview on the *Charlie Rose* show in March 1996, Schroeder stated that she was almost a "lifer" in Congress, and remarked that she had toilet-trained her last child and gone through menopause on the floor of the House. She believes, however, that she can be more effective at this point in her life outside the political arena and will go on to teach at the Woodrow Wilson School of Government at Princeton University. Yet she has only signed on for a year and acknowledges that she may consider another run for office in the future. She looks forward, she says, to the opportunity to be a recovering politician for a while, and to "be with people who think rather than react and scream."

SARAH RAGLE
WEDDINGTON

1945 –

S ARAH RAGLE WAS BORN IN ABILENE, TEXAS, AND GREW UP IN A
series of west Texas small towns. Sarah was raised according to
the frontier ethic that stressed individual accomplishment rather than
social status. The daughter of a Methodist minister, she had a traditional upbringing, in which she sang, played the organ, and served as
a youth leader at church. But Sarah never envisioned herself in the
customary role of wife and mother. Her rebellions were small but
foreshadowed her future—take, for instance, her role as drum major
(not majorette) of the high school band. Then she challenged the
rules of girls' basketball, which prohibited full court running. When
she pressed a physical education instructor for an explanation of the
odd rule, she was told, "Young women must preserve their reproductive capacity. It is their meal ticket." Sarah vowed early that this
would not be the meal ticket for her. In her book, A *Question of
Choice*, she quotes Barbara Jordan: "To be a leader, you must be comfortable feeling different."

After graduating from high school, Sarah enrolled in McMurry College in Abliene, Texas, a small Methodist liberal arts school. There her leadership role began to blossom. She was active in student government and drama and graduated with secondary-education credits for English and speech. Yet she dreamed of attending law school. The dean at McMurry had discouraged Sarah from such a pursuit; it would, he cautioned, be "too strenuous." That was all Sarah needed to convince her to pursue a career in law. In 1965, she and her younger brother John moved to Austin to work for the Texas legislature.

Sarah adored Austin, with its impressive capital buildings, beautiful campus, intellectually progressive atmosphere, and "live and let live" ideology. During her work for the legislature, she would often go to the house floor to watch the Texas legislature in action. She was appalled at the crude behavior of many members, and even more so at their lack of interest in what was taking place on the house floor. This experience confirmed for her the old adage about how those who are fond of sausage and the law should not see either being made.

After the session ended and her brother returned home, Sarah entered the University of Texas Law School. The school provided a separate women's lounge, and students bonded together to study and support one another. When it came time to interview for a job after graduation, like so many women of her era Sarah found no offers forthcoming. Fortunately, Professor John Sutton, who had always encouraged female students, offered her a job on the committee of the American Bar Foundation that was revising the code of ethics that governed attorneys. Sarah found it fascinating and stimulating work.

During her youth, Sarah lived what she characterized as a very proper life. Yet she learned early lessons in the importance of reproductive freedom. During the early sixties, she met mothers who had been given the drug thalidomide and knew their babies would likely be severely deformed. As a result, some had to travel as far as Sweden to obtain a safe abortion. When she was faced with her own unplanned pregnancy, it took her entire life savings to pay for the procedure.

Sarah recalls her 1967 trip, as a scared student accompanied by her fiance, to a dusty Mexican border town. But she was one of the lucky ones, she recalls, with a kind and competent doctor to perform the procedure. Many others she would encounter were not so fortunate.

Sarah has frequently written of the days before abortion was legalized, when Los Angeles County Hospital had to maintain a sixty-bed infected obstetrics (IOB) ward, where many women died after attempting to obtain back-alley abortions. When a few states began to legalize abortion, those who could afford to travel flocked to these sites, but poor women still had no options. Between 1970 and 1972, almost 350,000 women went to New York, one of the few places a nonresident could get a legal abortion.

Sarah married Ron Weddington in 1968, shortly after he entered law school. At the same time, she became involved with local women's groups. Law school and personal experiences had made Sarah more aware of the special legal problems faced by women. Seeing discrimination in a broader light, she steadfastly refused to accept that "that's the way it is." When a company refused to give her a credit card without her husband's signature, even though she was an attorney and the primary breadwinner in the family, she refused to do business with them. She often heard similar stories from the women in her groups.

Some of Sarah's friends began to work on *The Rag*, an alternative newspaper that published hard-to-find information on contraception and abortion, with plain talk about which methods were safe and which were not. She learned of various underground efforts to help women locate doctors who were willing to perform safe abortions. Recollecting her own experience, Sarah founded, with a group of other women and cooperative clergy, a project to get information to women who needed it. Existing state laws banning abortion, they agreed, only forced desperate women into crime, danger, and death.

The impetus for *Roe v. Wade* began at a garage sale to raise money for one of the women's groups with which Sarah was involved. The established network was becoming frustrated at having to conduct a covert operation. The referral project was overloaded and possibly illegal, yet still not reaching all women who needed it. She began doing legal research and considering strategies that might be effective to change the existing laws.

Sarah had been raised with a Methodist ideology that stressed Christian social concern, and she had always felt a responsibility to help others. Her father and her church had emphasized the importance of acting out of a concern for others. She wanted to find a case that could be taken to federal court, so as to affect the law of all states. She teamed up with her old friend and classmate Linda Coffee to get the wheels rolling. Coffee, then working in a bankruptcy firm, agreed. As Weddington explains in her book, *A Question of Choice, Roe v. Wade* started as a little case and ultimately became a vehicle to protect the reproductive rights and free choice for all American women. She was overwhelmed and humbled as she slowly realized the magnitude of her efforts.

Weddington and Coffee soon found a woman who was pregnant and was willing to sign on as the plaintiff in their case. They filed a complaint and took *Roe v. Wade* before a three-judge panel of the United States District Court in Texas. James Hallford, a licensed physician who had recently been charged with a crime for performing an abortion, teamed up, along with his attorney, with Weddington and Coffee.

The Fifth Circuit ruled that the Ninth Amendment protected the right of choice as to whether to have children, so the Texas abortion laws were ruled unconstitutional. The court further held that the laws were too broad and vague for physicians to follow. Yet the court did not issue an injunction against the laws to back up its declaratory judgment. As a result, both sides appealed and sought the permission of the United States Supreme Court to proceed directly to Washington D.C. to argue the case. The court agreed, and both sides began gearing up for the tough battle ahead. Sarah Weddington, who had virtually no trial experience prior to her appearance before the lower court in *Roe,* decided to argue the case before the United States Supreme Court herself.

When the U.S. Supreme Court convened to hear *Roe v. Wade* on December 13, 1971, Weddington was awed by the majestic setting. It reminded her of church, she later commented, with spectators seated on pews and rules prohibiting gum chewing, talking, writing, and other transgressions.

Proceedings before the court were long and convoluted, with both sides fielding tough questions by the justices. Following argument, deliberation among the justices began, with opinions spanning the spectrum. In 1972, the court announced that *Roe*, as well as a Georgia case on abortion, would be held over for reargument. By this time two new justices had been appointed.

Weddington and other pro-choice advocates were deeply disappointed by the court's announcement. Two years had already been committed to this case, and now it would drag on even longer. Nonetheless, Weddington, Coffee, and their assistants went back to work quickly writing a new brief and raised a new issue, based upon the national trend in cases involving abortion that supported their position.

Rehearing of the case was finally set for October 1972. Many speculated that the court would rule against the plaintiffs. Finally, following reargument and more waiting, the decision came in January 1973. It established a right to privacy broad enough to include a woman's decision to terminate a pregnancy, based on Fourteenth Amendment concepts of personal liberty and the Ninth Amendment's reservation of rights not enumerated in the Bill of Rights, including the right of privacy.

The court added a restriction to protect what it called "potential life," thus allowing states to limit the right to abortion to protect a woman's health in the second trimester and to prohibit abortion except to save a woman's life during the third trimester, when the fetus was presumably viable.

Not surprisingly, the decision left pro-choice advocates elated and antiabortionists outraged, paving the way for an intensified battle between the two groups. Those who opposed the right to abortion mobilized to try to sidestep the decision, with efforts to limit government funding for abortion being the most successful. In response to pressure, many states tried to erect roadblocks, including waiting periods, requirements that second-trimester abortions be done in hospitals, and other tactics.

The pro-choice camp mobilized as well. According to a 1988 NBC poll, 64 percent of the population wanted to keep abortion legal. Yet several later decisions of the United States Supreme Court eroded the abortion rights gained in *Roe v. Wade*. A 1990 decision upheld the constitutionality of state laws requiring a pregnant minor to inform both parents before getting an abortion. Another upheld a gag rule that prohibited employees of government-funded clinics from counseling pregnant women about abortion as an option. Perhaps the most ironic of the post-*Roe* developments has been the increase in violence by "pro-life" extremists, who have murdered doctors and other people working in clinics providing abortion.

Weddington has expressed trepidation since the appointment of Clarence Thomas to the Supreme Court in 1991 that *Roe v. Wade* would be overturned. Yet she was heartened when President Clinton, in one of his first acts after the 1992 election, ordered the gag rule preventing federally funded clinics from counseling women about abortion to be lifted. Clinton has taken a stand as a pro-choice president to support other protections of abortion rights as well.

In *A Question of Choice*, published in 1992, Sarah Weddington expressed her astonishment that she was still required to put every ounce of energy into preserving American women's right of choice, some twenty years after *Roe v. Wade* overturned the Texas antiabortion laws and made abortion legal throughout the United States.

Yet her life has not revolved solely around *Roe*. Her experiences have been broad, varied, and challenging. While the Fifth Circuit had placed the *Roe* appeal on hold, pending the decision by the U.S. Supreme Court on whether the case would be heard, Weddington went to work as the first female assistant city attorney in Fort Worth. When the Supreme Court accepted *Roe v. Wade*, however, her boss forced her to choose between pursuing the case and continuing her employment. She left to do what she felt was more important work.

Between 1973 and 1977 Weddington served three terms in the Texas House of Representatives. In 1974, Ron and Sarah divorced amicably. They still practiced together in the same building for a year and remained friends. During the years between 1975 and 1977, future Texas governor Ann Richards served as Weddington's administrative assistant.

Weddington left Texas in 1977 to work for the United States Department of Agriculture as general counsel. This job proved rewarding in diverse ways. Weddington, who loved riding horses and being outdoors, especially enjoyed a horseback camping trip in Montana with members of the U.S. Forest Service, when she was supervising legal work regarding the land and wilderness areas.

Later the same year, however, Weddington joined the White House staff as special assistant, then assistant to President Carter, a position that proved the most exciting job she ever had. She characterized the Republican election of 1980 and the subsequent changes it brought as one of the most difficult periods she ever faced. An anti-abortion administration was now in power, and anti-choice activists swelled in both numbers and visibility. Yet despite her fears, *Roe v. Wade* held its ground.

By 1989, the pro-choice camp had also increased its organization and visibility. Weddington was heartened to discover that people from many different walks of life actively supported choice, including nuns, cowboys, and actors. And in a 1989 Washington rally, as a U.S. Supreme Court decision on an important case attempting to narrow reproductive rights was pending, between 300,000 and 600,000 people turned out. Weddington called this "one of the most uplifting experiences of those otherwise dreary years." By 1991, she saw the shift moving back toward the pro-choice majority.

Despite her other commitments, Weddington feels she must be ever vigilant in preserving the rights won in *Roe*. She has served as president of the National Abortion Rights Action League, volunteered for Planned Parenthood, and has been actively involved with the pro-choice projects of many state and national groups. She continues to travel and speak on campuses. Weddington emphasizes that she is not for abortion, and cannot imagine that anyone is. She strongly believes, however, that it ought to be a personal legal choice. She often analogizes abortion to divorce, in that no one is "pro-divorce" but most believe it should be an option.

Weddington stresses that the best way to prevent an abortion is to prevent unwanted pregnancy. She notes that the rate of sexual activity is roughly equal for American and European teenagers, but teenage pregnancy occurs twice as often in the United States, in part because Americans are less candid about teaching human sexuality and contraception. She counsels abstinence and encourages contraception for those who are already active, pointing out that outlawing abortion would not end legal abortion but only serve to reinstate the horrors that existed before *Roe*. She agrees with Justice John Paul Stevens, who has said that there is no secular reason to outlaw abortion, and that theology is an improper reason to do so.

Weddington is moved by the stories she hears from those who have been touched by the trauma of illegal abortion. She hears many from men, whose mothers, sisters, or wives went through hell to end a pregnancy. She relates the story of a retired Episcopal priest who worked his way through seminary at an undertaking establishment. The first two bodies he saw were women who had died as a result of illegal abortions. Thereafter, he became a pro-choice leader in his community. Weddington reports that in most of Latin America where abortion is still outlawed, it is illegal abortion that remains the number-one cause of death for women eighteen to forty.

Determined to continue her efforts to preserve the right to legal abortion, Weddington invokes the old Texas saying that something will be done, "the good Lord willing and the creek don't rise"—in other words, if humanly possible. Advocates of choice will win in the long run, she believes, but those who support choice must remain vigilant. She reminds people that in the Supreme Court's recent *Casey* decision, *Roe* survived by a majority of only one vote.

HARRIET
RABB

1941 –

L ARGE LAW FIRMS, ESPECIALLY THOSE ON WALL STREET, LONG held the front lines of the old male-only guard. They strictly prohibited any female law graduate, even the best and brightest, from entering their ranks. In a 1950 article for *The New York Times,* Dorothy Kenyon recalled her own experiences and those of her classmates: "It's a lucky and nervy girl who can break through these barbed-wire entanglements and serve her law apprenticeship in an even reasonably good law office. It's still the rare exception to crash the gates of the gilded firms, the law factories that possess a monopoly of the big-business clients." Throughout the 1960s, little ground was gained. Many firms blatantly refused to even interview female candidates, sometimes writing "no women" across the top of interview sign-up sheets posted at the nation's leading law schools.

Prospects still remained dismal for women even twenty years after Kenyon's bitter indictment. In response to this persistent discrimination, Columbia Law School established the Employment Rights Project in 1969. In 1971, Harriet Rabb, a 1966 Columbia law school graduate and new faculty member, was appointed director of the project. Evidence was easily gathered by New York University and Columbia law students who had interviewed (or been denied interviews) with major firms. The records proved that women with equal or better qualifications than male students who were hired had been rejected on the basis of gender alone. The group filed numerous discrimination complaints with the New York City Commission on Human Rights, targeting ten large New York law firms. The charge was that each of the firms had established a pattern and practice of discrimination against female New York City law students.

As a result, a lengthy investigation was undertaken by the New York City Human Rights Commission. Commission attorney Eleanor Holmes Norton charged a group of firms with sex discrimination in recruitment, hiring, promotion, and treatment of female attorneys. Class-action civil-rights suits followed.

One of the suits settled fairly early when the firm named as the defendant agreed to a nondiscriminatory hiring formula. Another case, however, progressed toward litigation and was assigned through random judicial selection to Constance Baker Motley. The firm, Sullivan and Cromwell, one of the oldest and most prestigious, tried to have her disqualified, but the court of appeals upheld her right to hear the case. The case finally settled, with the firm adopting procedures to end discrimination in hiring. The battle, however, was far from finished.

Eventually, the firms named in the original 1971 complaint by the New York City Human Rights Commission agreed to adopt hiring guidelines that would assure women equal opportunity hiring and advancement. Such efforts by other female law students spread throughout the United States, through the filing of Equal Employment Opportunity Commission complaints, exposure of hiring practices in the press, and litigation. Thus the direction of Rabb's career and her far-reaching influence in her battle against employment discrimination was established.

Unfortunately, perhaps, Rabb was never to lack for work. Despite paper victories, the ornate doors and glass ceilings that kept women from gaining equal opportunities among the leading firms were slow to yield. In a 1980 *National Law Journal* article entitled "Wall Street's Sexist Wall," the *Journal* reported that it could find only 85 female partners among 3,987 partners at the nation's fifty largest law firms. Despite Rabb's lawsuit, Sullivan and Cromwell had *no* female partners at the time of the *Journal*'s survey. Moreover, it's attrition rate remained exceedingly high—hardly remarkable, given the dismal prospects for advancement.

Harriet Rabb's early years gave little hint of her future as a crusader. Born in 1941, she grew up in Texas during the days of gentility and segregation. Rabb's commitment to justice didn't gel until she was well into law school, the only political act in her early life occurring when she deliberately drank out of the water fountain reserved for blacks, in protest against segregation. Yet she came from a family of independent women. Both Rabb's parents were doctors. Her maternal grandmother helped her husband farm, in addition to running a dry goods store.

After high school, Harriet went to New York to attend Barnard, attempting to escape what she dubbed "southern bellism." At Barnard, the big political debates on campus revolved around such earth-shattering dilemmas as the appropriate length for Bermuda shorts. She majored in government and then continued on to Columbia Law School, where she was placed in a summer clerkship following her second year with a civil rights firm headed by civil rights pioneers William Kunstler and Arthur Kinoy. She later characterized the summer as extraordinary, with Kinoy becoming a mentor. Rabb was thus plunged into the exciting and brutal world of civil rights law in the sixties.

Harriet moved on for a year-long stint as Bess Myerson's special counsel to the Department of Consumer Affairs. When she and Bruce Rabb married in 1970 and went to Washington, Harriet joined a public-interest law firm to practice until the couple moved to New York the following year. Rabb then joined the faculty at Columbia University.

At Columbia Law School, Rabb joined the Employment Rights Project, which provided the vehicle for litigation in some of her best-known Title VII cases. In many of these cases, she combined her talents with those of such luminaries as tax lawyer George Cooper and civil rights advocate Howard Rubin.

Harriet Rabb has traveled far since her days as a teenager in Houston, when her most fervent wish was to be named a cheerleader. By the late seventies, she had become known as the foremost Title VII lawyer in practice, described as a "whiz kid" and "toppler of corporate giants." Her list of achievements on behalf of workers, especially working women, seems nearly endless. She negotiated a $1.5 million settlement in a 1977 suit against *Readers Digest* by its female employees. She scored a similar victory at *Newsweek*, another against New York Telephone, and then took on the formidable *New York Times*. But in legal circles she is still best known for lawsuits that shattered barriers at a number of prestigious, and persistently discriminatory, Wall Street law firms.

Rabb faced her own share of discrimination as a young lawyer, including one incident in which a judge who was unnerved by her obvious pregnancy asked her to sit down while arguing her summation. When Rabb respectfully declined, the judge insisted on standing as well. Rabb simply continued her summation until the weary judge sat down again.

While Rabb's work has been groundbreaking—some even consider it radical—she is reportedly both modest and conventional in her personal life. Having won respect for her tactful, nonthreatening style of litigation, she also enjoys a low-key family life.

Harriet Rabb is now general counsel for the Department of Health and Human Services in Washington, D.C. She has written on employment rights, co-authoring two books on fair employment litigation. She has also served on the boards of directors of the Ford Foundation, the New York Civil Liberties Union, the Lawyers Committee for Civil Rights Under Law, the NAACP Legal Defense Fund, the Mexican American Legal Defense and Education Fund, and worked on behalf of many other public-service agencies.

ANTONIA
HERNANDEZ

1948 –

A NTONIA HERNANDEZ WAS BORN INTO A TRADITIONAL MEXICAN family in 1948. As a child, she often worked in the fields and orchards picking crops alongside the rest of the family. Her parents and their six children immigrated to East Los Angeles when Antonia was eight years old. Manuel Hernandez worked as a gardener and laborer, while Nicolasa Hernandez took in odd jobs to contribute to the family's support. Antonia, the oldest child, helped with her younger siblings and took on other tasks as needed, including such unconventional chores as auto maintenance. The family was poor but loving, happy, and close.

The Hernandez family gave their children a strong sense of identity and pride as Americans of Mexican heritage. Her father once pointed out a sign on a restaurant wall that read, "No Mexicans and No Dogs." He urged the children to remain proud even in the face of such bigotry. They were taught the rich history that gave them a strong foundation built upon centuries of Mexican culture. But their parents also instilled in them the belief that serving the public interest was a noble thing to do. All of the Hernandez children earned college degrees, and several became teachers. Antonia initially pursued a career in teaching and counseling as well, but eventually came to realize that it was difficult to help the kids as teachers unless something was done about the laws that were holding them back.

Hernandez chose to attend law school at UCLA so she could remain close to her family. While she didn't earn stellar grades, Hernandez impressed her law professors as bright and articulate and having a knack for diplomacy. Hernandez placed a higher priority on service to organizations she served, such as the admissions committee, California Legal Rural Assistance, and Chicano student groups. She considered being a well-rounded person an important aspect of being a top lawyer, especially one in the public sector.

After graduating, Hernandez began her career with the East Los Angeles Center for Law and Justice, where she handled a wide variety of cases, many involving police brutality. This led her to a special interest in civil rights law. She soon became directing attorney of the Lincoln Heights office for the Legal Aid Foundation. In this position of considerable responsibility, she directed a staff of six other lawyers, litigated cases, and worked for passage of bills in the state legislature. She loved her work, which centered on poverty law.

Hernandez maintained close ties with her family and continued to follow cultural traditions, even as her career climbed. In 1977, she married Michael Stern, a lawyer in private practice—but not before the couple received Manuel Hernandez's blessing. When she was offered a job as staff counsel to the United States Senate Judiciary Committee in 1978, she initially declined, because it would mean a move to Washington, D.C., and she was reluctant to leave her family. But she knew the position would provide valuable experience, so she capitulated, becoming the first Hispanic to hold such a post.

The job proved highly rewarding. Hernandez developed a specialty in immigration and human-rights law. But after two years, the Democrats lost control of the Senate, and Hernandez lost her job.

Within days she was offered a position in the Washington Office of the Mexican American Legal Defense and Education Fund (MALDEF).

Hernandez began as associate counsel for MALDEF and quickly progressed through the ranks. She served as director of the employment litigation program and helped defeat the Simpson-Mazzoli immigration bill, which would have required Latinos to carry identification cards. She assisted in many cases that brought about historic changes for the Hispanic community. Additionally, her life in Washington, D.C., gave her a broader perspective on the diversity among the American Hispanic communities, bringing her into contact with Puerto Ricans, Cubans, and other Latino cultures. She often worked to increase cooperation among civil rights organizations across all racial and ethnic lines.

Hernandez eventually rose to the office of president and general counsel of MALDEF. She gained national visibility as an effective advocate for America's Hispanics and was frequently interviewed on such issues important to Hispanics as immigration rights, employment discrimination, educational inequities, and voting rights. During her tenure with MALDEF, she worked for increased employment of Hispanics in government and the private sector. She initiated several lawsuits that required employers to compensate bilingual workers for their special skills with a second language, when these capabilities were a part of their job.

Hernandez has faced her share of upheaval at MALDEF, however. In 1987, she was abruptly terminated by an executive committee, who questioned her abilities in administration and leadership. She was immediately replaced by former New Mexico Governor Toney Anaya—himself no stranger to controversy—at a salary 40 percent higher than Hernandez had been paid. Undaunted, Hernandez refused to accept the decision, and went to court. She successfully argued that only the full board was empowered to make such a decision and was reinstated when the board convened. Since that time, she has continued as the mainstay and top spokesperson for MALDEF, working not only to win in the courtroom but to implement changes in the human arena as well. As she told *La Paloma* magazine in 1991, "A court victory is important but just the beginning of the process. It must translate into empowerment. It is the people that have the power to give life to those court victories."

Family remains a priority for Hernandez. She and her husband, along with their three children, whom she describes as her greatest accomplishment, have returned to California. Although of Jewish descent, Michael Stern speaks Spanish and has embraced Antonia's culture. She credits his accommodating nature with helping her balance the many commitments in her life.

Community service remains important to Hernandez, and she serves on the boards of numerous organizations, including California Leadership, Quality Education for Minorities Network, and the Latino Museum of History, Art and Culture. She was appointed by Los Angeles mayor Tom Bradley to the Rebuild L.A. commission after the 1992 riots. She has put tremendous effort into recruiting others into community service as well, especially immigrants and Hispanics.

HILLARY RODHAM
CLINTON

1947 –

NO FIRST LADY IN AMERICAN HISTORY HAS DONE MORE TO profoundly change the image of the wife of the American president and her role in the White House—nor has any first lady been so besieged by controversy—as Hillary Clinton. "If I am going to be criticized for doing what I believe in," she remarked in 1994, "I might as well just keep doing what I believe in."

Given Clinton's position in history, such a credo is no doubt essential to her sanity and survival. Even when she has forayed into such areas as children's rights, a subject generally considered "appropriate" to the interest of a first lady, she has set off a storm of controversy. Since the first day of the Clinton administration, for her it's been a matter of "damned if you do and damned if you don't."

Clinton grew up in the middle-class, traditional world of Park Ridge, Illinois, outside Chicago. Throughout her youth she was involved in the Methodist Church, a congregation that emphasized social activism. As a teenager, she volunteered for inner-city programs and cared for the children of migrant farmworkers. Her years at Yale Law School (at that time the Ivy League choice for idealists who viewed the law as a tool of social reform) strengthened her commitment to public service. Throughout her career, she has worked and lobbied for the rights of children. "There is no such thing," she has often declared, "as other people's children."

Unlike virtually all of her predecessors, Hillary Clinton entered the White House as an accomplished professional woman. Many admired the new couple at the head of American politics: a balanced, egalitarian, complementary team reflecting the structure of more and more of the nation's families. The growing majority of American working women saw a first lady to whom they could relate—a woman who juggled the often conflicting demands of work, motherhood, and support of a husband's career. Many of these women had both high hopes and high expectations that Clinton would use her role to do something about problems close to their hearts, and to hers as well: health care, day care, and better government support for working families.

The first baby boomer in the White House, Clinton brought a fresh image to the position, much as Jacqueline Onassis had done nearly thirty years before her. She was part of the generation that came of age in the 1960s, a first lady who would dance onstage at the inauguration to the music of Fleetwood Mac. Clinton was expected by many to be a role model, actively involved in her career as a lawyer and public servant rather than slipping into the supporting role of the traditional first lady.

But others of a more conservative bent were wary. A high-powered lawyer in the role of first lady proved threatening to those who distrusted the Clinton agenda and feared that Hillary might use her influence excessively or inappropriately. Above all, most Americans seemed to expect from Hillary that modern and often near-impossible balance, between the soft, nurturing, family-focused woman and the shrewd, cool, consummate professional.

Conflicting public expectations came to a head early in the

administration when Hillary Clinton spearheaded the drive to establish a program of national health insurance. These efforts drew both
hearty praise from those who appreciated the gratis efforts of a brilliant professional and loud grumbling from others who resented a
first lady's activeness in a political endeavor. Many complained that
they had elected Bill Clinton—not Hillary Clinton—ignoring the
obvious fact that elected officials are in turn free to appoint a staff.
Later, when Clinton stepped back from active legislative policy
involvement, she was lambasted by a different group, who accused
her of bowing to pressure and not hanging tough.

Some believe that the criticism of Hillary also reflects a persistent distrust of women in positions of high power. When allegations
surrounding the Whitewater scandal began trickling into the press,
there were smug nods of "I told you so." And the harshest criticism
was leveled not against the president but his wife.

Yet Hillary Clinton has maintained grace and dignity through
unrelenting scrutiny and a ceaseless stream of harsh commentary.
Her talents as a leader and motivator cannot be denied. In 1988, she
chaired the ABA Commission on Women in the Profession. A longtime proponent of equality for women under the law, she has written
a weekly newspaper column discussing political and family issues.

In 1994, Clinton released her book, *It Takes a Village and Other
Lessons Children Teach Us,* whose title comes from the African proverb
"It takes a village to raise a child." Keeping her focus on her personal
agenda, especially her work on behalf of children, Clinton's book combines practical advice on child raising with a discussion of government
child-development programs over the past thirty years. Something
of a missionary, with a strong calling to do good—especially for
children—since her teenage years, she has taken to heart her church's
admonition to "be doers of the world and not hearers only."

Clinton is a study in contrasts. She is known as fun loving, enjoying such antics as wearing a holiday necklace with flashing Christmas
lights. She reportedly roams the White House after hours in jeans
and a ponytail, spouting such quips as "What's up, buttercup?" On
the other hand, she can be formidable in her professional role. She

expects and receives absolute loyalty from her largely female staff. As of early 1996, only two of her original sixteen members had left, one because of illness in the family. Clinton's perfectionism can make her demanding, and she is fiercely protective of her daughter, Chelsea, shielding her from the limelight. Reportedly, the rule in the White House with regard to Chelsea's involvement in political publicity is "Don't even bring it up."

Generally she ignores her detractors as much as possible and refuses to let them interfere with her duties; although as the Whitewater and "Travelgate" barrage escalated during 1996, she has more often felt compelled to respond, sometimes admitting misjudgments, sometimes intensely defending against unfounded accusations.

Yet Clinton is more concerned with getting on with what she believes to be far more important work. This attitude is viewed by some as evasiveness, by others as a cool and professional grace under tremendous pressure. She was deeply moved by the tragic suicide of deputy White House counsel Vince Foster, one of her closest friends. Clinton has told interviewers that she intends to cooperate in the investigation of her work at Little Rock's Rose Law Firm for Madison Guaranty Trust, a failed savings and loan. The records have, in fact, been opened. She frequently emphasizes such facts, overlooked by the Whitewater pundits, as her family's own loss of money in the deal and the strict attorney-client privilege that prohibits lawyers from revealing confidential matters until the client specifically waives the privilege. Though she generally hides her resentment well, her frustration occasionally shows, as when she remarked, "Remind me, have I ever done anything right in my life?"

The recent difficulties have, if anything, improved Clinton's political savvy. She now presents her agenda in what has been characterized as a more "politically correct" manner. Some have spoken with regret at what they see as a retreat into the more traditional role of first lady. Gloria Steinem has remarked that she misses "the old Hillary." Others have noted the waste of talent, of skill that could be put to more direct use. Many believe Clinton bowed to pressure from her husband's political advisers, who considered her outspoken nature a liability. "I hate to see her silenced," one woman has commented.

Yet others insist the decision to take a more low-key role was Clinton's alone. Her book may well represent a quieter, yet no less emphatic and effective means of pursuing her mission. Clinton is proud, dedicated, and determined, and it seems unlikely that she could ever be influenced to deviate from her chosen route. The means of her more recent activities may be different, but the message remains the same.

It Takes a Village makes clear that Clinton's dedication to health care for everyone is far from abandoned. She points out that ten million children, most with working parents, do not have health insurance. She also notes that this number will rise if Medicaid is cut, and characterizes as deplorable the fact that even those who can well afford private health coverage cannot find insurance companies that will write policies for children with conditions like cystic fibrosis.

In her book Clinton also writes of the overwhelming love and responsibility she felt upon becoming a mother herself, a turning point in her life and her work. She emphasizes that parents have primary responsibility for their children, but many others can play a role in shaping lives and helping young people reach their potential. She compares her own family to the fifties television show *Father Knows Best.* Hugh Elsworth Rodham ran a small business, screen printing and selling drapery fabrics. She describes her mother as traditional, devoted, encouraging, and affectionate. Though the family was financially stable, her parents, who grew up during the Depression, constantly worried about money. Yet the Rodham family enjoyed the support of a "village" that included grandparents, aunts, uncles, cousins, and many others who affected the children's lives in positive ways.

Another contrast many have noted in Clinton is between her politics, generally considered liberal, and a personal code so conservative she has been called a prude. She advocates sexual abstinence until the age of twenty-one, and believes that divorce is too easily available for parents. Clinton acknowledges rocky times in her own marriage, times she had to will herself to stop and count her blessings, to compromise both personally and politically.

Clinton's views on divorce are controversial yet based on sound reasoning. She advises parents to consider carefully what more could be done to salvage a marriage before dissolving it. At the same time, she is quick to acknowledge that violence and abuse, as experienced by women like her mother-in-law, Virginia Kelly, should not be endured by any parent or child.

Clinton's words throughout her book are compassionate but strong. She urges early-education programs for disadvantaged children and their families and offers scientific data on child development to support the value of such programs. Clinton reflects on her own frustrations as a new mother in discussing the importance of prenatal care. She emphasizes her belief that our highest priority as a nation should be educating and empowering people to be the best parents possible. "It is a national shame," she states, "that many Americans are more thoughtful about planning their weekend entertainment than about planning their families." She urges parents and the rest of the "village" to form a partnership to raise expectations of student achievement, and of public education. She discusses her strong belief that discipline and order must be maintained in schools, and that children should be educated early about the reality of sex and procreation. She cites statistics proving that sex education does not increase sexual behavior; on the contrary, it can include encouraging abstinence, an essential message, as well as realistically recognizing that some adolescents will choose to be sexually active and must receive straight talk about contraception and sexually transmitted diseases. She urges communities to provide supervised activities for children whose parents are still at work during after school hours, echoing Janet Reno's concern on this issue.

Clinton's book presents an intelligent discussion of her view of the role of government in supporting families. She believes in balance and emphasizes the essential nature of both personal and mutual responsibility for our children at all levels of society. "Let us use government," she states, "as we have in the past, to further the common good."

LINDA
FAIRSTEIN

1948 –

L INDA FAIRSTEIN HAS BEEN DESCRIBED MANY TIMES AS A paradox. Tall and elegant, she is an impeccable dresser with a classic education and suburban origins. Yet she has devoted her life to a job that would make many stout-hearted people cringe in horror. Since 1976, Fairstein has served as chief of the Sex Crimes Unit in the Manhattan district attorney's office. She deals with hundreds of cases each year, involving some of the most vile behavior attributed to humanity.

The unit Fairstein heads is the country's oldest legal bureau specializing in sex crimes. Fairstein has now worked on the frontlines of the war against rape for over two decades. She has been praised for her combination of toughness and sensitivity, and the compassion with which she treats the victims of sexual violence. Fairstein has never become desensitized to the horror of the crimes she prosecutes. What helps her cope is the opportunity to offer both justice and solace to the victims. As she told *People* magazine, "Helping them restore their well-being and mental health is enormously rewarding."

Cool and intelligent, Fairstein is respected as unrelentingly tough in the courtroom. Born in 1947, she grew up in Westchester County, New York, the daughter of a physician and nurse. She studied English at Vassar, then followed her brother to the University of Virginia Law School. When she joined the Manhattan D.A.'s office in 1972, she was one of six women in an office of two hundred attorneys. She often relates a story from early in her career, when she returned from an especially brutal day in court in tears. Her male supervisor, chagrined to see a D.A. weep, snapped, "For God's sake, Linda, stop crying! Go to the john and throw up like a man!"

Fairstein soon found her niche and earned the admiration of both colleagues and opponents for her phenomenal memory, her ability to think on her feet, and her innovative techniques. Fairstein takes pride in both a remarkable conviction rate and the fact that most of her plea bargains garner sentences only slightly shorter than what could be expected following a jury trial.

Fairstein is admired for her thorough preparation of each case, as well as a barely perceptible undercurrent of moral outrage that runs through her efficient courtroom presentation. She often works with rape crisis counselors, teaching them to prepare victims for testimony. As New York University law professor and former ACLU director Burt Neuborne told *The New York Times Magazine* in a 1990 interview, "If there were more people like her it would be an infinitely juster system." He noted that Fairstein never fights dirty, but always fights hard.

During her tenure as head of the Sex Crimes Unit, Fairstein has seen many changes and improvements in the law governing prosecution of sex crimes. Prior to 1972, the law of New York State did not consider the victim of a sexual attack to be an independently credible witness. Corroboration was required as to both the identity of the attacker and the nature of the assault. Fairstein has often pointed out the absurdity of such rules. Under the old law, a woman who had her purse stolen and was then raped by the assailant could, by her testimony, convict him of the theft but not of the rape. Fortunately, this law was modified in 1972 and thrown out completely in 1974. Another change in the law—which Fairstein helped bring about—put an end to a requirement that the woman prove "earnest resistance" to the attack by displaying injuries, torn clothing, or similar evidence. Fairstein credits the change in attitude that paved the way for such reforms to the women's movement, giving special praise to Susan Brownmiller, who brought the public's attention to the reality of sexual assault in her 1975 book, *Against Our Will: Men, Women and Rape.*

Fairstein is a persistent crusader against misconceptions. Frustrated by victims who decline to seek prosecution of their rapists because they do not believe their word alone will be enough to gain a conviction, she has made it her mission to educate the public so more victims will prosecute. Fairstein emphasizes that a woman's past sexual conduct may no longer be considered evidence in a case of sexual assault unless she had a prior relationship with the assailant, so the old practice of putting the victim on trial has been reduced to a great extent.

Fairstein acknowledges that convictions are often difficult to win in some sexual assault cases because of persistent public stereotypes. She has found that it is more difficult to convict a good-looking defendant, and harder to convict one who knew his victim. Fairstein laments that women tend to be less sympathetic as jurors than are men, and points out that rape is the only crime in which people tend to blame the victim rather than giving her sympathy and support.

Fairstein has handled a number of notorious cases. In 1978 she prosecuted Marvin Teicher, a dentist who was convicted of sexual abuse in the first degree for molesting his patients while they were under anesthesia. She also won the conviction of Russell West, the infamous "Midtown rapist," who sexually assaulted eighteen women before being arrested. Her most gratifying cases, however, aren't necessarily the ones that wind up in the newspapers. "They are the ones," she told an interviewer, "where the victim expects little from the system and says, 'But it's just my word against his.' Not only can I tell her that's all the law requires now, but very often I can take the case to trial and get her rapist convicted." A good deal of her work involves counseling victims, assuaging their fears and guilt. She provides the support that is too often lacking from friends and family, who may unfairly blame or embarrass the victim.

Her sense of fairness extends to defendants as well, and she carefully screens witnesses to be as certain as possible that a case is legitimate before she decides to prosecute. Yet the decision to deep-six a case is never made lightly. Not only have alleged victims made embarrassing public complaints, Fairstein painfully recalls a case in which the accused defendant was released due to serious problems with witness credibility, and then went on to assault and murder a nurse.

Fairstein's sense of humor helps see her through the gruesome subject matter that fills her days. She reportedly once remarked, "Anything between the knees and the waist goes to me," when asked about the parameters of her job. She also acknowledges the blessings of a rich and full personal life, relatively free of trauma and tragedy. She is close to her family, including Justin N. Feldman, a civil litigator whom she married just before the most famous trial of her career. The couple live in a gracious apartment on the Upper East Side of New York and spend summer weekends at their 175-year-old house on Martha's Vineyard. She and her husband are active in a number of legal and human-rights organizations.

Fairstein has a unique ability to compartmentalize her professional life away from her personal time. In a 1993 interview, Fairstein's friend Michael Goldberg remarked, "Linda can try a rape case in the morning, drink with cops after work, and end the evening at the ballet. In each situation she is completely herself."

Fairstein was thrust into the national limelight when she prosecuted Robert E. Chambers Jr. in the infamous "preppie murder trial." Chambers, young, handsome, and privileged, was charged with brutally raping and murdering eighteen-year-old Jennifer Levin in Central Park in August 1986. After the thirteen-week trial, including nine days of jury deliberation, Chambers pled guilty to manslaughter in the first degree. The Chambers case was Fairstein's first homicide trial. Because she did not have a living victim with whom to work, Fairstein interviewed Jennifer Levin's friends and members of her family to get to know the young woman.

The plea bargain was a disappointment for Fairstein, who had hoped for a murder conviction. She was also frustrated by the persistence of stereotypes. One juror on the case remarked that Chambers didn't look like a killer, while a black juror commented that had Chambers been poor and black, he would have been convicted in fifteen minutes.

Fairstein is often frustrated by the reluctance of witnesses to become involved in a case, and appalled by the selfishness of their reasons. When she was prosecuting the Chambers case, one man refused to let his son, a friend of the victim, testify because he believed it would be bad for his business if his son's name were seen in the newspaper.

Fairstein loves to read murder mysteries and has long enjoyed writing herself when the unrelenting demands of her job allowed her time. Given her passionate commitment to her work, this would seem unlikely. Yet Fairstein's first book, *Sexual Violence: Our War Against Rape*, published in 1994, drew accolades from critics and readers alike for its engrossing stories based on cases she had handled, and intriguing explanations of such potentially dry subjects as how evidence is collected in a criminal case. It also helped her crusade to eliminate misconceptions about the crime of rape, the justice system, and why victims should come forward.

In *Sexual Violence*, Fairstein explains the history and recent changes in the laws surrounding rape and walks readers through the legal process in straightforward language. Her view of the criminal justice system has been described as "cautiously optimistic," as the treatment of victims has continued to improve and justice is more often served. In 1996, she realized her longtime dream of writing fiction, when *Final Jeopardy*, her crime novel, was published to rave reviews.

Fairstein has been one of the leaders in bringing to light the reality, as well as the prevalence, of date rape. She also confronts persistent myths, such as the idea that rape does not happen to nice girls, or that victims who dressed a certain way or went to bars alone brought the assault on themselves.

Fairstein is pleased to see attitudes changing, and credits the women's movement, women's magazines, even television movies with raising public awareness of the facts about sexual assault. She has seen a dramatic increase in effective prosecution of date rapists in recent years. Perhaps the most innovative feature of *Sexual Violence: Our War Against Rape* is its vivid description of the brutal reality of these acquaintance rapes. As reviewer Kathy Young stated in the February 1994 issue of *Reason* magazine, "Fairstein's vivid descriptions of these crimes—a terrified secretary raped at knifepoint on the cold floor of a ladies' room, a dancer running for help half-naked after being violently overpowered by her date—make any comparison to being nagged into unwanted sex almost obscene." She goes on to commend Fairstein for devoting a chapter to the "politically incorrect" subject of false rape claims. As Fairstein points out, "Each false accusation makes too many skeptics think that every accusation is a false one— which is a danger that cannot be overstated."

While she hesitates to generalize, Fairstein believes that men almost never rape in order to have sex, and points out that many rapists have willing sex partners available. In 1989 she told *Cosmopolitan,* "What never ceases to amaze me are the differences among rapists—they come from every ethnic and social background. Their victims range from eighteen-month-old babies to eighty-year-old women. I don't think we have even begun to understand the psychological reasons for rape." Emphasizing that rape is a crime of opportunity, she urges women not to be too trusting of men they do not know well. She also stresses that while rape is a crime of violence, it is different than other traumatic crimes because it is so much more intimate.

After the preppie murder case, Fairstein was characterized in *Barrister* magazine as the best-known female prosecutor in America—barring fictional prosecutor Grace Van Owen of TV's *L.A. Law.* Suddenly a role model for people throughout the nation, she was portrayed in television movies, consulted by directors and actresses portraying prosecutors, and fictionalized, along with some of her well-known cases, in a novel. Fairstein has become legendary for both her high rate of convictions (around 80 percent) and for her courtroom flair. She was even interviewed by the Clinton administration for the post of attorney general, before the decision to appoint Janet Reno was made.

Fairstein's efforts to help women have extended to other attorneys. Today, nearly half the prosecutors in the Manhattan D.A.'s office are women. At the same time, she cautions women that prosecution is not for everyone, that it is difficult and demanding and requires sacrifices—including a starting salary that is a fraction of what private law firms generally offer.

NANCY J. MINTIE

1954 –

NANCY MINTIE REPRESENTS A NEW BREED OF PUBLIC-SERVICE attorney, carrying on traditions established by predecessors working for suffrage and other human-rights issues during the nineteenth and early twentieth centuries. Mintie is director of the Inner City Law Center in Los Angeles, which serves and advocates for the city's homeless population, estimated at over 35,000.

Mintie grew up in a large, conservative, working class Catholic family in Orange County, California. She supported Nixon and the Vietnam War during her youth. Her early career aspirations centered on music, and she studied piano while attending a Catholic girls' high school and began college at Loyola Marymount University on a music scholarship, aiming for a career in music. She supported herself as a waitress, as a night operator for an answering service, and selling stagecoach tickets at Knotts Berry Farm.

After a year at Loyola, however, she began to feel pulled in a different direction. "I couldn't stand to see people hurt or the victims of injustice," she told *Student Lawyer* magazine in 1985. "I wanted to do something about it."

As Mintie was reconsidering her plans, her brother became a social worker on skid row with the Catholic Worker Community. When she visited him on the job she was shocked at what she saw, never having been exposed to true poverty. She began to meet and befriend homeless people and was deeply moved by their kindness and dignity, despite the squalor of their existence. She was appalled to see human beings living in vermin-infested slums, or on the streets, and was devastated when an older homeless man she had befriended was murdered.

Mintie was also deeply disturbed when she learned the extent of the red tape and other bureaucratic barriers that prevented the poor from receiving government aid for which they were qualified. She also heard horror stories about slum landlords, exploitative employers, and other predators who contributed to the desperation of the poor, even when they could find work and shelter.

Mintie began law school at UCLA and got a part-time job as an advocate in a state mental institution to help pay tuition. At first she planned to take the more familiar route of working with a law firm to effect change within the system, but she eventually realized that she wanted to make a personal contribution, to go out and help the poor in a more direct manner.

Upon graduating from UCLA, she set up a legal clinic at the Catholic Worker Community's free medical clinic, living at the shelter and soup kitchen on skid row. From the first day she opened her office in the corner of a converted garage, she had more clients than she could handle. Mintie's practice grew steadily, and after three years in her crowded corner she eventually moved up to her own office—not the plush and glitzy suites in skyscrapers visible from skid row, occupied by many of her classmates, but a secondhand trailer decorated with graffiti. It sat between a soup kitchen and a collection of dwellings constructed by the homeless from available debris in a settlement that had been dubbed "Justiceville." The interior of Mintie's office also featured unique decor. Rather than the usual potted palms, her office boasted a piano, alongside a stack of jars containing enormous rats floating in formaldehyde—essential evidence in cases against the slumlords she frequently sued.

Mintie soon began to recruit volunteers, but the work was overwhelming—even dangerous at times, when a disturbed individual would lose control. Clients of the center were required to check their weapons at the door. Additionally, Mintie had to bear up under the despair of constantly seeing her clients victimized by the violence of life on the streets. Some were killed, and virtually all of the homeless women she encountered had been raped. Yet Mintie persevered. She developed a specialty in suing slum landlords in an effort to achieve safe, legal, habitable housing for their tenants. In one case, she faced off against three of the top law firms in the city. With a minuscule budget of her own, Mintie won $200,000 from a landlord, the largest settlement in the history of Los Angeles during the early 1980s. Mintie's greatest victory to date came in 1990, when she settled a case against an especially callous slumlord on the eve of trial for $1.25 million. After devoting three years to the case, she was thrilled to watch her clients use their winnings to move from the crumbling vermin-infested building into safe, sturdy homes.

Mintie's cases aren't limited to substandard housing, however. In one case she represented a defendant who had been falsely charged with a crime in order to cover up police misconduct in a racially motivated beating. Mintie so successfully revealed the dishonesty of the police that the prosecution dropped the case in the midst of the trial to avoid further embarrassment.

By 1985, Mintie was able to acquire a partner, move to a storefront office, and pay herself and her staff a modest salary. Mintie and her husband, a photographer, moved into a warehouse loft several blocks from the center. When their daughter Michelle was born, Mintie expanded her staff in order to cut back on her own caseload. By 1994, the Inner City Law Center had grown to include a team of four lawyers, three advocates, and several volunteers; now housed in larger quarters, but still in the heart of downtown Los Angeles.

Mintie finds deep satisfaction in simply helping her clients find their way back to a stable life, after literally pulling many of them out of the gutter. Some of her efforts focus on one individual at a time, while others have more far-reaching consequences. In one case, for example, she challenged a common practice of eviction in which landlords illegally locked families out of their dwellings. She achieved a verdict for the people she represented, awarding them over $40,000 in damages. The case also sent a strong message to other slumlords, who subsequently stopped the illegal practice.

Mintie has also taken an activist role in such efforts as Tent City, a homeless settlement erected in the winter of 1985 directly across from Los Angeles City Hall. Public pressure convinced the county to build a new shelter.

In the 1980s, Mintie was one of the founders of the Homeless Litigation Team (HLT), a group of public interest lawyers that brought lawsuits against the County of Los Angeles to force it to live up to its legal obligations to provide for the homeless. Under the leadership of brilliant poverty law attorney Gary Blasi, HLT filed suits that broke down the bureaucratic barriers that kept large numbers of homeless people from obtaining county shelter and services, improved the quality of those services, and made special assistance available for the homeless mentally ill.

Mintie views homelessness in America as both unacceptable and completely unnecessary. Her boundless optimism and belief in human compassion spurs her continuing efforts to educate others about the true nature of the condition. She also advocates the economic benefits of what she calls the "social-service safety net" to prevent people from losing their homes, rather than the more difficult and expensive task of trying to turn back the tide of homeless people and their ever-increasing disabilities.

Mintie identifies three primary causes of homelessness: alcohol or drug problems, mental illness, and the simple inability to earn enough money to afford shelter. In the years she has worked on skid row, she has seen significant shifts in the homeless population. In the beginning, most were addicted to drugs or alcohol. By the late eighties, however, there were far greater numbers of the mentally ill, released from institutions by those who believed they could be better cared for in community centers. Yet these alternative-care facilities were seldom funded. Mintie emphasizes that emotional disease can strike anyone, citing the example of a middle-aged man she met who at first appeared delusional when he claimed to be a NASA scientist. On further investigation, however, she learned that he had indeed been a brilliant scientist and inventor, who had worked in conjunction with the space agency until a series of mental breakdowns had left him disabled.

Mintie is deeply troubled by the number of healthy people who are on the street simply because they are unemployed or cannot earn enough money to afford shelter. She emphasizes that few of the homeless are lazy. She often encounters ill or disabled clients who aggravate their condition by working at whatever jobs they can find, often hard physical labor. She has also represented clients who work full-time jobs but are paid only minimum wage and must live in their cars or on the street because they cannot afford any available housing.

Mintie has been widely praised by colleagues for her willingness to tackle any problem, from obtaining a birth certificate to taking on a class-action lawsuit. Though bright, creative, tenacious, and extremely thorough, many believe her most extraordinary skill is her rapport with the homeless. Not only has she won the trust of a notoriously suspicious clientele, she has become an eloquent advocate, often speaking before government agencies on their behalf. While she doesn't always achieve her goals, few who have heard her speak with her customary sincerity and authority come away without a new perspective. Her work has earned her many awards, including the California Bar President's Pro Bono Service Award, and honors bestowed by the Los Angeles County and Beverly Hills Bar Associations, the American Bar Association, UCLA, and the Caring Institute, among others.

Mintie is known to her friends as consistently pleasant, fun loving, and a talented poet. But she considers her most important accomplishment (sharing credit with the Center) as establishing a place where homeless people—who have had other doors slammed in their face—can find someone who will talk to them, care about their needs, and advocate for them in a world where they are almost always ignored.

The center never charges its clients a fee. Its funding depends on grants from the city, legal aid foundations, private donations and percentage shares from court victories and settlements. Lawyers and law students also offer volunteer assistance. Fund-raisers have included a concert by local new-wave musicians and an aerobics marathon at a health club. Yet funding is a constant worry. As she remarked to *Student Lawyer,* "We just hope we don't become homeless lawyers for the homeless."

Mintie laments the lack of government support for those who need it most. "The government has cut every program designed to help them break out of the poverty cycle," she told *Student Lawyer.* "There are fifty people living in Justiceville. Some of them are working. Others are going to school. You can see children doing homework in the afternoon. They are trying to pull out of this, but there is no bathroom there, no running water. Can you imagine going to school under those conditions?"

Mintie also represents those who are employed but exploited by day-labor agencies that run "slave pools" and frequently fail to pay workers at all. Additionally, she represents many recent immigrants, whom she admires for their bravery and sense of community and mutual support. She calls Los Angeles "the New Ellis Island."

The Inner City Law Center also operates an outreach program to help the local community become familiar with the center's services. This is especially important for non-English speaking immigrants and mentally or physically disabled people who must have an advocate to assist them in finding their way through the government bureaucracy.

Mintie is gratified to know that she is making a contribution in an area where no one else has been willing to go. Determined and pragmatic, she simply does the work she knows must be done. "I am constantly treated to the sight of people living in the most deprived circumstances who have somehow managed to hold onto their human dignity and generosity," she told *Esquire* magazine in 1986. "As I get to know them, I realize that their pain is the same pain that is inside everyone—it's a lack of love and acceptance."

MARCIA CLARK

1953 –

M ARCIA CLARK WAS A SUCCESSFUL BUT LITTLE-KNOWN
assistant district attorney for Los Angeles County when she
was suddenly catapulted into the spotlight with the opening of the
O.J. Simpson trial in 1995. As she daily found herself in the public
eye, Clark soon became what many considered the quintessential
female American attorney—with all of the blessings and curses associated with that role.

The Simpson trial became both a cultural phenomenon and a
soap opera, but Clark brought an unmistakable touch of class to the
often squalid proceedings. In her twelve years with the Los Angeles
district attorney's office, Clark had built a reputation for being both
tough and compassionate, especially in her dealings with crime victims and their families. She had tried more than twenty homicide
cases and had not lost one in ten years. Clark also developed a passion for the high-pressure drama of courtroom work. Shortly before

the Simpson trial, she gave up an administrative job with higher pay and lower stress to return to the trial work she loved, work many of her colleagues were so anxious to escape.

Though it was the Simpson case that first brought Clark to national attention, she was no stranger to notoriety. When Rebecca Schaeffer, a young actress starring in the popular television series *My Sister Sam*, was murdered in 1991, Clark won a conviction, plus a life sentence without the possibility of parole, for the killer. She garnered the praise and admiration of the Schaeffer family, not only for achieving justice but also for her attentive kindness throughout their ordeal. In a system where many feel victimized a second time, the family commented that they knew they were in the best possible hands.

Marcia Kleks was born in 1953 in Berkeley, California, where her father, an Israeli immigrant, worked for the U.S. Food and Drug Administration. His job required many moves for the family, so Marcia learned early to be adaptable. Her family were liberal Democrats, and Marcia developed an interest in justice and politics early in life. Adolescent friends who knew her when the family lived in a San Francisco suburb in the 1960s remember the emphasis on good grades, though Marcia still found time to attend Hebrew school after regular classes and sail her dinghy in the bay.

After high school, Marcia entered UCLA as a political science major, where she also studied dance and drama. She married Israeli backgammon professional Gabby Horowitz, but the couple divorced shortly after Marcia graduated from the Southwest University School of Law in Los Angeles in 1979. She married her second husband, Gordon Clark, a short time later. In a bizarre twist of fate, the lay minister who performed the second marriage was also a friend of Marcia's first husband, and was involved with him in a shooting accident ten years later.

Clark's first job after law school was with a small Los Angeles criminal defense firm. But given her strong sense of justice, Clark could not stomach work that often freed vicious criminals on legal technicalities. After a short stay with the firm she joined the Los Angeles County District Attorney's Office. She had soon settled into

an active practice, and she and Gordon had two sons. The couple separated in late 1993, however, and their divorce became final just days
before Nicole Brown Simpson and Ronald Goldman were murdered.

Though a veritable army of lawyers paraded before the cameras
in the often lurid coverage of the Simpson trial, much of the public
focus from the very start centered on Marcia Clark. The nature of the
attention she received demonstrated, in many ways, that the public
still does not know quite what to make of female attorneys. The hair-
styles and wardrobe choices of male attorneys are rarely noticed
unless they are especially outrageous or flamboyant. But continuing
in the best tradition of the nineteenth-century tabloids, the press
often seemed to pay more attention to Clark's personal style than to
the substance of her work. Even the ubiquitous Mr. Blackwell, best
known for his annual lists of best- and worst-dressed people, earnestly
offered his unsolicited advice on her wardrobe choices.

The scrutiny of Clark's appearance and the nature of observers'
comments revealed a great deal about public perceptions of women
attorneys in the 1990s. Columnist Ellen Goodman pointed out that
a woman practicing in the courtroom, especially a prosecutor, must
constantly walk a fine line between being sufficiently tough and
acceptably warm. Clark's short skirts and curly hair at the beginning
of the trial brought accusations of fluff and frivolity. Yet when she
switched to darker colors and straight hair, she was accused of being
"abrasive" and of adopting a "prosecutorial style." As head of the
prosecution team, although handicapped by the daunting task of
prosecuting an American hero, Clark was expected to be strong and
persistent in her pursuit of justice. Yet the sentiment that any show
of aggression is inappropriate for a woman is so ingrained that female
attorneys are expected to keep courtroom adversity in a murder trial
on a contained and gracious level. On one occasion when Clark displayed anger toward defense attorney Johnnie Cochran, supposedly
an old friend, Cochran resorted to a common low blow by calling
her "hysterical."

Through the course of the seemingly endless trial, nearly all of
the familiar sexist labels used against assertive women were hurled at

Clark. She was called "shrill" when she fought back against inappropriate actions by the defense team. She was accused of being "obsessed with winning," in spite of a track record that indicated she consistently put justice above victory. As writer Jimmy Breslin astutely observed in a 1995 *Esquire* article, "She's trying to convict a guy for murder and they want her to be a hostess seating people." Clark was alternatively urged by countless unsolicited advisers to "soften" her style, both in appearance and behavior, and to "nail him"!

Clark's tenure in the spotlight also brought into sharp focus the public expectations—and hypocrisy—regarding working mothers. In the midst of the trial, Clark's estranged husband filed for temporary custody of his sons. He accused her of giving her career priority over her children, yet sought a change in custody only after Clark had asked the court to reinstate his original child-support payments, which had been reduced when he moved into a bigger home. Whether these two events were related remains open to speculation, but the custody dispute exemplified some of the most difficult and heart-wrenching dilemmas faced by working women in all careers.

Marcia Clark found herself in an impossible situation. When she asked Judge Lance Ito to make moderate scheduling adjustments to accommodate her child-care provisions and allow her to spend time with her sons, she was accused by opposing attorneys, among others, as inappropriately using her children in a trial strategy ploy.

Yet throughout many months of what must have been nearly intolerable pressure, Clark conducted herself with remarkable patience and grace. She resisted the urge to make any public comment on the custody battle, wisely choosing to put the best interests of her children first. In maintaining her dignity, Clark drew praise from many. Ellen Goodman characterized Clark as a perfect portrait of the balance women are expected to maintain as they go about their work lives.

Clark is known to have an outstanding sense of humor, and it proved an invaluable survival tool during the Simpson trial. She consistently found amusement in the endless prattle over her appearance, once laughing at a gawking crowd shouting fashion comments as she entered the courtroom and advising them, "Get a life"! On another occasion, a pilot circled the courthouse in a small plane trailing a banner that complimented her new hairstyle and invited her for a lunch date.

Clark gained many admirers, both male and female, during the course of the trial. *Esquire* named her 1995 woman of the year, billing her "the prosecutor who never rests." In fact, Clark was simply continuing a long history of hard work, rebelliousness, and running her life without apology. A study in contradictions, she smokes cigarettes, drinks scotch, and hangs out with cops in bars, but also manages to be a compulsive fitness enthusiast. She is a devoted mother and undeniably feminine, yet as Los Angeles deputy district attorney Paul Turly remarked to *People*, "I think it is well documented she can out-shout and out-cuss any fleet of sailors." Approachable and down-to-earth, she nonetheless has a cross-examination technique that people have compared to a spear in the chest.

For four years before the Simpson trial, Clark worked in the Special Trials Unit of the L.A. prosecutor's office, handling the most complex and sensitive cases. Such work requires a combination of intelligence, stamina, and dogged perseverance. Prosecutors must choreograph every detail of their trials and cope with unwilling and unpleasant witnesses, constant uncertainty, complex scientific evidence, and the anguish of seeing criminals walk away.

Many attorneys find such work intoxicating for a while but eventually burn out and seek a less demanding position. Clark is one of a relatively small number of "lifers," clearly possessing the dramatic instinct, fire, passion, and mental stamina to do her job consistently and well. Clark's colleagues admire her dedication to justice, and even defense attorneys who have opposed her have praised her ethics. Her compassionate devotion to the families of victims has won her the enduring respect of the Brown and Goldman families, to whom she introduced herself as "your prosecutor."

Clark is also known for her obsessive preparation and solid legal skills. Both focused and articulate, she is expert at putting together the blocks—research, evidence, legal scholarship, police, experts, and witnesses—to build a solid conviction. Though demanding of her colleagues, she is renowned for her wit and was described by one as "a very funny workaholic." Clark's feisty but straightforward style in the courtroom earned the admiration of many viewers who were put off by the grand-standing and questionable tactics of other players in the spectacle. Her honesty, intensity, enthusiasm, and tenacity have won her praise as the consummate professional.

Though defeated in the O.J. Simpson trial, Clark hardly emerged a loser. After the verdict, she took a well-deserved six-month leave of absence from the district attorney's office, to spend time with her two sons, six and three, and to write what is expected to be the definitive work on the trial. She found she could command fees as high as $22,000 for speaking engagements, and pursued a long-neglected personal life.

A 1996 article in *People* described an incident that shows the scope of her appeal. When Clark arrived backstage at a recent speaking engagement, she rushed through the backstage corridors with two police escorts, while a pair of cleaning ladies put down their mops to applaud and cheer.

Many who know her have characterized Clark as fearless, uninhibited, and independent. She clearly has the ability to fashion her own life and find a certain integration of its many elements. After her close friendship with fellow prosecutor Christopher Darden became public knowledge during the Simpson trial, speculation about a possible romance ran rampant. Clark simply chose not to comment, while Darden, in his book about the trial, stated that it would not be "gentlemanly" to divulge any details.

Yet Clark has not shied away from the notoriety that followed the trial, instead adapting it to her own agenda. She has drawn sold-out crowds to her appearances, where she discusses issues important to her, deploring domestic violence and promoting self-esteem. Many working mothers have found a comrade who publicly grappled with the challenges of a demanding career and personal upheaval, and did so with balance and poise. At the same time, her admitted imperfections, such as her tendency to run up high credit-card debt, make her a role model very much grounded in reality.

RESOURCES AND
SUGGESTED READINGS

Adams, Joshua B. "My Mentor, Myself." *Town & Country Monthly* (August 1994): 60.

Allen, Florence Ellinwood. *To Do Justly.* Cleveland, Oh.: The Press of Western Reserve University, 1965.

Allen, Mel R. "The Straight Shooter." *Yankee* (May 1992): 64.

American Bar Association Committee on Women in the Profession. *Options and Obstacles: A Survey of the Studies of the Careers of Women Lawyers.* Chicago: American Bar Association, 1994.

Amron, Cory M. "Chair's Column." *Perspectives* 3, no. 2 (summer 1994): 2.

Anderson, Paul. *Janet Reno.* New York: John Wiley & Sons, 1994.

Angelo, Bonnie. "An Ethical Guru Monitors Morality." *Time* (June 3, 1991): 9.

Bailey, Patricia P. "The Accomplishments of WCL Founder Ellen Spencer Mussey." *American University Law Review* (spring 1983): 619-621.

"Barbara Jordan's Ideals." *The New York Times* (January 19, 1996): 28.

Barnes, Thomas Garden. *Hastings College of Law: The First Century.* San Francisco: Hastings College of Law Press, 1978.

Beck, Melinda. "The Voice of the Victims." *Newsweek* (January 23, 1995): 48.

Becker, Peter. "Three Survivors' Comeback Strategies." *Working Woman* (July, 1992): 11.

Berkman, Ted. *The Lady and the Law: The Remarkable Life of Fanny Holtzmann.* Boston: Little, Brown, 1976.

Blum, Bill. "Toward a Radical Middle." *ABA Journal* (January 1991): 48.

Bodine, Larry. "The Taxman is After L.A.'s Lady in Purple." *The National Law Journal 2* (June 9, 1980): 35.

Bonenberger, Lynne M. "The Changing Practice of Law." *Ohio Lawyer* (July/August 1993).

Borger, Gloria. "The Child Star's New Role." *U.S. News & World Report* (September 14, 1992): 35.

Bouton, Katherine. "Linda Fairstein v. Rape." *The New York Times Magazine* (February 25, 1990): 21.

Brant, Martha, and Evan Thomas. "First Fighter." *Newsweek* (January 15, 1996).

Breslin, Jimmy. "Women We Love: Women of the Year: The Prosecutor Never Rests." *Esquire* (August 1995): 48.

Bretton, Tracy. "Being a First is Becoming a Habit for R.I.'s New Attorney General." *The National Law Journal* 7 (December 17, 1984): 6.

———. "New R.I. AG to Probe Predecessor." *The National Law Journal* 9 (February 2, 1987): 41.

Brown, Dorothy M. *Mabel Walker Willebrandt.* Knoxville, Tenn.: University of Tennessee Press, 1984.

Brown, Drollene P. *Belva Lockwood Wins Her Case.* Niles, Ill.: Albert Whitman & Co., 1987. (Highly recommended for young readers).

Carlin, David R., Jr. "Facing the Canons: Two Sisters Seek Office." *Commonweal* (January 27, 1984): 38.

Carlson, Margart. "The Law According to Ruth." *Time* (June 28, 1993): 38.

Carson, Rachel. *Silent Spring.* New York: Simon & Schuster, 1962.

Charlie Rose Show, PBS interview with Patricia Schroeder, March 28, 1996.

Chen, Edwin. "Rose Bird Runs for Her Life." *Nation* (January 18, 1986): 42.

Clines, Francis X. "Barbara Jordan Dies at 59: Her Voice Stirred the Nation. *The New York Times* (January 18, 1996): 1.

Clinton, Hillary Rodham. *It Takes a Village and Other Lessons Children Teach Us.* New York: Simon & Schuster, 1996.

Chambers, Veronica. "Antonia Hernandez, President, Mexican American Legal Defense and Educational Fund: She's In with Washington Even if Her Causes Are Way Out." *George* (September 1996): 113.

Cohn, Ellen. "And Then There Were None." *Village Voice* (November 23, 1993): 11.

Cook, Blanche Wiesen, ed. *Crystal Eastman: Women and Revolution.* London: Oxford University Press, 1978.

Cool, Lisa Collier. "The New Leadership." *Cosmopolitan* (May 1994): 206.

Copeland, Irene. "The Big Time! Eight Who Got Where Only Men Got Before." *Cosmopolitan* (May 1994): 208.

Cottle, Mation Weston. "Prejudice Against Women Lawyers: How Can It Be Overcome?" *Case & Comment* (October 1914): 371.

Cox, Gail Diane. "Skid Row Lawyer Fights to Regain Funding from City; Appeal Set Today." *The Los Angeles Daily Journal* 97 (September 6, 1984): 1.

Crowley, Susan L. "Children Under Siege: Marian Wright Edelman Fights to Keep Hard-Won Benefits." *AARP Bulletin* (July 1996): 16.

DeBenedictis, Don J. "Restrictive Abortion Law Upheld." *ABA Journal* (January 1992): 16.

Drachman, Virginia G. *Women Lawyers and Origin of Professional Identity in America: Letters of the Equity Club, 1887-1890.* Ann Arbor, Mich.: University of Michigan Press, 1993.

Dunne, Philip. "Men, Women and Tears." *Time* (September 30, 1991): 84.

Dusky, Lorraine. "Women Who Would Be President." *McCall's* (June 1990).

Eastman, Max. *Enjoyment of Living.* New York: Harper, 1948.

Ebron, Angela. "Defeating Slumlords." *Family Circle* (February 1, 1995): 19.

Edelman, Marian Wright. *Families in Peril: An Agenda for Social Change.* Cambridge, Mass.: Harvard University Press, 1987.

———. *The Measure of Our Success: A Letter to My Children and Yours.* New York: Harper Perennial, 1992.

Ehrenreich, Barbara. "Why Women Are Finally Winning." *Time* (June 22, 1992).

English, Dierdre. "Politics: The Ordeal of Rose Bird." *Ms.* (November 1986): 71.

Epstein, Cynthia Fuchs. *Women in Law.* New York: Basic Books, 1981.

Fairstein, Linda. *Sexual Violence: Our War Against Rape.* New York: William Morrow, 1993.

Farrow, Tiera. *Lawyer in Petticoats.* New York: Vantage Press, 1953.

Ferraro, Geraldine, with Linda Bird Francke. *Ferraro: My Story.* New York: Bantam Books, 1985.

Ferraro, Susan. "What Makes Gerry Run?" *The New York Times Magazine* (March 22, 1992): 46.

Fields-Meyer, Thomas, et. al. "O.K. After O.J." *People* (March 18, 1986): 85.

Flexner, Eleanor. *Century of Struggle: The Women's Rights Movement in the U.S.* revised edit. Cambridge, Mass.: The Belknap Press of Harvard University, 1975.

Foerstel, Karen. "Number of Female Departures Means Loss of Seniority." *Congressional Quarterly Weekly Report* 53 (December 9, 1995): 3760.

Foote, Donna. "You Have to Care for the Kids." *Newsweek* (April 7, 1995): 35.

Forster, Margaret. *Significant Sisters.* New York: Alfred A. Knopf, 1985.

Frank, Jerome. "Women Lawyers." *Good Housekeeping* (December 1944): 43.

Franks, Lucinda. "Backstage at the O.J. Trial." *People* (March 27, 1995): 70.

Friedan, Betty. "Comment: Children's Crusade." *The New Yorker* (June 3, 1996): 5.

Friedman, Jane M. *America's First Woman Lawyer: The Biography of Myra Bradwell.* Buffalo, N.Y.: Prometheus Books, 1993.

Gandee, Charles, and Vicki Woods. "Fear and Clothing." *Vogue* (September 1995): 550.

Gardner, Ralph, Jr. "Cosmo Talks to Linda Fairstein, Dauntless D.A." *Cosmopolitan* (October 1988): 158.

Giles, Isabel. "The Twentieth Century Portia." *Case and Comment* (October 1914): 353.

Gilbert, Lynn, and Gaylen Moore. *Particular Passions.* New York: Clarkson Potter, 1981.

Ginger, Ann Fagan. *Carol Weiss King.* Niwot, Colo.: University of Colorado Press, 1993.

"Ginsburg Adroit, Amiable, But Avoids Specifics." *Congressional Quarterly Weekly Report* 51 (July 24, 1993): 1982.

Ginsburg, Ruth Bader. "Speaking in a Judicial Voice." *New York University Law Review* (December 1992): 1185.

Gleick, Elizabeth, and Joyce Wagner. "Her Day in Court." *People* (July 18, 1994): 34.

Goldberg, Stephanie, and Henry J. Reske. "Talking with Attorney General Janet Reno." *ABA Journal* (June 1993): 46.

Goldberg, Stephanie B. "The Second Woman Justice." *ABA Journal* (October 1993): 40.

Goodman, Ellen. "Marcia Clark: Her Case Illustrates Child Custody Issues." *The Pantagraph* (dist. by Washington Post Writers Group) (March 9, 1995): A9.

———. "Putting Down Women in Put-On Trial." *The Boston Globe*, 1995.

Gray, Kevin, et. al. "Straight Shooter." *People* (June 12, 1995): 67.

Green, Michelle, with David Chandler. "Pat Schroeder's Ambition to be First Lady in the Oval Office nears the Moment of Truth." *People* (September 7, 1987): 48.

Griffin, Lynne, and Kelly McCann. *The Book of Women: 300 Notable Women History Passed By.* Holbrook, Mass.: Bob Adams, Inc. 1992.

Groller, Ingrid. "Law in the Family." *Parents* (March, 1995): 91.

Harrington, Mona. *Women Lawyers: Rewriting the Rules.* New York: Borzoi/Alfred A. Knopf, 1994.

Harris, Barbara J. *Beyond Her Sphere: Women and the Professions in American History.* Westport, Conn.: Greenwood Press, 1978.

Haskins, Jim. *One More River to Cross: The Stories of Twelve Black Americans.* New York: Scholastic, Inc., 1972 (for young readers).

Hays, Ed. "Law Be a Lady," *Interview* (June 1989): 48.

Heilbrun, Carolyn G. *Gloria Steinem: The Education of a Woman.* New York: The Dial Press, 1995.

Hentoff, Nat. "The Two Ruth Bader Ginsburgs." *Village Voice* (July 20, 1993): 20.

"Her Days in Court." *The Los Angeles Daily Journal* 95 (December 31, 1982): 4.

Herda, D.J. *Roe v. Wade: The Abortion Question.* Springfield, N.J.: Enslow Publishers, Inc., 1994. (For young readers.)

Hewitt, Bill, et. al. "Feeling Supreme." *People* (June 28, 1993): 49.

"Hillary's Chicago." *George* (September 1996): 132.

Hine, Darlene Clark, ed. *Black Women in America.* New York: Carlson Publishing, Inc., 1993.

Howard, O.O. *Third Annual Report.* Washington, D.C.: Howard University, 1870.

Hynes, Patricia M. *The Recurring Silent Spring.* New York: Pergamon Press, 1989.

Idelson, Holly and Jennifer S. Thomas. "Ginsburg's Abortion Anamoly: Support for Rights, Not Roe." *Congressional Quarterly Weekly Report* (July 17, 1993): 1874.

Ingrahm, Claire R., and Leonard W. Ingrahm. *An Album of Women in American History.* New York: Franklin Watts, 1972.

Jackel, Molly, and Steve Manning. "Long March to Equality." *Scholastic Update* (March 12, 1993): 12.

James, Edward T., ed. *Notable American Women 1607-1950: A Biographical Dictionary.* Cambridge, Mass.: The Belknap Press of Harvard University, 1971.

Jordan, Barbara, with Shelley Headon. *Barbara Jordan: A Self Portrait.* New York: Doubleday, 1979.

"Justice Ginsburg: U.S. Supreme Court Justice's Daughter Pays Tribute to Mother." *Perspectives* 3, no. 1 (fall 1993): 1.

Kaplan, David A. "Take Down the Girlie Calendars." *Newsweek* (November 22, 1993): 34.

Karpen, Lynn, "Taking It Personally." *The New York Times Book Review* (September 19, 1993): 42.

Kennedy, Florynce. *Color Me Flo: My Hard Life and Good Times.* Englewood Cliffs, N.J.: Prentice-Hall, Inc., 1976.

Kenyon, Dorothy. "The Case (By One of Them) for Women Lawyers." *The New York Times* (February 19, 1950).

Kohn, Allan. "Bankruptcy Judges Have Same Philosophy." *New York Law Journal* 188 (September 7, 1982): 1

Lacayo, Richard. "The Justice in the Middle." *Time* (July 9,1990): 27.

Lease, Mary Clyens. *The Problem of Civilization Solved.* (1895)

Leive, Cindi. "A New Wave of Women Judges." *Glamour* (May, 1995): 106

Lewis, Neil A. "Balanced Jurist at Home in the Middle." *The New York Times* (June 27, 1993).

Lewis, Shawn D. "The Bench Cannot Be Bullied!" *Barrister* (spring 1983): 26

Lilly, Mary M. "A Message to Lawyers." *Case & Comment* (October 1914): 379.

Litwak, Mark. *Courtroom Crusaders.* New York: William Morrow & Co., 1989.

Longstreet, Dana and Cynthia Moekle. "Nothing Succeeds . . . Like Justice Served." *American Health* (April 1989): 66

Machlowitz, David. "Sex Crimes and the Preppie Murderer; As a Manhattan Prosecutor, Linda Fairstein Has a Unique Specialty." *Barrister* (summer 1991): 35.

Mall, Elyse. "Ferraro Goes Private—For Now." *Working Woman* (October 1993): 18.

Manna, Sal. "Trouble in Paradise: Skid Row Lawyer Nancy Mintie Helps Her Clients Battle Poverty in a City of Plenty." *Student Lawyer* 14 (September 1985): 12–13.

Margolick, David M. "Wall Street's Sexist Wall: Barrier to Women Partners: A Case Study." *The National Law Journal* 2 (August 4, 1980): 1.

Martindale-Hubble Law Directory. New Providence, N.J.: Martindale Hubble/Reed Reference Publishing Co., 1996.

McCarthy, Abagail. "My Brilliant Career." *ABA Journal* (April 1, 1988): 138.

Moran, Terence. "The Court's Other Woman." *Mirabella* (September 1993): 40.

Morello, Karen Berger. *The Invisible Bar.* New York: Random House, 1986.

———. "Women's Entry Into the Legal Profession." *The American University Law Review* 32 (spring 1983): 623.

Mussey, Ellen Spencer. "The Child's Court." *Case & Comment* (October 1914): 367.

New Mexico Women's Bar Association. *Women JDs: Traveling a Successful Career Path.* Albuquerque, N.Mex.: State Bar of New Mexico, 1994.

"Newsmakers." *Perspectives* 3, no. 1 (fall 1993): 3.

"Newsmakers." *Perspectives* 3, no. 2 (summer 1994): 5.

"1990 Women of the Year." *Glamour* (December 1990): 96.

"Not Women of the Year." *Nation* 225 (October 5, 1992): 345.

Parks, Rosa, with Gregory J. Reed. *Quiet Strength.* Grand Rapids, Mich.: Zondervan Publishing House, 1994.

Parks, Rosa, with James Haskins. *My Story.* New York: Dial Books, 1992.

Pia, Audrey. "Founding of the Washington College of Law." *The American University Law Review* 32 (spring 1983): 617.

Primm, Wilson. "Death and the Bar: The Woman Lawyer." *Wilson Primm Scrapbook.* St. Louis, Mo.: St. Louis Historical Society, 1870.

Rapp, David. "States' Rights and Sandra Day O'Connor." *Governing* (December 1992): 59.

Reed, Susan. "Linda Fairstein." *People* (September 27, 1993): 77.

Reibstein, Larry, et. al. "And Now, The Trial." *Newsweek* (January 23, 1995): 44.

———, et. al. "Disorder in the Court." *Newsweek* (April 17, 1995): 26.

Reske, Henry J. "Two Paths for Ginsberg." *ABA Journal* (August 1993): 16.

Rice, Cy. *Defender of the Damned: Gladys Towles Root.* New York: The Citadel Press, 1964.

Roberts, Edith Lampson. "Justice Ruth Bader Ginsburg." (Courtesy of Ruth Bader Ginsburg.)

Roberts, Steven V. "The Two Lives of Ruth Bader Ginsburg." *U.S. News & World Report* (June 28, 1993): 26.

Robinson, Lelia J. "Women Lawyers in the United States." *The Green Bag* 2 (1890): 10.

Romney, Ronna, and Beppie Harrison. *Momentum: Women in American Politics Now.* New York: Crown Publishing, 1988.

Rosen, Jeffrey. "Make Up Our Mind, Justice O'Connor." *The New York Times* (December 26, 1995).

———. "The Book of Ruth." *New Republic* (August 2, 1993): 19.

Salter, Stephanie. "Rose Bird Wings it Again." *Savvy Woman* (May 1988): 14.

Sapinsky, Barbara. *The Private War of Mrs. Packard.* New York: Paragon House, 1991.

Schaffer, Thomas L. "The Ethics of Dissent and Friendship in the American Professions." *West Virginia Law Review* (summer 1986): 623.

Schlesinger, Arthur, Jr. "Hillary Rodham Clinton, First Lady: Get Used to Her, She's the Future." *George* (September 1996): 105.

Schroeder, Patricia. *Champion of The Great American Family: A Personal and Political Book.* New York: Random House, 1989.

"Schroeder Plans to Retire From Congress Next Year." *Wall Street Journal* (November 30, 1995).

Schwartz, Mortimer D., et. al. "Clara Shortridge Foltz: Pioneer in the Law." *Hastings Law Journal* (January 1976).

Scott, Niki. "Working Woman: Double Standard Brought to Light in Clark Case." *The Pantagraph,* 1995.

Shoop, Julie Gannon. "Gay Rights Case Prompts Heated Debate in High Court." *Trial* (December 1995): 12.

Sicherman, Barbara, Carol Hurd Green, and Ilene Kantrov, and Harriette Walker, eds. *Notable American Women: The Modern Period.* Cambridge, Mass.: The Belknap Press of Harvard University, 1980.

Smith, Betsy Covington. *Breakthrough: Women in Law.* New York: Walker, 1984. (For young readers.)

Smith, Jessie Carney, ed. *Notable Black American Women.* Detroit: Gale Research, 1992.

Snell, Marilyn Berlin. "The Politics of Family: State's Rights Feminism." *New Perspectives Quarterly* (winter 1990): 4.

Sochen, June. *Herstory: A Woman's View of American History.* New York: Alfred A. Knopf, 1974.

Sperling, Gene. "Justice in the Middle." *Savvy Woman* (March 1988): 26

Steinem, Gloria. *Outrageous Acts and Everyday Rebellions.* New York: Plume/New American Library, 1983.

———. *Revolution from Within.* Boston: Little, Brown, 1992.

Stewart, David O. "Holding the Center." *ABA Journal* (March 1993): 48.

Sylvester, Nancy. "Women and Public Office: Creating Alternative Approaches." *Catholic World* (November 1991): 265.

Telegen, Diane and Jim Kamp, eds. *Notable Hispanic American Women* first edit. Detroit: Gale Research, 1993.

Terry, Wallace. "Make Things Better for Somebody." *Parade* (February 14, 1993): 4-5.

"The Reckoning for Simpson." *U.S. News & World Report* (January 23, 1995): 32.

"Three Incumbents, Two New Judges Named for Bankruptcy Court." *New York Law Journal* 193 (April 19, 1985): 1.

Toobin, Jeffrey. "True Grit." *The New Yorker* (January 9, 1995): 28.

Truman, Margaret. *Women of Courage.* New York: William Morrow & Co., 1976.

"2,000 Celebrate Women in Law." *Perspectives* 3, no. 2 (summer 1994): 4.

Uglow, Jennifer S. *The Continuum Dictionary of Women's Biography* expanded edit. New York: Continuum Publishing Co., 1989.

Urbanek, Mae, and The Western Writers of America. *The Women Who Made the West.* Garden City, N.Y.: Doubleday, 1980.

Urbanska, Wanda. "Top 10 Women Presidential Contenders." *New Woman* (November 1990): 112.

Van Gelder, Lindsy. "Harriet Rabb: Scourge of Corporate Male Chauvenism." *New York Magazine* (June 26, 1978): 38.

Verhovek, Sam Howe. "At Funeral, Praise for Barbara Jordan." *The New York Times* (January 21, 1996): 18.

Violet, Arlene, with Suda J. Prohaska. *Convictions: My Journey from the Convent to the Courtroom.* New York: Random House, 1987.

Walsh, Kenneth T. and Ted Guest. "People to Watch." *U.S. News & World Report* (December 30, 1991): 67.

Weddington, Sarah Ragle. *A Question of Choice.* New York: G.P. Putnam's Sons, 1992.

Weisberg, Ed, and D. Kelly. *Women and the Law: A Social Historical Perspective* vol. II. Cambridge, Mass.: Schneckman Publishing Co., Inc, 1982.

Wiehl, Lisa. "Interview: Mona Harrington." *Perspectives* 3, no. 2 (summer 1994): 7.

Will, George F. "Her Sound-Bites Draw Blood." *Newsweek* (August 17, 1987): 76.

Wines, Michael. "Representative Schroeder Plans to Quit." *The New York Times* (November 30, 1995): 16.

"Wise Choice." *The New Republic* (July 5, 1993): 7.

"Women Lead the ABA: A Reason to Celebrate." *Perspectives* 3, no. 2 (summer 1994): 1.

"Work as Destiny: What Did You Expect?" *Esquire* (December 1986): 273.

Wortman, Marlene Stein, ed. *Women in American Law: Volume One: From Colonial Times to the New Deal.* New York: Holmes and Meier Publishers, Inc., 1985.

Young, Cathy. "Rancorous Liasons—The Morning After." *Reason* (February 1994): 57.

Zimmerman, Mary H., ed. *75 Year History of the National Association of Women Lawyers.* Lansing, Mich.: Wellman Press, 1975.

INDEX